Global Financial Markets series

Global Financial Markets is a series of practical guides to the latest financial market tools, techniques and strategies. Written for practitioners across a range of disciplines it provides comprehensive but practical coverage of key topics in finance covering strategy, markets, financial products, tools and techniques and their implementation. This series will appeal to a broad readership, from new entrants to experienced practitioners across the financial services industry, including areas such as institutional investment, financial derivatives, investment strategy, private banking, risk management, corporate finance and M&A, financial accounting and governance, and many more.

Titles include:

Erik Banks
DARK POOLS, 2nd Edition
Off-Exchange Liquidity in an Era of High Frequency, Program, and
Algorithmic Trading

Erik Banks
LIQUIDITY RISK, 2nd Edition
Managing Funding and Asset Risk

Daniel Capocci
THE COMPLETE GUIDE TO HEDGE FUNDS AND HEDGE FUND STRATEGIES

Sandy Chen
INTEGRATED BANK ANALYSIS AND VALUATION
A Practical Guide to the ROIC Methodology

Frances Cowell
RISK-BASED INVESTMENT MANAGEMENT IN PRACTICE, 2nd Edition

Jawwad Farid
MODELS AT WORK
A Practitioner's Guide to Risk Management

Guy Fraser-Sampson
INTELLIGENT INVESTING
A Guide to the Practical and Behavioural Aspects of Investment Strategy

Michael Hünseler
CREDIT PORTFOLIO MANAGEMENT
A Practitioner's Guide to the Active Management of Credit Risks

Felix Lessambo
THE INTERNATIONAL CORPORATE GOVERNANCE SYSTEM
Audit Roles and Board Oversight

Ross K. McGill
US WITHHOLDING TAX
Practical Implications of QI and FATCA

David Murphy
OTC DERIVATIVES, BILATERAL TRADING AND CENTRAL CLEARING
An Introduction to Regulatory Policy, Trading Impact and Systemic Risk

Gianluca Oricchio
PRIVATE COMPANY VALUATION
How Credit Risk Reshaped Equity Markets and Corporate Finance Valuation Tools

Applied Financial Macroeconomics and Investment Strategy

A Practitioner's Guide to Tactical Asset Allocation

Robert T. McGee

APPLIED FINANCIAL MACROECONOMICS AND INVESTMENT STRATEGY
Copyright © Robert T. McGee, 2015.

First published in 2015 by
PALGRAVE MACMILLAN®
in the United States—a division of St. Martin's Press LLC,
175 Fifth Avenue, New York, NY 10010.

Where this book is distributed in the UK, Europe and the rest of the world,
this is by Palgrave Macmillan, a division of Macmillan Publishers Limited,
registered in England, company number 785998, of Houndmills,
Basingstoke, Hampshire RG21 6XS.

Palgrave Macmillan is the global academic imprint of the above companies
and has companies and representatives throughout the world.

Palgrave® and Macmillan® are registered trademarks in the United States,
the United Kingdom, Europe and other countries.

ISBN: 978–1–137–42839–4

Library of Congress Cataloging-in-Publication Data

McGee, Robert T.
    Applied financial macroeconomics & investment strategy :
 a practitioner's guide to tactical asset allocation / Robert T. McGee.
      pages cm
    Includes bibliographical references and index.
    ISBN 978–1–137–42839–4
    ISBN 1–137–42839–2
      1. Investments. 2. Business cycles. 3. Asset allocation. 4. Monetary
policy. 5. Investment analysis. I. Title. II. Title: Applied financial
macroeconomics and investment strategy.
HG4521.M224 2015
332.6—dc23   2014039839

A catalogue record of the book is available from the British Library.

Design by Newgen Knowledge Works (P) Ltd., Chennai, India.

First edition: April 2015

10 9 8 7 6 5 4 3 2 1

Printed in the United States of America.

To Alice and Phil

Contents

List of Exhibits

Preface

Professional investment strategists tend to come from a variety of backgrounds. Many started as equity analysts covering companies in a particular sector. Since investment strategy involves cross-disciplinary insights from finance, economics, and business, financial sector analysts have an especially good vantage point to become macro strategists as they are more tuned into the monetary policy, credit, and interest rate cycles given their outsized effects on the earnings of the companies they follow. Finance majors learn many of the basic principles that are useful for valuing assets, an important skill for investment strategists. Economists, on the other hand, usually have more relative strength in analyzing the business cycle and the macroeconomy, as well as monetary and fiscal policy, which have significant impacts on investment performance. Indeed, some Wall Street strategists, like myself, were initially professional economists, with an economic forecasting and monetary policy focus.

Still, probably most practicing strategists learn on the job after finishing their MBAs, CFAs, or undergraduate academic degrees. This book is designed as a practical guide for investment strategists and finance students intending to pursue asset management careers. The aim of this book is to bring together insights from finance and macroeconomics that are useful for investment strategists concerned with asset allocation decision-making. This is the basis for the title, *Applied Financial Macroeconomics and Investment Strategy: A Practitioner's Guide to Tactical Asset Allocation.*

The absolute and relative performance of broad asset classes is systematically related to macroeconomic trends, both cyclical and secular. Among these trends are those of inflation, interest rates, real gross domestic product (GDP), profits, and income growth. The business cycle includes a monetary policy cycle, a profit cycle, credit cycles, inventory cycles, and cycles in housing and durable goods demand. Each business cycle has a pattern that rhymes, while not exactly repeating, the pattern of other cycles. In other words, "every cycle is the same except for what's different." For successful investment strategy, it is usually just as important to know "what's different this time" as it is to know where the economy is in the cycle.

In different economic environments, the financial characteristics of an asset class are important determinants of its relative return performance. At different stages in the business cycle, these characteristics may help bonds, for example, and hurt stocks. The crux of good investment strategy is to understand how the financial characteristics of an asset class are likely to interact with the economic backdrop.

This requires accurate insight about both the economic outlook and its likely market impact on different investments. In fact, the regularities in the business cycle are one of the most useful sources of information about the economic outlook and likely asset performance. This makes business cycle analysis a powerful tool for investment strategy. The book will focus on how business cycle patterns relate to investment strategy, such as which sectors do well in which parts of the business cycle, when do equities beat bonds and vice versa, and why. These considerations are key inputs for deciding when to overweight or underweight particular assets.

In addition to exploiting the regularity of patterns for investment performance, it is crucial to recognize "what's different" in each cycle and the implications of these differences for relative return performance. Examples of differences across business cycles illustrate this point. In the 2002 to 2007 economic expansion, residential real estate and financial engineering applied to mortgage lending created the primary cyclical excesses. In the 1992 to 2000 expansion, excessive technology company valuations combined with overinvestment stimulated by Y2K[1] worries to shape the main areas of cyclical excess. These differences played out in massive overvaluations followed by destabilizing crashes of particular assets.

Secular economic trends can create headwinds and tailwinds for assets that are also important to understand. Secular trends shift over longer stretches of time, causing secular bull and bear markets. For example, major bull and bear markets in equities, bonds, and commodities are often associated with long-term trend shifts in key macrovariables such as inflation and interest rates. Globalization has created secular trends, causing rising income inequality in the developed world, while

---

[1] Y2K refers to the worries that technology infrastructure would be severely disrupted by the inability of many computers to make the transition to dating the new century. Massive preparation and investments were made to avoid a catastrophe. This helped fuel excessive animal spirits around technology, media, and telecom stocks just as the Internet, with its unlimited potential, began to accrue critical mass.

lifting living standards for the world's poorest people at the fastest rate in human history. Accelerating technological change speeds up creative destruction and globalization, with important implications for the strategic allocation of wealth. As important, reversals of secular trends can be associated with the unwinding of economic excesses and heightened volatility.

There are always analysts predicting disasters. In rare instances they are correct. Generally, the best places to look for likely disasters are the sources of cyclical excesses. Cyclical excesses tend to arise in areas in which credit or valuations are expanding unsustainably because of a systemic breakdown in prudential standards for lending and/or investing. The financial crisis of 2008 provides an example of extreme ex-ante tail risk come to ex-post fruition. Analysis of its causes includes short-term cyclical influences, like the housing crisis, secular trends in leverage, and the interplay between politics, the private sector, and government officials affecting regulatory oversight. Sorting through the confluence of factors behind the crisis shows how the culmination of several trends and cycles can bring seemingly remote possibilities to reality. What's more, legacy effects from the crisis have implications for the investment environment going forward.

With this in mind, the first three chapters elaborate on cycles and trends as concepts used in this book (chapter 1); describe the business cycle, including its stages and subcycles (chapter 2); and focus on the major role that monetary policy plays in managing and causing business cycles (chapter 3). The second part of the book relates the financial characteristics of broad asset classes to the economic cycles and trends that are particularly important to their absolute and relative return performance. Chapters 4, 5, and 6 are divided to focus on: the bond market and credit conditions over the cycle, including interest rates and risk premia on fixed-income instruments (chapter 4); the profits cycle and equity market, including relative sector performance (chapter 5); and real assets, including the commodity markets' response to secular and cyclical economic conditions (chapter 6).

While longer-term trend (secular) impacts are discussed in each case, short-term business cycle influences are the main focus, as tactical asset allocation generally makes the most sense in a business cycle context. Trends are useful for long-term thematic investing. Chapter 7 discusses the role of globalization and technological change in shaping long-term trends that are driving some important investment themes for strategic asset allocation.

All of these insights are combined in chapter 8 for a case study of the 2008–2009 financial crisis to illustrate the multiple ways in which events converged to create the worst financial crisis since the 1930s. The purpose is not to create a definitive version of what caused the crisis, but rather to show how the approach developed throughout the book helps to understand how so much could go wrong at the same time, with important implications for asset allocation.

Acknowledgments

A book that focuses on the intersection of macroconomics and investment strategy seems in retrospect like an obvious topic. Yet it only
slowly dawned on me that in an age of countless books and blogs
about these subjects, there did not seem to be one with a holistic treatment of that intersection. This became increasingly apparent after the
financial crisis when, like the blind men touching the different parts
of the elephant, many investment professionals seemed lost in the
dark about how macroeconomic trends and cycles impacted their
universe.

Special thanks to my colleague Irene L. Peters, CFA, for constantly
reminding me that the topic was a useful subject for a book. Her
research and editorial support made this project possible. Of course,
responsibility for any errors and shortcomings remain mine.

This book would also not have been possible without the questions
and insights provided by all of the portfolio managers, strategists, and
other investment professionals with whom I have had the pleasure to
work over the years.

The simple fact is, either by default or design, investment managers
need an economic framework to do their job. This book is an attempt
to help with that process.

1

Cycles and Trends: History Does Not Repeat Itself, but It Does Rhyme

The daily news shapes the public conversation and dominates media discussion of financial market and economic trends. For example, early every month, when the US Department of Labor reports the jobs growth number for the previous month, a flood of commentary attempts to judge the strength of the labor market with a myopic focus on that particular number.

This focus on a snapshot in time outside the broader context often creates a consensus of meaningless information. When payrolls grow by 160,000 in a month when 200,000 jobs were expected, a lot of negative commentary follows, as if a 40,000 miss tells us something about the strength of the labor market. Every month in the United States, several million new jobs are created, and several million old jobs end. A net gain of 160,000 or 200,000 is a very small percentage of that massive churn, and the 40,000 difference is a statistically insignificant piece of information. Yet the reporting that the public hears inevitably focuses on this meaningless and often misleading "noise" rather than the more important underlying trend. In fact, given the wide confidence intervals around the initial estimates, subsequent revisions commonly change that initial interpretation by 180 degrees. By that time, however, the news has moved on to the noise in the next month's estimate.

This misinterpretation of noise as "signal" confounds professionals as well as the public. Market professionals pontificate in the media as if there is an important kernel of information in the latest noise. An extreme example of this pattern occurred in September 2013, when the August payroll number was first reported as a superficially disappointing 169,000 increase. This was taken as a sign the economy and labor

1

market were softening. The Federal Reserve had set the markets up to expect an imminent decision to taper its bond-buying program known as quantitative easing (QE3) based on the substantial labor market improvement over the prior year. Instead, the Fed surprised the markets by deciding to postpone the tapering based at least partly on worries created by the negative noise in the August jobs data. With more comprehensive data, the payroll gain was subsequently revised sharply higher to show a robust gain over 200,000, and gross domestic product (GDP) growth for the quarter was also reported well above consensus expectations at just over 4 percent, numbers that would have easily justified a September tapering had the Fed known them at the time. By its December meeting, the clarified picture of a stronger labor market contributed to the Fed's decision to vote in favor of reducing its QE3 bond-buying program. This about-face surprised market participants who had by then talked themselves into a much-delayed tapering schedule. This example illustrates how noise in the data creates volatility in markets. While traders exploit these misinterpretations, longer-term investors need to look through the noise to the underlying signals from the data to make sensible investment decisions.

The explosion of information made possible by modern technology has intensified the need to develop methods for better analysis and interpretation of data. In addition to useful information, the blogosphere has also created a platform for ill-informed pseudo experts of all sorts. Bad analysis has proliferated with the ease of access to information and expanded channels for mass communication, contributing to waves of pessimism or optimism in financial markets. A misleading focus on the noise in the data to the detriment of the signal is just one example of the pitfalls of the Information Age. Indeed, because noise is random, it allows commentators to always have a basis for advocating both sides of an issue. Negative noise supports the weak economy viewpoint, while positive noise supports the strong economy view. That's why on any given day, the financial news airwaves sow confusion. The bulls and the bears both are talking their respective cases "knowledgeably," with rationales culled selectively from the noise in the data. Successful investors must distill the signal from the noise.

Cycle and trend analyses take advantage of the information explosion to extract signals from noisy data. They attempt to find useful patterns for anticipating future developments by throwing out the noise and using the remaining signal. Exploiting systematic relationships between *cycles* in asset returns and economic variables is useful for tactical asset allocation. Likewise, exploiting relationships between *trends* in asset returns and economic variables is also useful. However, this cannot be done mechanically, without regard to the underlying economic and policy backdrop. For example, different monetary policy regimes can create or reverse particular trends in inflation and interest rates, which in turn affect trends in asset-class performance, both relative and absolute.

Trends are often segments of very long cycles. The rise of inflation from the 1960s to the early 1980s lasted long enough to be regarded as a trend by investors during that time. Likewise, the decline in inflation since the early 1980s has been a key trend affecting the relative performance of various asset classes. For example, it drove the long bull market in bonds.

From a longer-term perspective, these two trends—rising inflation (1965–1982) and falling inflation (1982–2008)—can be regarded as a very long cycle that restored price stability after it was disrupted in the 1960s (Exhibit 1.1). Assuming monetary policy continues to preempt deflationary forces, inflation has made a round-trip back to subdued 1950s levels. Looking forward, if the Fed remains committed to price stability around 2 percent, inflation would largely be cyclical around

Exhibit 1.1 Round-Trip Back to Normal

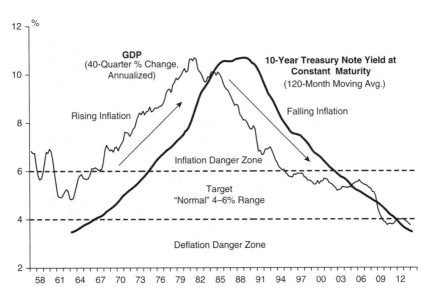

Source: Federal Reserve Board, Bureau of Economic Analysis/Haver Analytics. Data as of April 18, 2014.

a trendless 2-percent rate. This example illustrates the importance of historical and fundamental knowledge about what causes inflation as well as quantitative modeling of trends and cycles.

The ongoing evolution of the structure of the economy, combined with the fact that policy settings differ from cycle to cycle and some key relationships may be different in each cycle, help explain Milton Friedman's famous maxim that the lag between a change in monetary policy and its effect on the economy *"is long and variable."* It is also the case that the policy-impact lag varies for different parts of the economy. For example, real GDP responds more quickly to monetary stimulus than inflation, which exhibits more inertia. Given the variability in lags from cycle to cycle *and* the difference in lags across economic variables, it is not surprising that econometric models based on statistical averages over multiple cycles have a hard time forecasting accurately. Add to this the fact that lags in the impact of one variable on another also fluctuate with changes in preconditions and structure, and it is not hard to see why forecast models often have so much difficulty. This explains why well-informed consideration of "what's different" about a particular cycle can sometimes be more useful than the best econometric models.

That said, the limitations of models do not mean that they should be abandoned. If they are, the result is what we see in the mass media, in which both sides of any particular issue about the economic outlook seem to have compelling stories to tell. Models add insight to help distinguish signal from noise. While not precise by any stretch of the imagination, they can be very useful for getting the direction of change right. By itself, that can be a big advantage, especially when the market is looking the other way or is extremely uncertain about direction.

These considerations are behind the approach taken in this book. Rather than a formal modeling or theoretical approach to these issues, the method is to show how *the art* of economic forecasting can be applied usefully to investment strategy. This means we have to steer clear of precise mathematical definitions and organize our vocabulary around concepts that are fuzzier but that better serve the purpose for which they are intended. With that in mind, let's talk about cycles and trends.

Time horizon and frequency of observation are necessary assumptions for any practical application of data to the concepts of cycle and trends. Cycles in interest rates, profits, equity prices, and economic growth are generally related to the underlying business cycle, which we discuss in depth in the next chapter. As with all the cycles we discuss, business cycles vary in duration. Since World War II, for example, expansions have been longer and recessions less frequent than was the case for the business cycles in the prior century. We will discuss why that has been the case in chapter 2. With the time frame of a business cycle in mind, the easiest way to define a cycle is the pattern of movement in an economic or financial variable, such as corporate profits, over the course of an economic expansion and recession. Profits generally rise during expansions and fall during recessions.

In some cases, cycles in particular variables do not mesh with the business cycle. For example, consumption spending and housing investment grew through the 2001 recession instead of contracting in the usual fashion. In the case of housing, it grew from 1995 to 2006 throughout two business cycles. This allowed an unusually long time for excesses to accumulate. Generally falling interest rates, easy mortgage-credit conditions, and the pent-up demand left over from the deep housing recession in the early 1990s helped power residential real estate through the 2001 recession. It was the collapse in technology-sector investment that was the main weak point in that downturn.

This illustrates the flexibility necessary to use the term *cycle*. Generally, it can be regarded as a period in which a particular variable, say GDP, starts rising, continues to rise, and then starts to decline and bottoms before a new ascent. Similarly, an interest-rate cycle begins when rates rise off the prior cycle's low point, then peak and fall before rising in the next cycle. Within a business cycle, which will generally be our reference cycle, there can be multiple cycles in some of the variables we discuss. For this reason, and because it is a good framework for investment strategy, we will usually orient cycles of particular variables over the business cycle defined by the National Bureau of Economic Research (NBER) cycle-dating committee.

For the momentum trader, a *trend* can be six months or less. For a historian, it may span centuries. Here we use the term to refer to periods when a variable of interest is moving up or down *through at least a few business cycles*. The example of inflation (up 1965–1982, down 1982–2008) illustrates the practical application of the trend concept. Another reason why econometric modeling is limited is that variables switch from trending (or nonstationary) to cyclical (stationary), and the statistical procedures that apply depend on this distinction. However, timing the distinction right can be difficult when structural and policy shifts move a variable from one category to the other. For example, inflation was a nonstationary variable during the period when it trended up and down. It is not a coincidence that econometric tests for stationarity got a lot more attention starting in the 1970s. That's when some key macroeconomic variables were becoming non-stationary. We believe inflation has recently become stationary as part of the Fed's successful shift to targeting a 2-percent rate.

Some methodological considerations: Economists express their sense of humor by using decimal points

Applying econometric forecasting to investment strategy puts more focus on what works for that objective compared to more academic deductive theoretical reasoning. In the latter case, economists are concerned with formulating theories and testing them empirically. While some microeconomic theories lend themselves to relatively precise empirical estimations, macroeconomic theories are more likely to have conceptual and measurement issues, making modeling less reliable.

Aggregate measures, such as GDP and employment, are much harder to tally, or even define, compared, for example, to direct measures of individual company metrics. There are exceptions, especially with price data, including interest rates, in which direct measurement is easy. Generally, financial data are more timely and precise than aggregate macro data. Arguably, finance theory is also more representative of the underlying phenomena that determine asset values, compared to, say, macroeconomic theories of what determines GDP. Put another way, there is more room for dispute in macroeconomics than finance.

In the early days of building big econometric models, there was more of a sense that a stable structure through time could represent macroeconomic variables and provide a good basis for forecasting. By the 1970s, it was becoming clear that this was a naive expectation, as more focus turned to the sort of issues raised by the Lucas critique, which argues that it is naive to try to predict the effects of a change in economic policy entirely on the basis of a relationship observed in historical data, especially highly aggregated historical data.

One example of why this is the case is embodied in Goodhart's Law, which refers to the notion that "when a measure becomes a policy target, it ceases to be a good measure." This is a social science variant of the Heisenberg uncertainty principle, the idea that the more closely we can measure the position of a subatomic particle, the less precisely we can measure its momentum. Put another way, if we get very close to an object in order to describe it, we lose perspective on how it fits into the dynamics of its broader environment. We abandon that dynamic perspective to move in on a fixed perspective that maximizes our view of the object itself. Importantly, however, by doing this, we can also change the dynamics (e.g., the effect of the policy target on the economy). These measurement and conceptual difficulties with traditional economic forecasting and applied macroeconomics are probably behind the fact that investment strategy professionals tend to lean more toward the camp of economic forecasting that comes out of the empirical business-cycle approach to following the economy. Basically, the business-cycle approach has proved much more useful for investment strategy than theoretical models.

This distinction between the deductive theoretical approach to macroeconomics and the inductive business-cycle approach is illustrated by Greg Mankiw's review of Alan Greenspan's book *The Map and the Territory: Risk, Human Nature and the Future of Forecasting.* Rather than examining Greenspan's ideas, Mankiw focuses on the fact that the former Fed chairman is different from what passes as a traditional academic economist: "he is driven less by theory, more by data and practical experience."[1]

Greenspan's practical bent is a good way to describe how investment strategists use economics. Greenspan was a student of Arthur Burns and Geoffrey Moore, who both built on the work of Wesley Mitchell and Simon Kuznets, who guided the NBER in its first decades with a focus on measurement, empirical work, and business cycles. Over the years, in academia, the business-cycle focus of the NBER has largely been overshadowed by the sort of macroeconomics that deductive theoretical economists prefer. Milton Friedman was an interesting exception to this parallel universe of macroeconomists, achieving great success in both realms. His *Monetary History,* written with Anna Schwartz, was heavily influenced by the business-cycle approach to macroeconomics that he learned from Burns, who encouraged Friedman to look at monetary policy from a business-cycle perspective.

Because the business-cycle approach to macroeconomics has lost influence in the academic community, investment strategy is generally learned practically on the job by people from various backgrounds. As noted above, this book tries to help with that process. Ultimately, the business-cycle approach becomes a crucial element for applying economic forecasting to investment strategy.

---

[1] Greg Mankiw, "Things Didn't Go as Planned, Alan Greenspan's The Map and the Territory," The New York Times Sunday Book Review, November 14, 2013.

What does this mean in practice?

A flexible business-cycle-focused approach tends to characterize the way in which macro strategists forecast the economic outlook. It is not surprising that the Federal Reserve's policy-making committee, the Federal Open Market Committee (FOMC), also relies heavily on this approach, as can be seen by reading the minutes of their meetings. This means a lot of tea-leaf reading takes place, with different readers coming to different conclusions. Indeed, to go back to the signal and noise analogy, one forecaster's signal could be another's noise, causing the dispersion of analysts' outlooks to be wide and sometimes diametrically opposed.

In fact, some of the best investment opportunities arise when a strategist has confidence in a particular outlook when the market consensus is highly uncertain. Less often, and even more valuable, are cases in which the consensus is strong, but wrong. In this case, a strategist who sees why the consensus is wrong usually has the best opportunities to get into an undervalued asset class early.

A good example is the equity market in the winter of 2009. Early in the winter, the markets were in the depths of despair, with various credit indicators signaling defaults comparable to what had happened in the early 1930s. However, policymakers were clearly committed to preempting such an outcome and had begun implementing measures deliberately aimed at preventing a self-reinforcing down-spiral in aggregate demand such as that of the early 1930s.

Signs that this was going to work started to appear in various leading indicators. By March 2009, there was enough evidence to forecast that the recession would probably be over by the summer. In fact, it was. Stocks, which typically bottom well before a recession ends in anticipation of this dynamic, made their bottom in March, about four months before the recession ended.

A large number of useful quantitative indicators show what phase the economy is in within the business cycle. The most valuable opportunities for strategists are often at turning points, such as in March 2009, when the US equity market began one of the strongest bull runs ever, as both a cyclical and a secular bull market started. While that turning point was evident to some, most missed it. In fact, for the next few years, most Americans continued to believe the recession had not ended and many money managers acted as if that were the case. By the time that perception changed, the market had doubled. It's an old market adage that "they don't ring a bell at the top." Similarly with bottoms. There are, however, useful tea leaves that help.

The problem is that because "every business cycle is the same except for what's different," its starting point is somewhat different from the ones before. This means a flexible *weight-of-the-evidence* approach is often more helpful than *a rigid mix of indicators* rule. For example, while the stock market followed its typical leading indicator role in 2009, foreshadowing the end of the recession a few months later, this was not the case in 2002, when the recession had officially ended but equities continued to decline for a while longer as the fallout from the tech bubble's bursting weighed on the equity market even as the economy began to expand. As mentioned earlier, housing and consumption were less impacted than investment in that recession. It was "what was different" that helped explain why equities did not play their usual leading indicator role in that cycle's turnaround. Thus, to form a useful economic outlook for investment strategy requires a degree of flexibility within the framework of the typical business cycle as developed over the years by the NBER.

Another Wall Street adage claims that the most dangerous words for investors are "this time is different." However, these words can also be true and extremely valuable. The key is to know whether things are truly different or not. A useful paradigm in a world of macroeconomic regularities that vary from cycle to cycle is the gestalt approach to perceptual organization, combined with the notion that the economy is a self-organizing entity that reconfigures differently in each business cycle. As long as there is a business cycle, certain features of the macro economy recur in a way that is useful for forecasting. The mix and degree of these features vary across cycles, often for reasons that are key to understanding "what's different this time around."

No one sees this with perfect clarity as it's unfolding, however. Instead, the more astute observers are constructing a gestalt that slowly clarifies even as new events unfold to dissolve parts that seemed apparent for a while. To illustrate the process, think of the traditional picture used to represent gestalt theories of perception, an image that some perceive as an old crone, while others see a young woman (Exhibit 1.2). It's not one or the other, but rather, both, depending on the observer's bias.

To apply this analogy to the business cycle, let's associate the young woman's image with an expanding economy and the old woman's image with a recessionary economy. Now, the key point is that at any particular point in time there are trillions of data points about the

Exhibit 1.2 **What Do *You* See?** It is possible to see either a young woman or an old woman in this picture. Facial features like eyes, chins, and noses are recognizable depending on which woman you "see."

economy. Some are contracting and some are expanding. As more and more data become expansionary, we can better perceive the image of the young woman, while that of the crone fades. Then, as the expansion ages and more economic bits start to contract, the image of the young woman transitions to the aged crone. Still, at any point in time, some people mainly discern one image, while others see the alternative, depending on their perceptual organization of economic data.

In this analogy, turning points occur when the weight of the data tip the momentum from positive to negative, or vice versa. This way of looking at how data bits aggregate to macro concepts illustrates why perceptions about the same thing may vary and may even be diametrically opposed. It is also a paradigm that helps explain why the consensus of a bigger and bigger sample tends to home in on the correct image (i.e., the principle embodied in "the wisdom of crowds"). The analogy also suggests that as economic analytics for "big data" develop, economists might actually become better able to model the macro economy.

The other key aspect of this way of looking at the economy is the self-organizing principle. Underneath the macro picture at any point in time are trillions of bits of economic information. The dynamics of how they evolve depends on many influences. From an economic viewpoint, the most powerful drivers are *incentives*. These incentives drive the organizing of economic activity. Top-down coercion can force that organization, but historical evidence suggests that the long-term structural resilience of the US economy relative to other periodic contenders for its preeminent status probably arises from the more efficient resource allocation created by micro-incentive structures compared to top-down directives that almost by definition rule out efficiency in this framework.

Incentives change as the economy evolves, and the economy is constantly reorganizing in step with an ever-changing set of incentives. In this process, the business cycle creates a rhythm that is recognizable and therefore helpful for investors when properly applied. Weighing the evidence from business-cycle indicators is necessarily a combination of art (judgment) and science (based on observed repeatable patterns).

Viewed in this light, the business cycle reflects a macro pattern in the always-evolving sea of economic data. It shows that there is a recurring tendency to go overboard in one direction (recession) or the other (inflationary boom) as the dynamics continually unfold. Some of this tendency to go to extremes arises naturally in the private sector, while some of it is related to government policies, monetary and fiscal. Indeed, policies can work both to amplify and to dampen these cycles. Monetary policy is especially built into business cycles in a way we will elaborate throughout the book.

This cyclical dynamic suggests that individual responses to incentives tend to take on group characteristics that cause atomistic behavior to coalesce in collective directions. For example, as profits improve, firms eventually reach a tipping point at which more profits require more hiring and more capital spending to boost production. At the same time, new technologies are shifting the profit-maximizing capital and labor mix to stimulate new kinds of investment and incentives for new labor skill sets.

Likewise, age demographics, labor incentives, immigration, and wealth levels help determine who wants to work and how much. For example, one of the big misconceptions over the first few years of the recovery that began in mid-2009 that caused widespread misinterpretation of economic conditions and missed investment opportunities was a persistent association of declining labor force participation with a weak labor market and worker discouragement over finding jobs. Instead, a deep dive into the issue clearly showed a declining structural *trend* in labor force participation, mostly as a consequence of an aging population reaching retirement age.

The *downtrend* in the participation rate also reflects a changing set of incentives to work. For example, income benefits are substantially reduced if older recipients work too much and earn beyond a certain threshold. In the prime working-age population, participation is reduced because potential two-income households are penalized relative to one-income households by the tax code. The second income is penalized by a higher effective marginal rate because it generally means losing the earned income tax credit, incurring much higher child-care expenses, and various other costs of employment that the tax system additionally penalizes because of its progressivity. As a result, it has become relatively advantageous for median-income families to be one-income households. Finally, lower participation rates of young people reflect the social trends of extended childhood and education. In a wealthy society, more people can enjoy a longer, more carefree childhood without having to work. Waiting longer to work is a privilege that young people from rich countries have that is unimaginable in most of the poor parts of the world.

Just as important, the returns to higher education that defer labor force participation to an older age have increased dramatically relative to the returns to less education. Unemployment correlates strongly with education. On average, more education means less unemployment and a much higher lifetime income. This reflects the changing technology and skill set requirements in the modern workplace. It also is a natural result of increased globalization of the economy. The United States has a disproportionate share of the world's highly educated people. Their value is greatly enhanced by globalization, which on the other hand is driving rising inequality not just in the United States but throughout the developed world. In sharp contrast to the highly educated who benefit greatly from globalization, the less educated part of the US population has been thrown into a more intense labor market competition with a vast, similarly undereducated population around the world.

The point of this digression is that, looking over the past century, labor force participation has always varied according to the need to work and the incentives for work. While the demand for labor by business is quite cyclical, the supply of available labor depends on these structural considerations. When supply grows faster, demand does as well. A look at the relative performance of jobs growth over the post-World War II business cycles shows clearly that the growth of jobs ultimately depends on labor supply (Exhibit 1.3). This is a variant of Say's

Exhibit 1.3   Employment Gains Are Cyclical but Anchored by Labor Force Growth

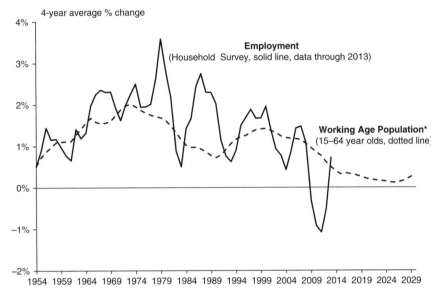

Source: BLS, *Bureau of the Census/Haver Analytics.
Data as of February 2014.

Law: In a well-functioning market economy, supply creates its own demand. While it's true that the profit motive drives business demand for labor over the business cycle, there is a positive feedback from the supply of labor side. More workers with more income feed back into more profits. Those who want and are able to work have historically found work in the United States, temporary cyclical difficulties notwithstanding. That's why all over the world, people are literally dying to come to the United States. This is easily understood by considering the *self-organizing-around-incentives* paradigm of the economy, which causes a natural waxing and waning of economic activity that creates the business cycle.

2
The Business Cycle

As Victor Zarnowitz observed in a 1991 NBER research paper,[1] "Business cycles have varied greatly over the past 200 years in length, spread, and size. At the same time, they are distinguished by their recurrence, persistence, and pervasiveness. They make up a class of varied, complex, and evolving phenomena of both history and economic dynamics. Theories or models that try to reduce them to a single causal mechanism or shock are unlikely to succeed."

Business-cycle analysis has proven to be a useful means for garnering insights that have practical relevance for the tactical asset-allocation process. For that simple reason, most strategists follow the economy and project an outlook based on a more inductive, data-driven approach rather than from the models that one finds in theoretical economic textbooks. It is also critical, however, to have a working understanding of the way policy, especially monetary policy, shapes the macroeconomic environment, and that is why in the next chapter we will focus on the macro policy environment's role in the business cycle.

Poorly conceived macro views, often influenced by political bias, are always competing with the best thinking that economists have developed over the years. Interestingly, that best thinking has largely developed out of historical experience rather than a priori theorizing. Ex-post reasoning applied to explain historical anomalies seems to account for the quantum leaps in macroeconomic understanding.

---

[1] *"What Is a Business Cycle?"* NBER Working Paper # 3863, October 1991. This is a comprehensive source of information on the history, international dimensions, and details of business-cycle analysis. Here we limit the analysis to a more applied look for investment-strategy purposes.

Fed Chairman Ben Bernanke's unorthodox response to the 2008–2009 financial crisis owed much to the largely empirical analysis done by economists like Milton Friedman, who focused on the lessons from the Great Depression of the 1930s. To be fair, the theoretical work of economists, like J.M. Keynes, also weighs heavily in the best thinking synthesis of how policy can preempt depressions. In a nutshell, the modern synthesis of appropriate economic policy boils down to avoiding deflation by keeping long-term inflation expectations stable at a slightly positive level.

A common mistake many money managers make is failing to appreciate the role that the business cycle plays in shaping relative returns across asset classes. The cacophony of viewpoints that one hears on any given day in the financial media is often striking in its lack of business-cycle context. Understanding where you are in the business cycle helps focus attention on the relative significance of the mix of data available on any given day. It also helps distinguish that significance for different categories of investments. Late in a cycle, attention necessarily turns to inflation. Signs of increasing price pressures are generally a necessary condition for tighter monetary policy, while early in the cycle inflation is less of an issue, so that the same monthly increase in the consumer price index (CPI) conveys a much different message, for example. For this reason, before we can apply the business cycle to investment strategy, we need to focus on the dynamics of the business cycle itself.

Business cycles have been around for over 200 years. As noted in the late professor Zarnowitz's statement quoted above, "they make up a class of varied, complex, and evolving phenomena of both history and economic dynamics." For example, as alluded to above, economic thought has evolved toward the modern policy response to economic fluctuations. The abolition of deflation has changed business cycles. The methodological approach cited in the previous chapter comparing the economy to a gestalt process of self-organization around changing incentives is more consistent with Zarnowitz's observations about the complexity and differences across business cycles, which are much harder to capture in a narrow, deterministic model of the sort that prevails in much economic theory.

Still, despite change and complexity, the notion of a business cycle implies some recurrence that shares important traits with prior occurrences. Exhibits 2.1 and 2.2 show the year-over-year growth rates of nominal and real (inflation-adjusted) GDP since 1900. In its simplest sense, the business cycle is the result of the fact that the economy does

Exhibit 2.1 US Business Cycle Much Milder since World War II

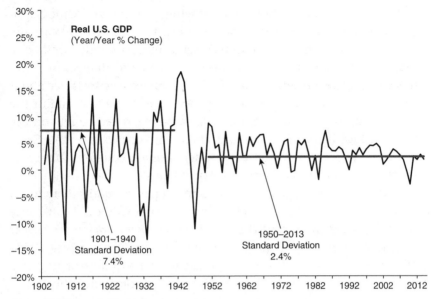

Source: BEA/Haver Analytics.
Data as of 3/27/2014.

Exhibit 2.2 US Business Cycle Much Milder since World War II

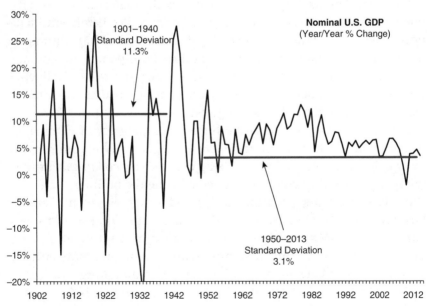

Source: BEA/Haver Analytics.
Data as of 3/27/2014.

not grow in a straight line. The ongoing evolution required by constantly changing incentives created by improving technology, demographics, and government policies means smooth trend growth is virtually impossible. The business cycle in its essence reflects the dynamics of a capitalist market economy that is always adjusting to change.

It is striking, nevertheless, that the historical experience since about 1950 is much less volatile than the experience in the first half of the twentieth century and before. Essentially, policy, based largely on the lessons deduced from Keynes' and Friedman's analyses of the Great Depression, has stopped the frequent deflationary collapses that characterized the US economy prior to World War II.

The absence of deflation in the modern era has dramatically reduced the amplitude of business cycles since 1950 (Exhibit 2.1). Because inflation has generally stayed positive, it has been rare to see a year of negative nominal GDP growth. In fact, the financial crisis of 2008–2009 and the associated recession was the first instance of negative nominal GDP growth since the 1940s and the worst since the 1930s, helping to explain the unprecedented and highly controversial policy response at the time.

The elimination of deflation has been a major factor behind the more muted business cycles of the past half century. As can be seen in Exhibit 2.2, the standard deviation of nominal GDP fluctuations, like real GDP fluctuations, is also about one-third of what prevailed before anti-deflation policy became the orthodoxy. While it is obvious that eliminating deflation curtails amplitudes in inflation cycles *if* policy also contains the upside moves in inflation, it is less obvious that real GDP fluctuations should be moderated by containing deflation unless the macro view that deflation risk hurts real growth in a persistent way is correct. This is the key message from the historical experience of eliminating deflation: both real and nominal GDP fluctuations have been substantially reduced by activist policy to stop deflationary collapses. Putting a safety net under the economy has helped tame the business cycle.

While eliminating deflation has played a key role in moderating business cycles, there are several additional factors that seem to have damped the amplitude of modern business cycles. Information technology has made real-time inventory management and more efficient supply chain management possible, largely eliminating one of the major sources of old-fashioned business cycles: much bigger under- and overshoots of inventory accumulation. Automatic stabilizers such as unemployment compensation help reduce the fluctuations in aggregate demand by helping to sustain consumption in periods of weakness. Countercyclical tax payments that are progressively based on income rise more as the economy accelerates and fall when the economy shrinks. Banking system collapses have been eliminated by deposit insurance. Monetary and fiscal policy have been more deliberately applied to governing the economy. Also, the structure of the modern economy is less cyclical as the goods-producing sector has shrunk relative to service-producing sectors. As we shall see, goods-producing, and especially durable-goods-producing industries tend to be much more cyclical than modern services industries, such as health care, education, and government. A bigger share of jobs in less cyclical industries helps smooth economic growth compared to an economy in which manufacturing jobs dominate. In sum, the structure of the postindustrial economy has combined with the much strengthened policy safety net to help moderate the modern business cycle.

Still, the business cycle lives. It has been tamed, not conquered. In fact, there is also a case to be made that the policy safety net has increased moral hazard in a way that allows reckless behavior to accumulate over cycles rather than purging it in each cycle as was the case in "the good old days" of more frequent recessions and depressions.

While there are lots of reasons business cycles vary over time, there are also features that they have in common over time. The gestalt self-organizing principle helps us understand the "sameness" dynamic. Essentially, a growing economy starts off with early adopters (new business models, new technology applications, for example) and restructured, more efficient operations in existing businesses buying into the notion that business conditions are turning up (usually helped by more stimulative interest rates as the Fed cuts short-term lending rates in recessions to help spur borrowing and economic growth) and progresses to the point where growth has created certain excesses that need to be corrected by a slowdown. A slowing economy feeds on itself until business conditions start to signal a sustainable level of activity has been reached.

Inertia in this dynamic seems to create overshoots and undershoots, with bandwagon effects bringing in too many optimists and pessimists in each phase. In addition, what seems a sustainable level of activity can be rendered unsustainable when conditions change. Clearly, if something cannot go on forever, it will stop.

In some cases, rather than over- or underproduction being exposed by changing economic conditions, it can also be a matter of changes in confidence or outlook, as in the housing boom in the early 2000s, when more and more people borrowed more and more money to leverage up in order to take advantage of home price gains that were increasingly perceived to be a sure thing. This relates back to the moral hazard comments about the downside risks from eliminating deflation risks from people's set of concerns. The absence of deflation over the prior half century was a major reason people, including many experts, felt that a nationwide decline in home prices was highly unlikely. After all, it had not happened since the 1930s, and most Americans had not experienced it.

Leverage is a one-way ticket to higher wealth if the leveraged asset only goes up in price. The housing collapse was a useful reminder that leverage works both ways. As confidence about the house price outlook waxed and waned, strong cyclical forces were unleashed in both directions. More generally, eliminating deflation risk biases economic rewards in favor of debtors at the expense of creditors, helping to explain why there was an unprecedented leveraging of household balance sheets through each successive business cycle from World War II until it peaked during the 2008–2009 financial crisis. The 2008–2009 crisis reminded people why their grandparents' generation had feared debt to the point of avoiding it irrationally.

The process of ebbs and flows in different macroeconomic variables through a business cycle tends to have certain common characteristics across cycles. Variables of interest for analyzing business cycles include employment, unemployment, household incomes, retail sales, spending on durable goods like automobiles, housing investment, industrial production, business orders, shipments, inventories, commercial construction, profits, revenues, consumer inflation, producer price inflation, wage inflation, productivity, unit labor costs, and GDP inflation, to name some of the main categories. In addition, financial variables, like interest rates, credit, and money supply are cyclical. We will discuss the business-cycle behavior of financial variables in the next chapter. Here we focus on the business-cycle patterns of some of the real variables as well as profits, labor costs, and inflation.

Business cycle indicators

There is no single measure that tracks a business cycle. The NBER is the official arbiter of the beginnings and endings of recessions. The period between the end of one recession and the beginning of the next one generally involves a recovery of output lost during the recession and an expansion beyond that level until the next recession begins. In addition to more moderate cycles since 1950, it is also a fact that expansions have been much longer and recessions much shorter on average in the modern era. The economy has spent a much larger proportion of time growing in the era of activist policy.

To track business cycles, in its early years the NBER developed a set of composite indicators that anticipate (leading indicators), date (coincident indicators), and follow (lagging indicators) the turning points from expansion to recession and recession to recovery. Because of the variability of cycles, no single indicator works as well as the composite indicators developed for timing cyclical turns. Over the years, the composite indicators have been refined to better serve their purpose.

In recent years, The Conference Board, "a global, independent business membership and research association,"[2] has assumed responsibility for publishing the Business Cycle Index data, which include three indexes: the Composite Index of Leading Indicators, the Composite Index of Coincident Indicators, and the Composite Index of Lagging Indicators.

The Composite Index of Coincident Indicators is made up of the main variables that help determine when recessions begin and end. There is a widespread public perception that a recession is defined by two sequential negative quarters of real GDP growth. This is a pretty good rule of thumb. However, in the United States, the Business Cycle Dating Committee of the NBER is the most widely accepted authority for dating recessions. The Committee relies heavily on the index of coincident indicators because the four components that it includes have been determined to best coincide with turning points in economic momentum. These four components are employees on non-farm payrolls, real personal income less transfer payments from the government, industrial production, and real manufacturing trade and sales. Basically, a recession involves a suitably prolonged decline in production, jobs, incomes, and spending. The Cycle Dating Committee has a bit of discretion in deciding the necessary duration and degree of decline, but generally speaking its decision will usually, but not always, coincide with the onset of at least two down quarters in real GDP, hence the attraction of that simpler definition.

The Composite Index of Leading Economic Indicators (LEI) is much maligned and often ignored by economists and strategists. Partly,

[2] www.conference-board.org.

that's because it is put together well after most of its ten components have already been released. Some call it the index of *mis*leading indicators. Paul Samuelson famously quipped that it had caused economists to predict *nine of the last five recessions*. Nevertheless, it does provide useful information about the economy's momentum. Unlike the coincident indicators, which largely tell us where the economy is, the LEI try to tell us where it will be a few months down the road, offering a useful, albeit relatively short, lead time. In fact, there are different classes of leading indicators that vary in their lead times—long leading and short leading. The financial market-related components of the LEI, especially credit conditions and the yield-curve spread (the difference between the ten-year Treasury note yield and the Federal funds rate), seem to have the longest lagged effects on the economy, while most real activity indicators, such as building permits, new orders, and unemployment claims, tend to have shorter lags.

Overall, there are ten indicators in the composite index of leading indicators published monthly by The Conference Board:

1. **Average weekly hours of manufacturing workers.** As noted above, manufacturing is more cyclical than the overall economy. Producers tend to trim or expand factory hours before laying off or adding workers, giving an early indication of changes in the direction of the economy.

2. **Average number of initial applications for unemployment compensation,** which gives an early read on rising or falling layoffs.

3. **Average consumer expectations for business conditions**, which combines results from surveys of consumer sentiment.

4. **Manufacturers' new orders, consumer goods and materials.** This is one of three orders-related indicators. Factory orders tend to rise and fall ahead of advances and declines in production (which is a key *coincident* indicator).

5. **Manufacturers' new orders, nondefense capital goods, excluding aircraft.** This indicator helps assess the outlook for business equipment investment.

6. **Institute of Supply Management (ISM) Index of New Orders.** Based on a survey of purchasing managers, this index reflects their views on whether orders are rising or falling.

7. **New building permits, private housing units.** This indicator gives an early read on residential investment, one of the most cyclical sectors of the economy.

8. **Stock prices, S&P500 index.** By anticipating changes in profit conditions, stock prices anticipate improving or deteriorating economic growth as business activity responds to the changing profits outlook.

9. **Leading Credit Index.** This indicator tracks credit conditions. Easing credit conditions generally fuel improving economic activity, while tightening conditions precede recessions. This component replaced the real M2 money supply, which seems to have lost its usefulness since 1990.

10. **Interest rate spread (yield curve spread), ten-year Treasury note yield minus Federal funds rate.** An inversion of this spread (lower ten-year yield than the Fed funds rate) has proved one of the most reliable precursors of recessions.

Leading indicators are especially important for investment strategy. The stock market itself is a leading indicator because it anticipates the twists and turns in all the different industries that make up the global economy. The mix of industries showing relative outperformance varies over the course of the business cycle, conveying information about where the economy is strengthening or weakening. Generally speaking, when weakening forces are getting the upper hand ahead of a recession, broad equity price indices usually decline from their cyclical peaks several months before the coincident indicators roll over and signal that a recession has begun. Lagging indicators are useful for gauging the contours of a business cycle and provide confirmation that business cycle dynamics are playing out. Also, when lagging indicators are showing more strength than coincident indicators, it is often a sign that the economy is losing momentum. That is why the ratio of the composite coincident indicators to the composite of lagging indicators is considered a leading indicator of economic momentum. If momentum is picking up, the index of coincident indicators rises relative to the index of lagging indicators.

The index of lagging indicators is composed of the following:

1. **Commercial and industrial loan volume:** as a business cycle progresses, businesses go from largely self-funding to relying more on bank credit, often becoming overextended as the expansion ages.

2. **Ratio of consumer installment credit to personal income:** as consumers feel more secure in their jobs and income, they tend to use credit more and, like businesses, can become overextended as the expansion ages.

3. **Average duration of unemployment (inverted):** as the labor market strengthens, it's easier to find a job and the duration of unemployment declines.

4. **Ratio of manufacturing and trade inventories to sales:** businesses tend to build inventories relative to current sales as they anticipate stronger future sales.

5. **Unit labor costs, manufacturing:** as the cycle progresses, labor costs begin to rise relative to productivity, a sign of a tightening labor market, which eventually tends to restrain profits growth and the expansion itself. Labor costs are a major determinant of profit margins.

6. **Average prime rate charged by banks:** as the economy strengthens, credit demand pushes interest rates higher.

7. **Change in the CPI for services:** compared to commodity prices, prices of services tend to respond to rising demand conditions with a much greater lag. This makes overall inflation a *long lagging* indicator.

These lagging indicators are less sensitive to the initial pickup in business conditions compared to leading indicators or coincident indicators. When a recession starts, they tend to keep rising for a while after the others have already rolled over. Exhibits 2.3 to 2.5 show examples of variables with coincident, leading, and lagging qualities, respectively. Industrial production, a coincident indicator, usually reaches its peak right as a recession (shaded areas) begins (Exhibit 2.3). Employment, another coincident measure of aggregate economic activity also tends to peak when recessions begin. For this reason, it is often the case that people feel best just when an expansion is ending. Conversely, they tend to feel the worst when a recession is ending because economic activity, measured by coincident indicators like industrial production and employment, for example, tends to be at its cyclical low point just as a recovery begins. This helps explain why crowd sentiment about the economy and the stock market tends to be a useful contrarian indicator at major cyclical turning points. In March 2009, for example, just as stocks were about to begin a major cyclical bull market, consumers were extremely bearish on the year-ahead outlook for equities. The signals from leading indicators (especially taking account of the lagged effects of the aggressive monetary policy stimulus and positive government measures to stabilize banking conditions) were positive, however, providing a great entry point for those investors focused on

Exhibit 2.3   Industrial Production Declines with Recessions

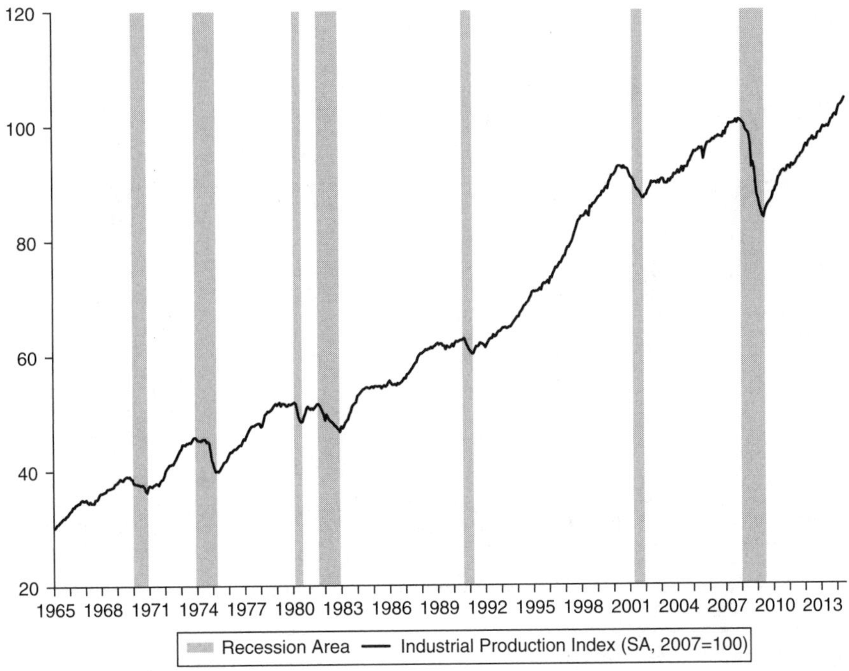

Legend: Recession Area — Industrial Production Index (SA, 2007=100)

Source: Federal Reserve Board/Haver Analytics.
Data as of August 2014.

future prospects rather than the dire readings from coincident eco-nomic indicators.

As shown in Exhibit 2.4, the yield spread is a good leading indicator of recessions. As noted above, when the yield curve inverts, the over-night federal funds rate is higher than the ten-year Treasury note yield, a situation that reflects tight monetary policy relative to economic con-ditions. For example, in the summer of 2007, the yield curve inverted after the Federal Reserve had raised rates from 1 percent to 5.25 percent over the prior few years. Despite lots of rationalization for why mon-etary policy was still easy, or at least not tight, the yield curve suggested otherwise, and six months later the economy was in recession.

Finally, Exhibit 2.5 shows the average duration of unemployment, a lagging indicator that often keeps rising after a recession has ended and a recovery has begun. Businesses tend to expand hours for existing employees before hiring new workers, so the average workweek is a *lead-ing* indicator. As businesses expand hours worked first, the growth in the

Exhibit 2.4   Inverted Yield Curve Leads Recessions

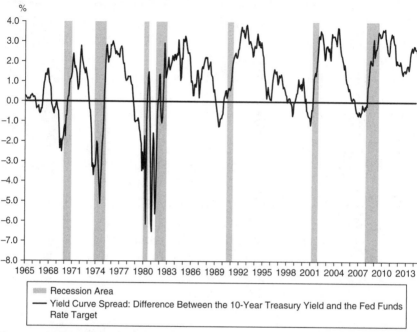

Recession Area

—— Yield Curve Spread: Difference Between the 10-Year Treasury Yield and the Fed Funds Rate Target

Source: Federal Reserve Board/Haver Analytics.

Data as of August 2014.

labor force often pushes the unemployment rate higher after a recovery has started. This was especially true in the 1970s and 1980s when the US labor force was growing rapidly. As the existing workforce resumes a normal workweek, businesses begin to hire to expand output, and the unemployment rate begins to fall. The average duration of unemployment continues to increase until employment grows enough to start absorbing the pool of unemployed workers that accumulated over the recession. As the labor market strengthens, it becomes easier to find a job, and the duration of unemployment declines. The average duration of unemployment peaked at about 40 weeks in 2011, more than a year *after* the recession ended in June 2009. The unemployment rate peaked at 10 percent in October 2009, just four months *after* the recession ended, and was down to 6.1 percent by September 2014. Waiting for the unemployment rate or other similarly intuitive but generally *lagging* indicators to start improving to position investment portfolios for a recovery can miss a large part of early-cycle risk-asset outperformance. Leading indicators are more useful from that vantage point.

Exhibit 2.5 Average Unemployment Duration Peaks *after* Recessions

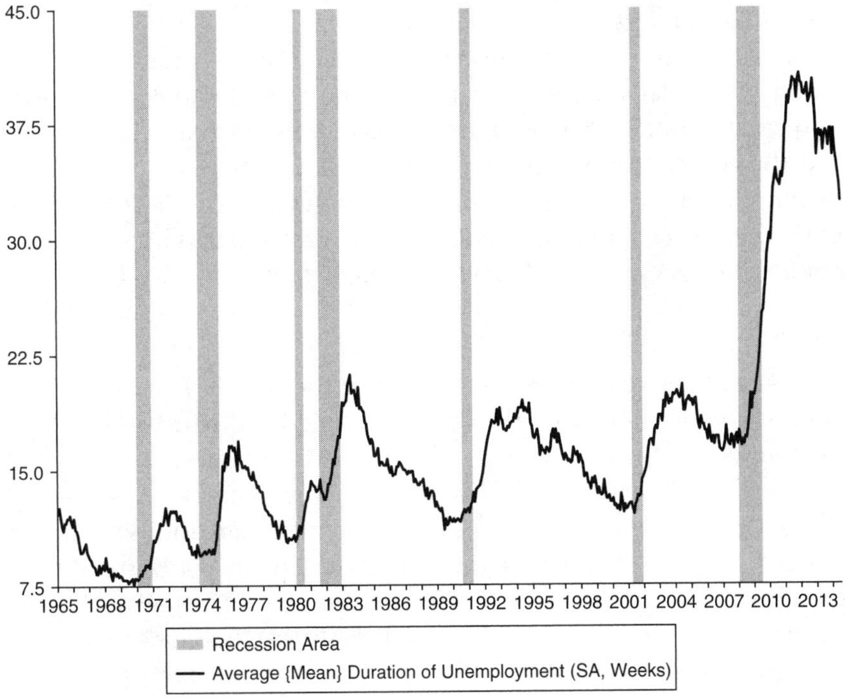

Source: Bureau of Labor Statistics/Haver Analytics.
Data as of August 2014.

Cycles within cycles

The components of the LEI provide insight into the drivers of the business cycle. Several reflect trends in orders, both for business equipment and consumer goods. This highlights the role that business spending on capital equipment and consumer spending on durable goods, such as automobiles, play in driving the cyclical fluctuations in the economy.

The housing cycle is another important force shaping the business cycle, and that's reflected in the fact that building permits are a component of the LEI. Finally, the labor market cycle is perhaps the most comprehensive cycle, as it reflects conditions in all the parts of the economy. That's why unemployment claims and the average workweek have proved to be good leading indicators of the business cycle.

These "real economy" cycles interact with financial cycles. Stock prices, credit conditions, and the shape of the yield curve are key financial variables in the composite of leading indicators. Because the cycle in financial variables is so wrapped up in the monetary policy cycle, we reserve the next chapter entirely for a discussion of monetary policy and its role in the business cycle.

Indeed, the more moderate business cycles of the post–World War II period have largely been governed by the necessity to contain inflation and avoid deflation, making monetary policy both the cause of and the governor of the business cycle in a way that was not so well defined in the more laissez-faire, pre-Keynesian era. Understanding the role played by monetary policy will be easier following some elaboration on the cycles in the real economy.

Business investment

Businesses have to constantly prepare for the future. Their orders for big-ticket equipment and investment in long-lived structures depend on confidence that economic conditions will require the services of any new equipment. By not investing enough, they face the risk of not having enough productive capacity to meet demand, thus losing business. On the other hand, too much investment is a waste of capital if it ends up as idle capacity. Over the course of the business cycle, confidence about the need for new investment fluctuates with the strength of the economy.

Coming out of a recession, there is a lot of excess capacity and relatively little demand for new equipment. During a recession, companies are in more of a survival mode, preserving cash flow to meet obligations by minimizing expenses, especially investment spending on big-ticket items. One reason recessions end is this caution about spending starts to appear excessive relative to the business opportunities still available or becoming apparent.

As overly cautious behavior is exposed, businesses, now leaner, probably reorganized and more efficient, realize the need to stop running down inventories, laying off workers, and cutting back investment spending. Replacement demand for aging equipment and consumer durable goods, as well as the introduction of new technologies all play a role in this process, as do more attractive interest rates compared to those at the peak of the business cycle. Slowly, the ship gets righted, and the dynamic shifts back to the expansionary side. Naturally, there is a self-reinforcing dynamic here, as a rising tide starts to lift all boats.

Helping to monitor the business investment situation and the strength of the economy is a report that shows manufacturing shipments, new orders, inventories, and the backlog of unfilled orders for capital goods every month. Data on shipments of nondefense capital goods, excluding aircraft, from this report are a key input for the calculation of the business equipment investment component of GDP.

Over the cycle, the relationships between new orders, shipments, and inventories fluctuate according to whether investment momentum is rising or falling. For example, going into a recession, new orders (a leading indicator) will slow first, while shipments (a coincident indicator) will maintain their pace for a while longer. As this mismatch grows, the backlog of unfilled orders begins to shrink. With waning demand, shipments start to decline, and inventories start to back up. Firms scramble to reduce inventories by cutting back on production. Eventually, inventories get too low, orders start to revive, and the process reverses.

Real-time inventory control has reduced the cyclical role of inventories and damped the amplitude of business cycles. Inventory excesses were a bigger force driving the business cycle before sophisticated information-processing and logistics technology existed. Nevertheless, inventory accumulation in the capital goods sector remains much more volatile (cyclical) than the overall economy (GDP).

One result of better inventory management is shorter inventory cycles within business cycles as excesses or shortages of inventories are flagged more quickly and redressed faster. A more muted cycle of inventory liquidation, within the overall expansion that began in 2009, occurred between 2011 and 2013. Global growth slowed over the course of 2011–2012 and capital-goods inventories were worked down. This loss of momentum bottomed in late-2012 and early 2013. Over the course of 2013, new orders growth outstripped shipments by a substantial margin, causing the backlog of unfilled orders to grow at an accelerating pace (Exhibit 2.6) and sparking an inventory turnaround as global economic momentum rose through 2013. By correcting inventory excesses before they become extreme, real-time information-processing technology has helped lengthen expansions and shorten recessions.

While useful, the monthly capital goods orders data are very noisy, perhaps the noisiest of the regular economic data, causing especially misleading interpretations of the trend in business equipment spending by economists who project too much significance on the big upward and downward movements around the underlying cyclical trend. Extracting the signal in the behavior of the inventories, orders, and shipments data requires smoothing out the noise. In especially noisy data like the orders statistics, looking at the past few months' changes can be highly misleading. Averaging the latest three months' data and comparing it to

Exhibit 2.6 Rising Backlog of Unfilled Orders Signaled Growing Economic Momentum in 2013

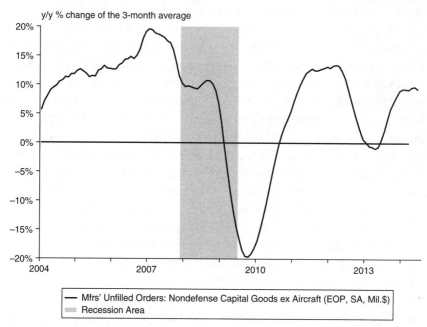

Source: Census Bureau/Haver Analytics.
Data as of August 2014.

the 3-month average 12 months earlier helps separate the trend (signal) from the meaningless noise that receives most of the sound-bite attention in the financial media. In general, the noisier the data series, the more it helps to smooth it with a longer-frequency procedure like this.

Longer-term investment in structures tends to lag behind other cyclical sectors like business equipment and housing over the course of the business cycle. Research by Alan Greenspan since the 2008–2009 financial crisis attributes most of the shortfall in the cyclical recovery after the crisis to the weakness in investment in long-lived assets like structures. One explanation for this reduced willingness to commit capital for long periods is low business confidence because of the long-term uncertainty around the sustainability of US government finances as entitlements are projected to grow much faster than revenues and political stalemate has prevented a solution. Another possible explanation for shortened investment horizons is the accelerated pace of technological change, which makes the economic future ever murkier. More rapid "creative destruction" makes a 20-year investment harder to evaluate. Finally, there is an ongoing transformation of the US economy from tangible, physical output and capital stock to intangible, knowledge-based output and capital. This transformation is evident in the growing role of intellectual capital that's now explicitly measured along with business equipment in the overall investment schema of GDP accounts. Rapid advances in information technology are transforming developed-world GDP from tangible to intangible output at an accelerating rate. It is not unusual to hear some analysts distinguish physical output as somehow superior to intangible output. In fact, since knowledge-based output accounts for most of the growth in the postindustrial stage of development, this bias is often the basis for critique of the modern economy's performance. However, this view ignores the fact that invisible output is valued according to its worth in the market, just like physical output. Otherwise, Bill Gates would not be one of the world's richest people.

Consumer durables

Spending on big-ticket items tends to be the first to stop when times are tough. That's true not only for business equipment spending but also for consumer spending on autos and houses. Day-to-day expenses tend to be a top priority. A willingness to loosen the purse strings and spring for a new car, boat, or appliance is much greater when the economy is humming.

Volatility in household durables spending is consequentially much greater than spending on everyday necessities. That's why consumer staple stocks are considered defensive plays for bad times, while consumer discretionary companies thrive in better economic environments. The financial crisis of 2008–2009 was particularly tough on consumer purchases of motor vehicles, which fell by about half from their average level of the 1995–2007 period as the financial markets seized up. The auto market was hit hard because auto loans were heavily securitized and the loss of confidence in asset-backed securities froze financing until the government created special programs to unfreeze lending to the sector. The Federal Reserve in conjunction with the Treasury introduced the Term Asset-Backed Securities Loan Facility (TALF) to support the securitization of loans to consumers and businesses. The program was announced in November 2008 and began lending in March 2009, three months before the recession ended. After that, auto sales grew steadily and consumer durable goods purchases showed their usual cyclical leadership in a recovery.

Housing

Consumer purchases of housing and automobiles became increasingly joined at the hip, with both sectors gaining steam from 1995, hardly flinching in the 2001 recession, and finally blowing up after the 2007 recession hit. As the secular decline in interest rates progressed, housing refinance and home equity loans allowed consumers to "cash out" some of their growing home equity and buy cars with the proceeds. By 2008, tapping the inflation in the home prices "piggy bank" came to an abrupt end. From 1995 to 2007 it was a growing trend.

The long uptrend in housing and motor vehicle purchases, with only a minor speed bump in 2001, illustrates the way business cycles differ. The 2001 recession was largely a correction of excessive business investment in technology in the run up to Y2K. Excessive valuations of technology stocks marked the end of the 1982–2000 secular bull market in equities. Housing and consumer spending barely flinched after the technology bubble burst, however, and went on to accumulate excesses that came home to roost in the recession that began in late 2007. In fact, housing activity had already been slowing for over a year before the recession began. Initially, in the first half of 2008, the recession seemed mild and contained. The rest of the global economy was doing well, causing oil and other commodity prices to surge and raising worries about inflation. The dollar was weak in foreign exchange markets. By the second half of 2008, when the US financial system threatened to implode after the collapse of Lehman Brothers, the whole world was in recession as the consequent freeze in finance caused the worst collapse in global trade since the 1930s.

Housing finance, which had dominated the credit creation process, had begun to unravel. Mortgage securities began to blow up in the first half of 2008, causing Bear Stearns to fail. The rescue of its credit obligations by its acquirer, J. P. Morgan, had the unfortunate side effect of making investors complacent about the debt obligations of other systemically important financial institutions. This created significant moral hazard as investors continued to ignore traditional credit valuation criteria on the presumption that the government would keep bailing out creditors.

As the contagion spread, policymakers decided that they could not stop the credit obligations of Lehman Brothers from failing in September 2008, which set off events that almost turned into a 1930s bankrun scenario. Fortunately, an aggressive government response pulled the economy back from that brink. While we will discuss this episode in more depth in chapter 8, this digression illustrates the dominant role played by housing and housing finance in the 2002–2009 business cycle. It also illustrates the point that *"what's different"* about a particular business cycle is often a function of where excessive financing has been applied. In this case, it was residential real estate. In the earlier 1992–2001 cycle, rather than excessive credit creation, it was excessive equity valuations that funded an investment boom. While the excessive equity valuations did set the stage for a secular bear market, the recession that followed the technology bust was relatively mild and short lived, unlike the 2007–2009 recession. The recovery that started in late 2001 was not preceded by a rising stock market. This is a rare instance in which the stock market failed as a leading indicator. This seems to reflect the unusually big role that equity overvaluation played in the late-1990s boom. Big corporate bankruptcies, including those of Enron and WorldCom, did not occur until 2002, just after the recession had "officially" ended. There were a lot of excesses still concentrated in the equity market well after the recovery began in November 2001. As noted above, consumer spending and housing investment were barely affected following the bursting of the tech bubble. The difference between these two cycles also illustrates the point that cycles funded more by equity valuation excesses are generally less damaging than those fueled by excessive debt growth. We will discuss this difference in more detail in chapter 8.

Additionally, we would note that the early 1990s recession marked the culmination of real-estate and junk bond-related debt problems that heavily damaged the savings and loan industry. *Each business cycle tends to be characterized by a unique mix of financial excesses.* Still, since housing has been the overwhelming source of finance for US consumers over the past 65 years, it has played an important role in most US business cycles during this time. The 2001 recession was an exception.

Homebuilding is a relatively small part of each quarter's GDP. Even residential investment, which includes the actual building of new homes, renovations of existing homes, and the real estate commissions generated by housing transactions, tends to fluctuate between just 2 percent and 6 percent of GDP. Despite their small shares of GDP, cyclical sectors such as housing can be the "tail that wags the dog" in a business cycle because their higher volatility can be combined with excessive leverage to generate disproportionate cyclical fluctuations around an economy's long-term trend.

Aside from the direct effect of volatility in the housing sector itself, there are indirect effects that impact other sectors. We already referred to the role housing wealth played in funding purchases of motor vehicles during the 1995–2007 period. Obviously, a new house needs to be furnished, creating a whole host of spillover effects throughout the retail sector. New housing developments need schools, local government, and businesses. Collateral fallout from the housing bust of 2008–2009 included a noticeable impact on small-business formation in the subsequent recovery. It turned out many entrepreneurs had been relying on home mortgage and other real estate financing as a source of funding for their businesses. When this source dried up, alternatives were slow to develop, especially as property values sank and credit evaluation for loans returned to more historically normal standards following the unusually easy standards during the prior cycle. In essence, real estate wealth made people creditworthy. When that wealth shrunk, so did their creditworthiness.

Building permits to start new residential structures are one component of the index of leading indicators. When new permits are high relative to actual starts, it's a sign that building activity will be picking

Exhibit 2.7   Big Variation in Housing Cycles but Permits Start Falling ahead of Recessions

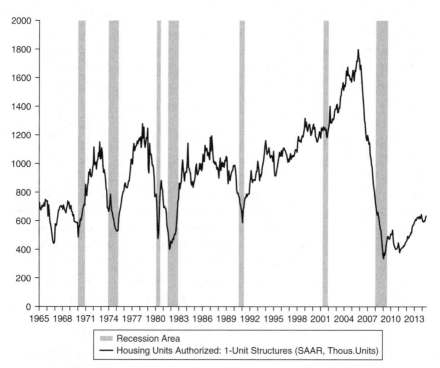

Source: Census Bureau/Haver Analytics.

Data as of August 2014.

Exhibit 2.8   Residential Investment Averages Just Around 5 percent of GDP but Is Very Cyclical

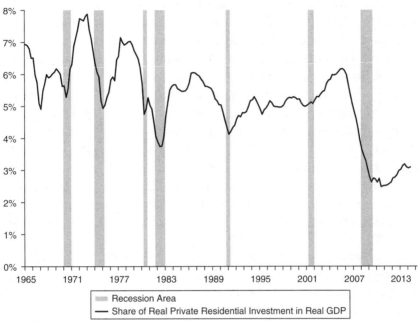

Source: Bureau of Economic Analysis/Haver Analytics.

Data as of Q2 2014.

up. It is the actual building that counts in GDP, so permits are a portent of a pickup in GDP. Exhibit 2.7 illustrates the cyclical behavior of building permits. Notice that the massive decline in permits began well in advance of the 2007–2009 recession, whereas in other instances permits showed a much smaller decline and generally shorter lead time before recessions (late 1980s are an exception). This is another example of the "variable" nature of business cycles. Exhibit 2.8 shows the share of residential investment in GDP. Note how high it got in 2006 relative to its historical average and how low it remained during the recovery out of the 2007–2009 recession. This illustrates the role excesses play in creating "booms" and "busts."

Employment

Business investment, consumer durables purchases, and housing are examples of especially cyclical parts of the economy. Aggregate employment is cyclical partly because it includes jobs in cyclical sectors and partly because aggregate activity moves up and down with the business cycle. Negative spillover effects from highly cyclical sectors can cause the overall economy to stop growing. These spillover effects vary from cycle to cycle. Housing spillover effects were greater during the 2007–2009 recession because of all the financial activity and related jobs and spending that the housing boom created. Tech stock spillover effects were unusually significant in the early days of the first Internet boom at the turn of the century.

Certain jobs are much less cyclical than others. In the 1930s Great Depression, teachers and government workers were widely regarded as fortunate beneficiaries of stable employment. In recent years, however, pressures on public finances have challenged this historic advantage and even caused fiscal policy more generally to become a destabilizing, procyclical force.

As a mix of cyclical and less cyclical jobs, overall employment is one of the best trackers of whether GDP is growing or not. That's why it is one of the four components in the index of *coincident* indicators. These four components are available on a monthly basis, making it possible to date recessions in the month they start and end. GDP is a quarterly measure, making a monthly dating scheme based on it impossible. Some analysts use monthly data to track a surrogate monthly GDP series. For example, the Chicago Federal Reserve Bank puts together a monthly national activity index (CFNAI) comprised of 85 economic indicators from four broad categories of data. The data are weighted in an index and normalized to show whether economic growth is above or below trend, and by how much (in standard deviations). The CFNAI is constructed as a coincident indicator of aggregate economic activity. When its three-month moving average falls below -0.7 standard deviations, the economy is usually in a recession. Employment-related indicators are one of the four broad categories of variables that make up this measure.

As mentioned in chapter 1, over long periods of time job growth seems to depend mainly on how many people are available to work, that is, the growth of the labor force. That's because the trend growth rate of the economy is determined by the labor-supply growth rate and the growth in its productivity. Interestingly, low labor-force growth seems to put pressure for stronger productivity growth. This seems to have been the case in the 1950s, when the low-birth cohort from the Great Depression came of age to work. Despite a slow-growing workforce, productivity was higher, and the economy grew at a respectable rate. Conversely, when the huge babyboom generation was coming of age in the 1970s, productivity growth dropped significantly, suggesting cheaper, abundant labor was substituted for relatively more dear capital.

More recently, forecasters have been surprised by the impact of retiring baby boomers on labor force participation rates. Indeed, there was a lot of confusion about the state of the economy in the first few years of the recovery from the 2008–2009 financial crisis, with many commentators attributing falling participation rates to discouraged workers dropping out of the labor force because of a weak economy. Deeper analysis made clear that the overwhelming reason was baby boomers' retirement.

Without a major liberalization of immigration, which has been a traditional source of strong US labor supply growth, demographic trends imply that the US labor supply will grow at a slower pace in the next few decades. While most observers assume that this implies a slower trend growth rate for GDP, the experience of the 1950s, along with current evidence of rising profit margins, suggests that increased capital intensity will help make up for at least some of the shortfall in labor supply growth. In fact, accelerating technological progress makes this alternative view even more likely. In essence, technology, artificial intelligence, and robotics are substituting for labor supply growth, keeping potential GDP growth healthier than basic demographics alone would suggest.

In any case, growth in employment can be viewed as the normal course in a capitalist economy, in which the labor force is absorbed until sufficient imbalances accumulate and eventually interrupt the process, causing a recession to correct excesses. Job losses during recessions are generally commensurate with the excesses that create the recession.

During the last 50 years, jobs have risen in about 80 percent of the months and declined in roughly 20 percent of the months. Better policy to sustain growth deserves a lot of the credit. These numbers were much less impressive in the "good old days." Even worse, the safety net to help unemployed workers barely existed in those days, making unemployment a much tougher experience than we can imagine in today's world.

Still, an upswing in the business cycle tends to build on itself, partly because a growing labor force that is finding jobs creates new incomes that increase demand for new goods and services, sparking a virtuous circle of rising jobs and incomes. This is the dynamic behind Say's Law, which as noted earlier, refers to the notion that supply creates its own demand. This dynamic works as long as the economy expands. Keynes' contribution was to highlight the need to support demand when confidence is low and this dynamic starts working in reverse. Say's Law seems to be asymmetric, working in good times and breaking down in bad (deflationary) times.

Useful measures of the cycle clock

Consumer sentiment

A multitude of indicators can help gauge where the economy is in any particular economic cycle. While any one indicator may vary in its pattern across different cycles from recovery through recession, a group of the indicators taken together can provide a rough, but accurate, idea of whether it is early or late in the cycle.

Within a business cycle, there are interrelated cycles in consumer sentiment, monetary policy, credit conditions, and inflation. Turning first to consumer sentiment, in the early stage of expansion right after a recession, business conditions are generally the worst of the cycle. For example, at the end of a recession just as a recovery is beginning, the unemployment rate is usually close to its cycle high point. On the other hand, there are usually some glimmers of hope that the worst is over as is reflected in the index of leading indicators, which is usually rising at this point in time, raising the possibility that the turn is underway. This mix of weak current conditions but an improving future outlook is captured in consumer surveys that ask opinions about the present conditions in the economy and expectations for the future.

Exhibit 2.9 shows the difference between an index of consumer expectations for the future and the assessment of present conditions from the monthly Conference Board survey of households. Notice that the gap reaches its cycle high point right after recession, in the early stage of an expansion. That is, expectations for the future are highest relative to current conditions when current conditions are coming off a bottom and the outlook is that things can only get better (and leading indicators are suggesting such is the case).

Conversely, right before a recession, when current conditions are the best, consumers recognize that the economy does not have as much room to improve in the coming months and the gap tends to be most negative (future expectations are below current conditions measures). *This is a good indication that things are as good as they get.* Notice that the historical extreme of this "as good as it gets" sentiment occurred in 2000 at the peak of the "dot.com" bubble and equity market "irrational exuberance." While consumers are generally overly optimistic

Exhibit 2.9 Expectations Tend to Lag Current Conditions Going into Recession

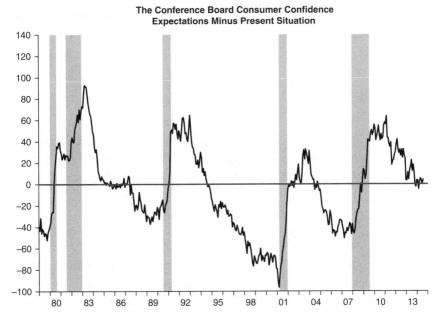

The Conference Board Consumer Confidence
Expectations Minus Present Situation

Source: The Conference Board/Haver Analytics.
Data as of August 2014.

going into recessions, this measure shows that they do recognize the economy is unlikely to get much better relatively. At this stage, they would be content if things stayed the same. Unfortunately, "staying the same" means not growing, which is what happens in a recession.

As can be seen, a balance between current conditions and future expectations (when the difference is zero in Exhibit 2.9) tends to occur one-third to halfway into a business expansion. From this vantage point, the economy was one-third to halfway through its expansion in March 2014. In baseball parlance, that's the third or fourth inning. Eventually, in the later innings expectations for the future begin to lag behind current conditions as they heat up.

Since World War II, expansions have been longer and recessions shorter, less extreme, and much less frequent than before World War II. Long expansions, like those of the 1980s and 1990s, set records for longevity, lasting about a decade in each case. Those cycles were also underpinned by the strongest secular bull market in equities in US history.

In our opinion, the economic expansion and equity bull market that began in 2009 marks the beginning of a new secular bull market in equities after the secular bear market from 2000 to 2009 that corrected the excessive valuations of the "dot.com" bubble that marked the end of the 1980s–1990s secular bull. This pattern suggests cyclical bull and bear markets in the context of a longer-term secular bull market through at least two business cycles going forward.

Monetary policy and inflation

One reason business cycles have been longer and recessions less frequent since World War II is proactive monetary policy. Over the course of the business cycle, monetary policy goes through a cycle from maximally accommodative to maximally restrictive. Generally, monetary policy is most stimulative in the first phase of expansion, when inflation is low and unemployment high. This is reflected in a very steep yield curve that embodies cycle lows in short-term money market rates along with higher rates in longer-maturity bonds that recognize that these short rates are temporary until the economy absorbs more of the slack in labor markets and production capacity.

Over the course of an expansion, the yield curve flattens, as the Federal Reserve raises short-term rates more than long-term rates rise, until at the extreme of maximum monetary restrictiveness the yield curve inverts and eventually precipitates a recession. This extreme in monetary policy restrictiveness occurs when inflation has become a problem and there is much less slack in the labor markets. As the recession worsens and the inflation rate falls, monetary policy usually moves rapidly to cut short-term rates, and the cycle begins anew.

Judged in this context, monetary policy in March 2014 remained in the early innings. That cycle saw a significant risk of deflation, and interest rate policy ran into the zero-rate lower bound. This prompted several rounds of quantitative easing to add additional monetary stimulus that helped bring down long-term rates. The Fed removed that quantitative stimulus by "tapering" its asset purchases. From this vantage point, maximum monetary stimulus ended in the spring of 2013, when then-Chairman Bernanke announced that the Fed would need to start paring its asset purchases by the end of that year. Ten-year Treasury note yields promptly rose 100 basis points, signaling the end of maximum monetary accommodation.

Taking account of the zero-bound and quantitative easing, which were new in that cycle, it seems best to consider that the Fed was about a year into its rate-normalization process in March 2014. This would also argue for the recovery to have been about in its third inning at most at that point.

This view is also confirmed if we look at Fed policy in relation to wage pressures, which fall and rise with the slack in the labor market. Ultimately, it is wage pressure that drives the cyclical fluctuations in inflation. Without higher wages, workers can't afford higher prices. To be more accurate, only wage gains above productivity growth generate inflation.

Exhibit 2.10 shows the relationship between the Fed's policy rate and wage growth. Compared to the prior two cycles, the Fed lagged behind wage acceleration by not raising its policy rate. In 1994 and 2004, it began to hike rates as wage growth picked up from its cycle bottom. This time around, *it began the tapering process* as wage growth accelerated. This was a precondition for the rate hikes that were expected to begin in 2015 after the tapering process had been completed.

In 1994, there were six years of expansion after the Fed began raising rates. In 2004, there were four years of expansion until the next recession after the Fed started raising rates. All in all, from an inflation vantage point, wages had accelerated normally for the stage of the cycle by 2014, suggesting that there was not as much slack in the labor market as Fed Chair Janet Yellen thought. Assuming that was the case, the Fed would

Exhibit 2.10 Inflation Pressures Pick Up with Wages. Tapering Substitutes for Initial Rate Hikes

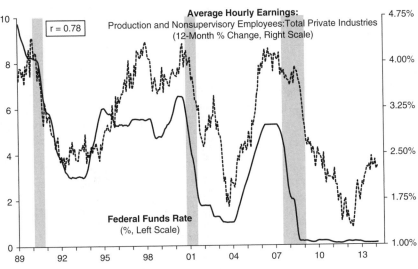

Source: BLS, Federal Reserve Board/Haver Analytics.

Data as of August 2014.

hit its 2-percent inflation target sometime during 2016. At that point, monetary policy would be about half way through the inflation cycle as the gradual transition from accommodation to restriction progressed.

Capacity utilization

Aside from labor market slack, there is slack in industrial capacity that varies over the business cycle. As can be seen in Exhibit 2.11, the capacity utilization rate in manufacturing tends to bottom at the end recessions with maximum slack available for growth. As industrial production (a coincident indicator) picks up, the slack in capacity utilization diminishes, and it tends to peak before, or at the beginning of recessions. Over the long haul, 80 percent has been considered a rough threshold for full capacity in manufacturing, although a secular decline in that figure is apparent in the exhibit.

Given the renaissance that we believe is underway in US manufacturing, we expect the secular decline through recent cycles in capacity utilization to reverse in coming cycles. The stalling of utilization in 2011 coincided with the global slowdown in trade precipitated by

Exhibit 2.11   Expansions End with High-Capacity Utilization

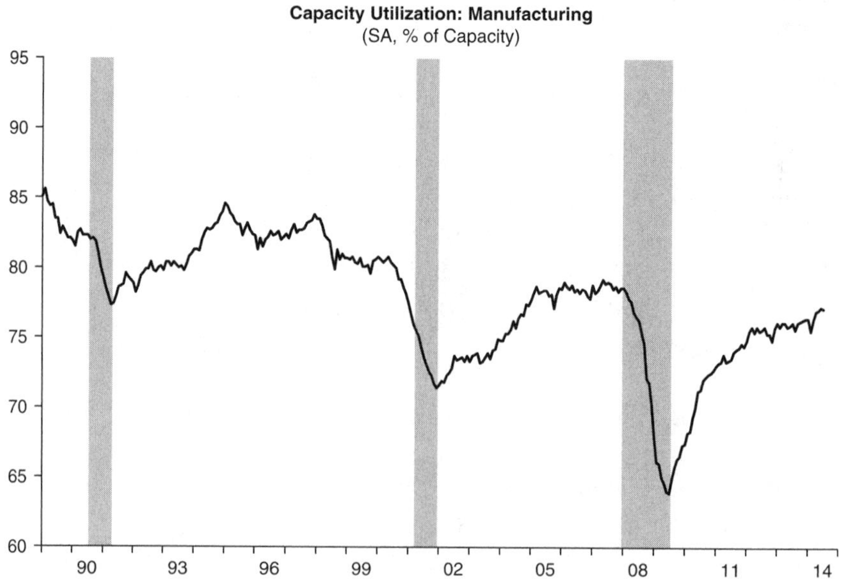

Capacity Utilization: Manufacturing
(SA, % of Capacity)

Source: Federal Reserve Board/Haver Analytics.
Data as of August 2014.

Europe's double-dip into recession. As global growth improved, capacity utilization rose and closed some of the gap left by the slowdown. Manufacturing is especially tied into global trade, and its pickup tends to have an outsized effect on US factory activity.

From a "cycle clock" vantage point, capacity utilization was not particularly high in mid-2014 from a historical perspective, and there seemed to be several years of growth possible before capacity constraints in manufacturing would pose a barrier to the expansion. Automation of increasing segments of manufacturing activity suggests bottlenecks are more likely to rise from materials costs rather than processing constraints. Automation limits the impact of higher wage costs in manufacturing as factories experience the loss of jobs that farms experienced over one hundred years ago.

Credit cycle indicators

Finally, a credit cycle clock tends to play out over expansions as borrowers start to tip their toes into the borrowing waters in the early days of recovery when lenders are typically most cautious. By the end of an expansion, the party is going full steam, with lots of over-imbibers of credit and lenders more than willing to indulge them.

This behavioral pattern over an expansion is evident in credit spreads. For example, as shown in Exhibit 2.12, the difference or spread between high yield (junk-rated) debt and ten-year Treasury yields tends to blow out in recessions, diminish as a recovery unfolds, and approach cycle lows later in an expansion before rising ahead of a recession. Overborrowing by low-quality businesses is a key feature of the excesses that ultimately create the conditions for a recession. In the late 1990s, this process of deteriorating (rising) spreads was well underway before the "dot.com" bubble burst. Probably that's partly because "Y2K" concerns kept the Fed on "easy street" longer than was typical.

The spread also started to rise in mid-2007 as an early warning sign of what was to come in the financial crisis. By the winter of 2009, junk spreads were discounting a level of credit defaults comparable to the worst part of the Great Depression. However, the government through its monetary and fiscal policy powers was committed to avoiding another Great Depression. The high-yield market turned out to be a screaming buy at that point as the anticipated defaults never materialized.

In mid-2014, the spread was back in complacency territory, suggesting that liquidity was abundant in credit markets. Notice that it moved

Exhibit 2.12   Credit Conditions Deteriorate before Recessions

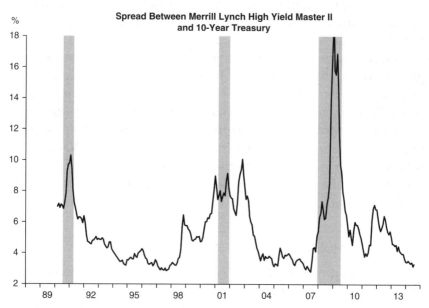

Source: Haver Analytics.
Data as of August 2014.

to new cycle lows after the flare-up precipitated by the euro's near-death experience in 2011. Essentially, at under 400 basis points, the spread was in a similar position to where it was in 1994 and 2004, similar to the Fed policy-wage inflation relationship. From that vantage point, the party was just getting started and had several years to run.

International dimensions of the business cycle

There is a global business cycle. While national business cycles get most of the analytical attention and have been scrutinized in great detail, the global business cycle is less documented. Partly, that's because of the nationalistic bias in economic and financial organization. Boundaries around economic data and their definitions have a heavily nationalistic orientation. Barriers to trade, labor mobility, investment, and other capital flows are most severe at the national level. In an information age, barriers to information flows are also being fortified at the national level. National leaders who control dissent to sustain their power are threatened by the possibility of a wide-open Internet. Open societies have a comparative advantage in the Information Age.

These limitations on commerce, mobility, and information flows have always existed. Technological progress, however, is increasingly eroding the artificial barriers that are justified in the name of nationalism. It is driving globalization, which in its essence means the dissolving of national barriers to business, culture, and ideas at an ever-increasing rate. As this happens, the global dimensions of the business cycle become more important for the analysis of the domestic cycle. As investors diversify away from the extreme home bias that is created by national barriers to capital flows, the international dimensions of the business cycle also become increasingly important for investment strategy.

Nations built from smaller tribal aggregations dominated the past few centuries. The future is about the globalization of humanity and what shape it takes. Technology is forcing this despite all the resistance embedded in the status quo. Societies that best facilitate this trend have tremendous economic tailwinds, which we'll discuss in more detail in our analysis of globalization. For now, suffice it to say that there are two extreme paradigms epitomized currently by the United States in the avant-garde, and North Korea in the about-to-be-extinct dinosaurs of national readiness for this new globalized world. That's why, with each passing day, the globalizing world economy looks more like the US economy and less like the North Korean economy. People prefer prosperity to starvation. They prefer hope for their children's future to a bleak stagnation. The United States is the largest, richest economic bloc, with the most integrated diversity of the world's people living in peaceful harmony under one government. That's what is needed for a successful globalization process to reach its logical conclusion. Logical, because it optimizes economic opportunities for the world's people. For many reasons, which will be elaborated in chapter 7, the US economy comes the closest of any of the major economies to being a prototype for a globalized world economy.

Because the organization of trade, capital flows, and currency regimes is always changing, rigid theoretical economic frameworks are even more limited at the international level. In addition to the ongoing incremental evolution of global economic arrangements, there are quantum leaps in institutional arrangements that create disruptive transitions, regime changes that redefine how economic forces influence trade patterns, and capital flows across countries.

The global business cycle faced a different set of constraints under the international gold standard era than during the Bretton Woods era or the post-Bretton Woods era of today. During the Cold War period, two big parts of the global economy operated largely independent of each other. Emerging markets used this bipolar competition to play the two sides against each other, extracting economic favors in the process. When the Iron Curtain came down, the two competing ideological blocs began to integrate economically. After 1979, China also began to integrate its economy with the West. Obviously, these momentous changes have had dramatic effects on the patterns of global trade and investment, and, consequently, the nature of the global business cycle.

This ever-evolving globalization process means traditional econometric models are unlikely to have fixed parameters to an even greater extent than they might in relatively stable domestic economic models. The gestalt paradigm of information processing shaped by ever-changing economic incentives is probably even more relevant for a global perspective. It allows for both structural and behavioral changes as institutions evolve, regulations adjust, and the weights of different populations shift in the aggregate economic pie. Patterns emerge in big global data sets. They shape and reshape as incentives change.

Our focus up to now has been on the United States and its business cycle. Partly that's because it is the world's biggest economy with a disproportionate share of the world's financial assets denominated in its own currency, which happens to be the world's premier reserve currency. For all these reasons, the US economy tends to play a significant role in the global business cycles.

To a large extent, the US business-cycle pattern is also reflective of the pattern in other countries that share similar economic structures, mainly other rich developed economies.

Together with the United State, these other developed economies with roughly 20 percent of the world's people, account for about half of world GDP and a much higher percentage of global wealth. In any event, the analysis of business cycles, while taking account of differences in the relative importance of underlying sectors, such as the degree of openness to trade, is not so different across the rich world. The degree of cyclical synchronization across countries, however, can vary quite a bit. For example, the United States went into a recession in December 2007, while the rest of the world, including Europe and most emerging markets, continued to grow in the first half of 2008. By late 2008, the biggest collapse in global trade since the 1930s had put the whole world in recession. With vigorous policy stimulus across the world, by 2010 the whole world was growing together at an above-trend rate. Then, in 2011, Europe and many of the emerging markets tightened their monetary policies. A two-year slowdown ensued, with the United States continuing to expand, Europe going back into recession, and emerging markets losing steam to varying degrees.

Just as there can be differences in the degree of synchronicity within a domestic business cycle, as credit, housing, investment, and trade cycles, for example, mesh somewhat differently in each overall cycle, there are differing degrees of lead and lag across countries, as just discussed, as well as differing degrees of relative strength in the sub-cycles. The global recovery from the financial crisis was highly synchronized. Then, in 2011, divergences arose for various reasons, including different policy approaches and the pressing need for structural reforms in major emerging markets, such as China. By 2013, a more synchronized global growth pattern began to emerge once again as the global trade and manufacturing cycle benefited from the end of Europe's double-dip recession.

China's growing role in globalization

These different patterns of global business cycles are evident in the last three economic cycles. China played a particularly prominent role in the 2001 to 2009 cycle. That cycle capped an extraordinary 30-year period that saw China grow from an isolated and insignificant part of the global economy to the second-largest economy in the world. China achieved a critical mass in many markets, especially natural resource markets, that played a major role in the commodity super-cycle that saw oil prices, for example, go from around $10 a barrel at its low point in 1998 to $140 a barrel at its peak in the summer of 2008. Many other commodities such as gold and copper saw gains of 500 percent or more during the Chinese growth boom in the first decade of the twenty-first century. We'll discuss other macroeconomic influences on commodity prices in chapter 6. Suffice it to say that Chinese demand became an especially large factor in the 2001–2009 commodity super-cycle.

The primary economic transmission channels across countries are trade flows and balance-of-payment financial flows. These shape the patterns of the global business cycle. Chinese growth influenced both types of flows in the first decade of the twenty-first century to an unprecedented degree. To continue its double-digit GDP growth streak, China increasingly relied on an ever-growing trade surplus. On the eve of the financial crisis in mid-2008, China's trade surplus had grown to about 10 percent of its GDP. By some measures, it had become the largest exporter of goods in the world. The financial surplus that China cumulated from its ever-growing excess of exports over imports allowed it to build up foreign exchange reserves in the world's main reserve currency, the dollar. Most of these dollars were stored in US government and agency securities. By 2008, China had accumulated about $2 trillion in foreign exchange reserves compared to only about $165 billion in 2000.

On the one hand, after the Asian currency crisis of the late 1990s, and as a growing economic superpower, China needed an adequate supply of foreign exchange reserves to protect itself against events such as that currency crisis. Indeed, a major feature of the 2001–2009 global business cycle was a growing current-account surplus across many of the Asian economies, not just China, as they all sought in the wake of the late-1990s currency crisis to fortify their national balance sheets with sufficient foreign-exchange reserves for future contingencies.

On the other hand, Chinese purchases of US Treasuries with its surplus trade receipts blocked one of the natural adjustment mechanisms that would have normally worked to rebalance trade and stop the ever-growing current-account imbalances in the global economy. Normally, an ever-rising Chinese surplus and US trade deficit would have caused the dollar to fall and the yuan to rise. This happened to some extent after the summer of 2005, when China finally began a controlled appreciation of the yuan, but China's massive reserve accumulation was a form of currency intervention that preserved some of its competitive advantage and allowed its trade surplus to grow and maintain a domestic growth rate above 10 percent.

For every trade surplus, there is a trade deficit somewhere else. The US business cycle during this period was characterized by an ever-expanding trade deficit that peaked at about 6 percent of GDP. This unusually big deficit enabled China to have an unusually large surplus. Other countries also facilitated this dynamic, with big trade deficits growing in Ireland, the United Kingdom, Spain, and a host of other countries. China's trade surplus recycled into global financial markets helped finance housing booms in many of the trade deficit countries. A trade deficit only becomes a problem when it is difficult to finance. Financing by China made it easy and in fact enabled unusually big trade imbalances to grow until the excesses in lending standards became so egregious that defaults on loans began to proliferate. All the housing booms eventually went bust.

The key point is that the global business cycle from 2001 to 2009 was dominated by ever-rising trade imbalances that eventually became unsustainable. Recycled surpluses helped finance excessive housing booms and bubbles to keep this particular global business-cycle dynamic going. This cyclical source of instability was a major contributor to the financial crisis.

The 2008–2009 crisis marked the end of that pattern of global growth. Since then, a new pattern has emerged. It is a pattern that has forced China to grow its domestic demand because it can no longer rely on an ever-growing trade surplus. In fact, China's current-account surplus has dropped sharply from about 10 percent of GDP in 2006 to about 2 percent of GDP in 2013. In the United States, the 6-percent trade deficit from 2006 has shrunk to about 3 percent. This general pattern of reduced trade imbalances is a key differentiator of the global cycle that followed the financial crisis compared to the one that preceded it. Reduced imbalances mean the subsequent cycle is more sustainable and less prone to be derailed by the dynamics that undermined the 2001–2009 cycle.

This changed dynamic is behind China's slower growth. Its five-year plan for 2011–2016 recognizes the need to transition growth away from exports and toward domestic consumption and investment. Reducing a surplus from 10 percent of GDP to 2 percent of GDP takes away eight points of growth. In the United States, in contrast, going from a 6-percent deficit on trade to just 2 percent adds four points of growth. The pattern of rebalanced trade narrows the gap between Chinese and US growth.

While it's an international business cycle with a more sustainable growth pattern, it's also a pattern with slower global trade as the structural adjustments making this transition possible have hit growth in other countries that benefited from exporting when the Chinese trade juggernaut was ascending. Many emerging markets, like Brazil, have had a hard time making this adjustment to the new pattern of global trade and investment flows.

For the United States, the timing of the adjustment was fortuitous in a couple of ways. The 4-percentage point drop in its current-account deficit between 2006 and 2013 was driven by two key factors. First, an energy revolution turned it from the world's biggest oil importer into one of the world's biggest producers. Oil imports were its biggest category of imports until recently, making this reversal a particularly big help for rebalancing trade. Rapidly increasing exports, including of energy products, further helped the rebalancing of trade. Second, an undervalued dollar combined with globalization and rising living standards in the developing world have made travel and tourism one of the most powerful economic trends in recent years. As per capita incomes have increased in the emerging world, the United States has seen its services account surplus rise from inbound tourism. This is another benefit of having such a diversity of people, including significant diasporas from all the major countries and cultures on the globe. The country's close ties with so many people around the world also create business connections around the world that offer the United States a major comparative advantage and bolster its claims to being a microcosm of the globalized world.

New risks are also arising from these new global business cycle dynamics. Indeed, it seems to be the case that when the US trade deficit becomes too small, say less than 3 percent of GDP, it reduces the growth in the supply of dollars to the rest of the world to a level that starts to strain finances in the world's balance-of-payment flows. That's because a small US trade deficit means slower growth in foreign holdings of the global reserve currency. This tends to put upward pressure on the dollar and cause financial strains in certain countries that find it harder to finance their balance of payments. In many ways, this was the dynamic that characterized the 1990s global business cycle, when the United States did relatively well, while a succession of emerging markets encountered problems in a strengthening dollar environment. For these reasons, it is not surprising that China and other emerging markets are having more difficulty in the postcrisis global business cycle. For the United States, on the other hand, global cyclical forces are much more favorable since the financial crisis.

Europe's incomplete institutional structure for banking, monetary, and fiscal policy, and governance has left it in limbo. In addition, while most of the world's formerly big trade surplus and deficit countries have restructured to much more balanced trade flows including Japan and China, Germany remains a glaring exception. Its trade surplus at about 6 percent of GDP in 2013 was the highest among the major economies and even marginally above its prior cycle peak in 2006 (Exhibit 2.13). This has severely hampered the ability of the rest of Europe to adjust to the new, more balanced nature of the current global business cycle. Aside from overly restrictive monetary and fiscal policy, Europe is hampered by an inability to rebalance its trade in line with the rest of the world because of its "one size fits all" currency system.

Exhibit 2.13   Rebalancing Trade Key in New Global Business Cycle

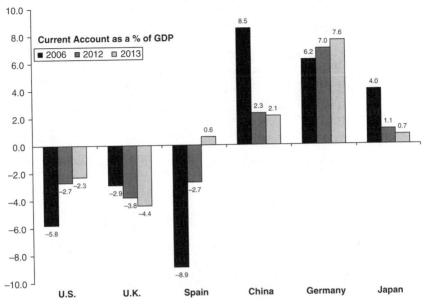

Source: OECD, Haver Analytics.

Data as of April 7, 2014.

These observations on recent patterns in the global business cycle illustrate the role of changes in trade patterns, investment flows, and exchange rate policies. They highlight the important new role China is playing in the global economy and illustrate some of the reasons why the US economy remains such a dominant force in the global economy.

3
Monetary Policy

Don't fight the Fed

The late legendary investor Martin Zweig was one of the first asset managers to apply the insights of modern academic monetary economics to Wall Street. Even as a professor, before becoming a prominent money manager, one of his maxims was "don't fight the Fed," an investment rule of thumb that continues to resonate, especially after the extraordinary monetary policies that followed the financial crisis of 2008–2009.

Those extraordinary actions prompted a host of armchair Fed critics to "fight the Fed." They were, however, overwhelmingly proven wrong as their dire predictions of roaring inflation and financial Armageddon failed to materialize. Instead, the Fed's policies worked to save the US economy from another Great Depression and by 2012 had put the economy on track for a fairly solid and normal business expansion. More importantly, investors who "did not fight the Fed" enjoyed one of the greatest equity bull markets of all time.

Former Fed Chairman Ben Bernanke's actions during the crisis will go down in monetary history as confirmation of what monetary economists learned during the half century after the Great Depression, by building on the insights of great economists like J.M. Keynes and Milton Friedman. Furthermore, the difficult experience of Japan in the two decades after its double bubble (real estate and equities) burst in the early 1990s and that of Europe, which lapsed into a double-dip recession in 2011 while the United States continued to expand, provide alternative monetary policy experiments that vindicate Bernanke's actions as the application of the best thinking in academic economics. In sharp contrast to Bernanke's enlightened measures, the tepid and always behind-the-curve policy responses in Japan and Europe did not follow this thinking and the results speak for themselves. In fact, it was only after Bernanke succeeded that the Japanese central bank belatedly adopted his approach to end the threatening deflationary undertow. Whether it will work at this late stage in Japan's fiscal crisis remains to be seen. In the meantime, the European Central Bank (ECB) repeated the Japanese mistakes of the 1990s, eschewing a proactive monetary policy for a minimalist "too little, too late" crisis-avoidance approach until 2015.

These assertions about the effect of monetary policy and the relative success of the US approach compared to that in Europe and Japan—where the ECB, under the influence of the German Bundesbank's traditional anti-inflation focus, and the Bank of Japan, which was also governed by a traditional pre-Keynesian, anti-inflation view until "Abenomics" forced it to change course in late 2012, have hindered a return to normal—will be developed through the book because they illustrate many of the principles discussed throughout. For now, suffice it to say that Japan's economy was stagnant for about a quarter century, and Europe's economy seemed to be following Japan under the influence of old-fashioned austerity policies six years after the Great Recession.

There is a reason why the chair of the Federal Reserve Board is often called "the second most powerful person on Earth." The US business cycle is heavily influenced by Federal Reserve monetary policy. As the dominant financial system in the global economy with between 30 percent and 40 percent of total financial assets denominated in its own currency, the United States tends to be a major driver of the global business cycle as well. A discussion of the US monetary policy rationale, mechanics, and role in the business cycle will make it easier to understand why it's not a good idea to "fight the Fed."

Monetary mechanics and learning from experience

The Federal Reserve celebrated its one hundredth anniversary in 2013. During the past century, its policy approach has evolved along with the US economy and knowledge about best monetary policy practices. Still, because monetary policy is generally poorly understood, including by many politicians, the Fed is a lightning rod for misplaced criticism and paranoid conspiracy theories.

The way the Federal Reserve conducts monetary policy today reflects the evolution of economic knowledge with a heavy dose of learning from experience. For example, out of the cacophony of ex-post rationalizations about the causes of the Great Depression a consensus evolved over time about how the mechanics of monetary policy broke down in those extreme circumstances in a way that demanded extraordinary action that was not forthcoming at the time. Eighty years later, in the wake of the 2008–2009 financial crisis, Federal Reserve policymakers led by Chairman Bernanke developed and implemented extraordinary measures that repaired the broken monetary mechanism sufficiently to avoid another depression and support an economic recovery. The lessons from the 1930s made that possible. So too, did the lessons learned from the inadequate Japanese response to its 1990s banking crisis and ensuing deflation.

As noted above, while the underlying theoretical basis for the Fed's postcrisis response reflects the best thinking in monetary economics, it perplexed many economists and non-economists, including many money managers with outstanding track records. Some of these money managers strongly criticized the Fed's unorthodox response and often belittled the Fed's "academic" orientation and lack of "market smarts." Six years after the crisis, it's pretty clear that the Fed's insights from the best academic thinking worked and the dire consequences predicted by critics failed to materialize. Indeed, it is precisely the orthodoxy of money managers with "street smarts" that has traditionally been shared by central bankers and caused them to fail in preempting prior debt-deflation fiascoes. In fact, it was this orthodoxy that lay behind the failures of the Bank of Japan and the European Central Bank to put their respective economies on a comparably successful track as the United States. What seems excessively easy and irresponsible monetary policy by normal standards is precisely what's required when a debt-deflation process threatens the economy and financial system.

Why Bernanke's therapy proved effective

The Great Disinflation trend that began in the early 1980s with Paul Volcker at the helm of the Federal Reserve inevitably brought an eventual brush with deflation. Inflation fell from well over 10 percent when he began to turn off the monetary spigots, to less than zero (deflation) in the wake of the Great Recession. Throughout the early 2000s, the Federal Reserve was already primarily concerned with stopping this powerful downtrend in inflation from becoming deflation. Because low real interest rates were necessary to prevent a deflationary apocalypse, US monetary policy was mainly in this reflation mode for about a decade before the Great Recession.

Still, the US economy fell into the deflationary danger zone during the 2008–2009 financial crisis for the first time since the Great Depression, and during the four years up to 2012, nominal gross domestic product (GDP) growth (inflation plus real growth) averaged just under 2 percent, something that also hadn't happened in the United States for such a long stretch of time since the 1930s depression (Exhibit 3.1). The lowest prior four-year stretch was just a tad under 4 percent in the period that ended in 1961.

For many reasons, 4 percent is the minimal growth rate the US economy appears to need to service its outstanding debt and still allow for real trend-like growth in the 2-percent to 3-percent range. Nominal GDP growth below 4 percent implies that trend real growth can only occur with inflation *below* the Fed's 2-percent target. On the other hand, nominal growth consistently above 6 percent has been associated with inflation above the Fed's target. Only nominal growth between 4 and 6 percent has been associated with stable inflation *and* trend-like real growth. This range is also the "sweet spot" for risk assets, as discussed

Exhibit 3.1 Fed Policies Have Helped United States Move Out of Deflationary Danger Zone

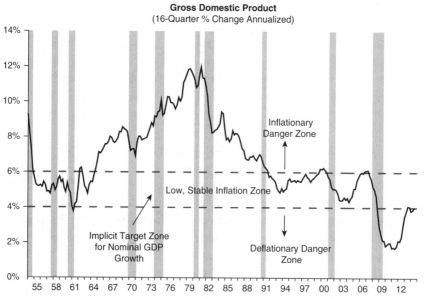

Source: BEA/Haver Analytics.

Data as of August 15, 2014.

in subsequent chapters. Here suffice it to say that nominal growth dictates the cash flows through the economy. If it's too low, companies and individuals will have a harder time servicing the debt that they have accumulated. The higher the debt, the harder it is to service.

Exhibit 3.2 shows that credit growth far exceeded nominal GDP growth during the 1980s and the first decade of the twenty-first century. These were "bubbles" in borrowing in the sense that debt growth was out of line with the capacity of the economy to repay the debt. Interest rates were declining throughout these years as inflation came down to the Fed's goal. Lower interest rates and greater relative economic stability induced people to borrow more. However, slowing nominal GDP growth increasingly reduced their ability to pay back the debt. Eventually, with very low nominal growth, debt levels became too high even at very low interest rates. The 2008 financial crisis ended the progressive leveraging that had built up over the prior 60 years.

The Fed's aggressive reflation effort succeeded in bringing nominal GDP growth back into the "normal" range, thus avoiding a debt-deflation collapse. Indeed, by the third quarter of 2013, the four-year average of nominal GDP growth rose above the critical 4-percent threshold for the first time since 2008. In the process, households managed to deleverage from their unprecedented overindebted position, and

Exhibit 3.2 United States Transitioning from Credit Bubble to Equity Bubble?

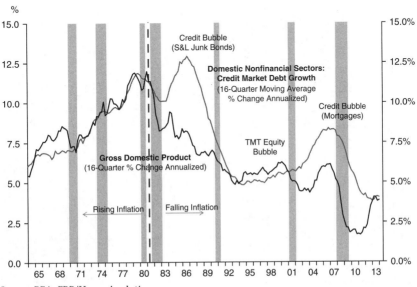

Source: BEA, FRB/Haver Analytics.
Data as of August 2014.

bank balance sheets were repaired. The unorthodox policies of Federal Reserve Chairman Bernanke supported the economy so that deleveraging could occur in a relatively orderly fashion with help from economic growth, unlike the debt-deflation debacles of the past, when policy actions were not forthcoming to stop the vicious, self-reinforcing down-spiral caused by ever-greater deleveraging pressures in an ever-worsening economic environment.

Bernanke's "muse," Milton Friedman

The policy response to the 2008 financial crisis was a Great Experiment, and the United States was fortunate to receive the therapy that proved successful. Basically, while it may be surprising to those who believe that the Federal Reserve was irresponsibly printing money, the Fed supplied just enough monetary base (reserves) to the banking system (Exhibit 3.4) to offset the collapse in the money multiplier (Exhibit 3.5), in order to maintain a stable growth rate in the money supply (Exhibit 3.3). Indeed, as shown in Exhibit 3.3, US money-supply growth was fairly steady in the 5-percent to 7-percent range over the

Exhibit 3.3   Unconventional Monetary Policy Kept Money Growth Stable...

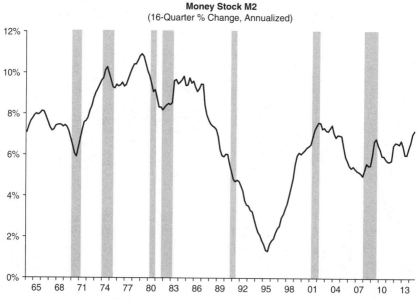

Sources: Federal Reserve Board/Haver Analytics.

Data as of August 2014.

Exhibit 3.4 ...By Flooding Banks with Reserves...

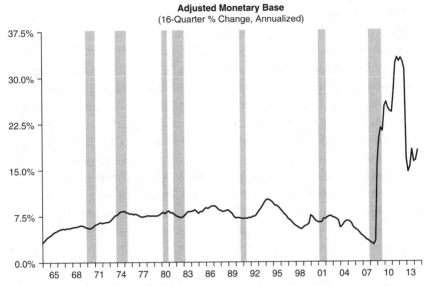

Adjusted Monetary Base
(16-Quarter % Change, Annualized)

Sources: Federal Reserve Board/Haver Analytics.
Data as of Q2 2014.

Exhibit 3.5 ...Sufficient to Offset the Collapse of the Money Multiplier

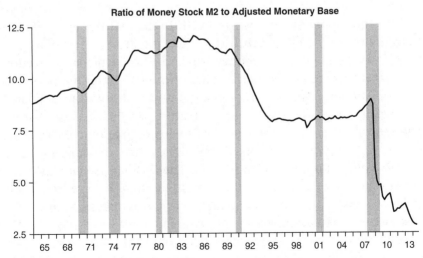

Ratio of Money Stock M2 to Adjusted Monetary Base

Sources: Federal Reserve Board/Haver Analytics.
Data as of Q2 2014.

period surrounding the financial crisis (2007–2009), which was essential to preclude a worse outcome given the surge in risk aversion and strong deleveraging pressures following Lehman's collapse.

Bernanke's actions drew upon Friedman's analysis of why the US economy collapsed in the 1929–1933 period. Back then, the Federal Reserve thought it was being sufficiently accommodative by expanding the monetary base. Unfortunately, the growth in the monetary base during the Depression was not sufficient to offset the collapse in the money multiplier, as banks that were worried about runs on deposits hoarded excess reserves instead of lending them out. The money supply shrank and the deflationary collapse ensued.

Thanks to Friedman's insights, Bernanke knew what to do this time around when the multiplier fell to less than half its precrisis value (before the crisis, a dollar of base money in the banking system supported about $8 of money supply in the economy; afterwards, it was closer to $3 of money supply for each dollar of bank reserves). By creating an environment for a relatively orderly deleveraging process, the Fed's extraordinary actions to offset the collapse in the money multiplier facilitated a much more benign adjustment process to the financial system shakeout. For example, while uncomfortably high, unemployment peaked at 10 percent this time around instead of the roughly 25-percent rate in the 1930s collapse. Indeed, it could have been much worse.

Banks weren't the only ones hoarding reserves out of fear after the financial crisis. In fact, the velocity of money—the ratio of nominal GDP to the supply of money—declined throughout the low inflation era (since the mid-1990s) as the risk of deflation increased (Exhibit 3.6). In this environment, more money is hoarded for principal protection and less is spent, so the average dollar of money supply supports less economic activity (GDP). Corporations, for example, have accumulated massive amounts of cash that are just sitting on their balance sheets. The velocity of money is slower. That's why, despite much alarm, the money-supply growth rate has been higher than the nominal GDP growth rate without causing inflation. The Fed has just provided the amount of money that allowed the economy to grow in a low, stable inflation range, which, as experience shows and as discussed later, is the best monetary environment for the economy to realize its potential.

As mentioned above, aside from the lessons of the Great Depression, Bernanke also learned from the Japanese experience of the 1990s. In this case, until "Abenomics" in late 2012, Japanese policymakers always thought that they were being accommodative. Yet, Japanese nominal

Exhibit 3.6   Hoarding of Liquidity Has Collapsed Velocity of Money

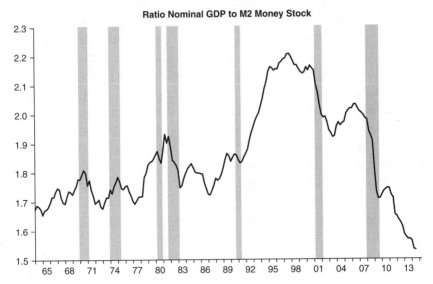

Sources: Federal Reserve Board/Haver Analytics.
Data as of Q2 2014.

GDP was lower in the third quarter of 2013 than in 1992. That's two decades without any growth in nominal GDP. During this period, real growth was less than 1 percent and inflation was negative, clear evidence that, while seemingly accommodative, policy never was easy enough to eliminate deflation and stagnation, and more needed to be done.

The Japanese case is especially surprising because Japan was one of the first countries to respond appropriately to the Great Depression crisis in the 1930s and, as a result, recovered well before the United States and most other major economies. The prescription it used was very close to the US policy response in 2009 that headed off a repeat of the 1930s experience.

The finance minister who orchestrated the successful Japanese response to the world depression was Takahashi Korekiyo, a fascinating character who is the subject of an excellent biography by the historian Richard J. Smethurst.[1] His legacy has been resurrected with "Abenomics." Unfortunately, it lay dormant through the 1990–2012 period of policy muddle. The monetary and fiscal policy mix

---

[1] Richard J. Smethurst, *From Foot Soldier to Finance Minister: Takahashi Korekiyo, Japan's Keynes* (Harvard University Press, 2007).

Takahashi concocted included leaving the gold standard, ending yen convertibility to gold, devaluation against the dollar and pound, deep interest rate cuts, and authorization to raise the Bank of Japan's (BOJ's) limit on bank note issuance. On the fiscal front, he increased spending without raising taxes by selling the increased debt to the BOJ.

According to Smethurst, "Takahashi's policies worked, and by 1935–1936, half a decade before the United States would, Japan returned to complete utilization of capacity and to full employment, and did so with an inflation rate of less than 3 percent per year."[2] Here we have another historical example of a social experiment validating the aggressive use of fiscal and monetary policy, including monetization of government debt, that successfully stopped a depression.

Europe is also vulnerable to this debt-deflation trap. In the four years after the financial crisis, Europe saw its nominal growth rate average less than 1 percent, risking a Japanese-like descent into deflation (Exhibit 3.7). Both Japan and Europe have shown a pickup since

Exhibit 3.7   Euro Area and Japan Moving away from Debt-Deflation Abyss?

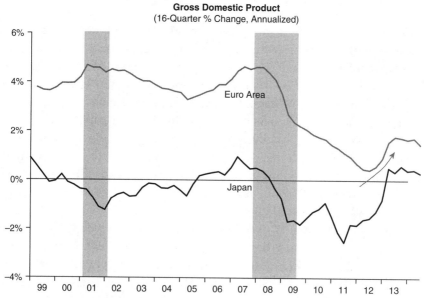

Gross Domestic Product
(16-Quarter % Change, Annualized)

Sources: EUROSTAT, Cabinet Office of Japan/ Haver Analytics.
Data as of August 2014.

[2] *From Foot Soldier to Finance Minister: Takahashi Korekiyo, Japan's Keynes*, page 239.

Exhibit 3.8 Deflation Risks Remain as Credit Continues to Contract in Euroland, Threatening Relapse

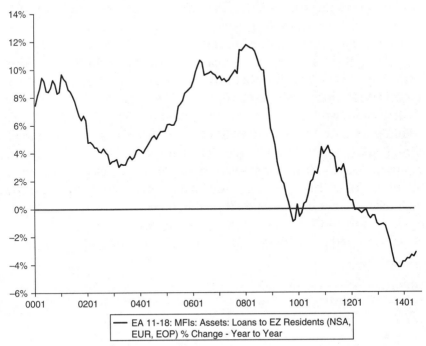

Source: European Central Bank/Haver Analytics.

Data as of August 2014.

the crisis, but both are far behind the United States in terms of successfully reflating their economies. Encouragingly, the first arrow of "Abenomics" included a strong reflation effort, and the ECB head, Mario Draghi, who took over the helm just in time to avert another crisis in late 2011 and who was trained in the United States by Bernanke's mentor, Stanley Fischer, has tried to overcome Bundesbank resistance to Friedman's lessons. Still, Europe's slow-moving policy response to deflation risks remained the biggest threat to sustained global expansion six years after the Great Recession (Exhibit 3.8). In 2011 and mid 2012, it threatened to derail the global recovery out of the financial crisis. Finally, in January 2015, Draghi took bold and aggressive action.

The yield curve rules

From an investment strategy perspective, the yield curve is one of the most useful metrics for gauging the thrust of Fed policy. When the yield curve is steepest, with the overnight money market rate determined by monetary policy very low compared to the long-term Treasury note yield, policy is most stimulative. Partly, that's because banks generally pay the short-term rate to gather funds that can be lent for longer terms at higher rates. The incentive to do this is strongest when the yield curve is the steepest (the spread between long and short interest rates is most positive), and that's usually the case in the early years of a recovery. In this phase, "don't fight the Fed" usually means "be long equities or be wrong."

Policy is tightest when the yield curve is very flat, or even inverted (when the ten-year Treasury rate falls below the Fed funds rate), as has been the case just before every recession in the past half century (Exhibit 3.9). In that case, "liquidity" is expensive: short-term rates are high relative to long-term rates. If banks are paying more for sources of funds relative to long rates, net interest margins are low, lending slows down, and credit gets tight. This also tends to be the part of the credit

Exhibit 3.9 Yield Curve Spread: Difference between 10-Year Treasury Note and Yield and Overnight Federal Funds Rate (shaded areas represent recessions)

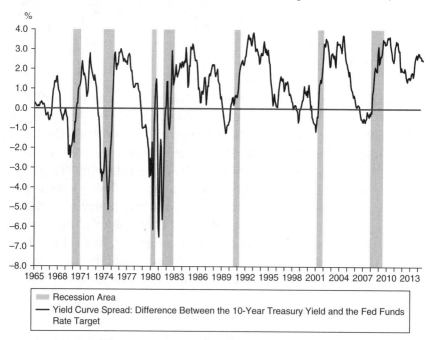

Source: Federal Reserve Board/Haver Analytics.

Data as of August 2014.

cycle when, as Warren Buffet famously said, we see who's swimming without trunks. Indeed, credit defaults rise and credit risk premia blow out to cycle highs. It's like a game of musical chairs, only instead of a chair being missing when the music stops, leaving a loser standing, missing liquidity means someone cannot roll over a loan or make a payment.

In the tight phase of the liquidity cycle, the inversion of the yield curve reflects a growing market judgment that policy rates are high enough to satisfy the Federal Reserve's tight monetary policy objectives (aimed at reducing elevated inflation expectations) and that subsequent policy moves are likely to be toward lower rather than higher rates in order to eventually re-stimulate the economy out of recession. Since longer-term rates reflect the future trajectory of expected short rates, an inverted yield curve is often a signal that tight policy has come close to its end. Generally, maximum restraint and the most inverted stage of the yield curve precede and even continue into the early stage of the recession, depending on how serious the inflation problem is. Then, as it becomes apparent that economic momentum is fading faster than the Fed desires and inflation is headed lower, the yield curve often enters its most aggressive steepening phase, with short-term policy rates dropping rapidly until policymakers feel comfortable that the recession is over and that policy will support a sustainable recovery.

When the yield curve is in the later stage of flattening and even inverting, the "don't fight the Fed" rule implies getting out of equities because a recession usually is on the way. Recessions are bad for equities because profits are very cyclical and tend to drop sharply in a recession. This, combined with tight credit conditions, raises the specter of growing credit defaults and bankruptcies. On the other hand, the best time to buy equities is when the recession has reached an extreme point at which its end is in sight. That's what happened for example in March 2009, when equities bottomed about four months before the recession ended. As is usually the case at that stage of the business cycle, pessimism about the outlook for both the economy and equities was extremely high precisely at the best time to invest in a recovery, as the steep yield curve was correctly indicating.

The key point is that the yield curve has been the most reliable gauge of whether monetary policy is tight or easy. Most other metrics of the policy stance have been much less reliable. For example, a common mistake is to gauge policy by whether the Fed is raising or cutting rates. The problem with this perspective is that monetary policy can be "behind the curve." This was consistently the case in the 1970s, when the Federal Reserve was too slow raising rates as inflation rose ever higher. Indeed, conventional wisdom at the time held that policy was tight because interest rates were rising. Inflation, however, does not keep rising for long in a truly tight monetary policy environment. Also, the money supply grew faster and faster even as interest rates rose. Partly, the problem was that while *nominal* interest rates (inflation plus the real interest rate) were rising, *real* interest rates were falling because inflation was rising faster than the Fed was hiking interest rates. This created an incentive to borrow money and buy real assets that appreciate with inflation (hence the accelerating money-supply growth and lack of impact on inflation until Paul Volcker pushed interest rates high enough above inflation to start reining it in).

A more recent example of how interest rates can be a misleading gauge of the monetary policy stance comes from the European experience following the 2008–2009 financial crisis. ECB officials and most market participants talked as if policy was very accommodative in 2012 and 2013 because interest rates were quite low and had been cut. A look at Exhibit 3.8 suggests otherwise. From about the time of the premature April 2011 ECB rate hike, the recovery in credit that had started in 2010 during the synchronized global expansion was halted in its tracks and a massive contraction of credit was set off. The central bank's role in this deflation of the financial system is evident in the contrast between the Fed and ECB balance sheets in Exhibit 3.16. The differential impact on the economy is evident in the contrasting behavior of the unemployment rate (Exhibit 3.15).

The evidence is overwhelming that despite low interest rates, ECB policy was too tight rather than accommodative. This classic mistake of associating low interest rates with easy policy breaks down in a deflationary world. This was a major point made by Milton Friedman and Anna Schwartz in their *Monetary History of the United States*, which they explained in great detail. Fifty years later, some policymakers still don't grasp this point, with grave consequences for their countries.

When the banking system is shrinking, the central bank's balance sheet is declining, the money growth rate is decelerating, and inflation is falling toward zero, these are all classic signs that policy is too tight regardless of the level of interest rates. If rates are at zero, then this scenario cries out for quantitative easing. Bernanke knew this. The Bundesbank orthodoxy ignored the obvious.

Conversely, as the Fed raised rates into the 2006–2007 period, the conventional wisdom claimed that policy was not especially tight because the Fed funds rate was "just" 5.25 percent, the dollar was weak, and commodity prices were soaring. Nevertheless, 5.25 percent turned out to be enough to invert the yield curve, strong evidence that a recession was coming. Since the bond market "thought" a 5.25 percent Fed funds rate was high enough in July 2007, the ten-year Treasury note yield was lower than that, at 5 percent. Within six months, the United States was in recession and the "trunk-less swimmers" began to multiply, culminating in the worst financial crisis since the 1930s.

The Fed's rationale—"the 2-percent solution"

While the yield curve is a good indicator of the monetary policy stance, it does not really tell us why the Fed has adopted that stance. For that, it's helpful to understand the longer-run goals and monetary policy strategy.

Since the Greenspan Fed began in 1987, monetary policy has become increasingly transparent, with more and more efforts to communicate the Fed's strategy to the general public. This process was largely completed during the Bernanke years, with regularly scheduled press conferences instituted after policy meetings to explain the Fed's views and reasons for its actions. Some have criticized this transparency as sowing more confusion than necessary. This was the case, for example, in the summer of 2013, when the Federal Open Market Committee (FOMC) tried to prepare the market for its eventual tapering of asset purchases as its third round of Quantitative Easing (QE) was to be phased out. Some argued that this attempt at greater communication backfired, creating more market volatility than necessary.

While there will always be pitfalls associated with communicating something as complex and potentially impactful as monetary policy, most scholars would argue in favor of more rather than less explanation of the thinking behind monetary policy actions. As we discussed in chapter 1, markets are big processors of information. The more accurate the information, the more efficient this processing can be. Without transparency, the markets would have to guess unnecessarily about various aspects of the policy outlook. In the past, this created a bigger cloud of uncertainty that presumably added to market volatility.

Nevertheless, the fact remains that the FOMC is often just as uncertain about the economic outlook as market participants are. This means that there is a natural limit to its policy transparency, a limit that is set by the possibility that the Fed may need to change course from what it currently expects. Indeed, confusion over policy is often the result of the Fed's own uncertainty about which way the wind will blow. When the wind surprises, both the Fed and the market need to adjust accordingly. The Fed is not omniscient, so there will naturally be miscommunication as a result. Nevertheless, a lot of the prior mystique around monetary policy before the era of transparency was an unnecessary source of confusion of questionable and probably negative value.

In any case, to better clarify its mission, the Fed now produces a Statement on Longer-Run Goals and Monetary Policy Strategy. The version amended effective January 28, 2014, is presented below. This is a concise summary of how the US central bank seeks to achieve its statutory mandate from Congress to promote maximum unemployment, stable prices, and moderate long-term interest rates.

While monetary policy attempts to address deviations from full employment in their cyclical context, it acknowledges that the maximum level of employment is largely determined by nonmonetary factors that affect the structure and dynamics of the labor market. On the other hand, economists believe that the inflation rate over the longer run is primarily determined by monetary policy, and hence the Committee has the ability to specify a longer-run goal for inflation. That goal is 2 percent, as measured by the annual change in the price index for personal consumption expenditures.

Statement on longer-run goals and monetary policy strategy[3]

As amended effective January 28, 2014

The FOMC is firmly committed to fulfilling its statutory mandate from Congress of promoting maximum employment, stable prices, and moderate long-term interest rates. The Committee seeks to explain its monetary policy decisions to the public as clearly as possible. Such clarity facilitates well-informed decision-making by households and businesses, reduces economic and financial uncertainty, increases the effectiveness of monetary policy, and enhances transparency and accountability, which are essential in a democratic society.

Inflation, employment, and long-term interest rates fluctuate over time in response to economic and financial disturbances. Moreover,

[3] www.federalreserve.gov/monetarypolicy/files/FOMC_LongerRunGoals.pdf.

monetary policy actions tend to influence economic activity and prices with a lag. Therefore, the Committee's policy decisions reflect its longer-run goals, its medium-term outlook, and its assessments of the balance of risks, including risks to the financial system that could impede the attainment of the Committee's goals.

The inflation rate over the longer run is primarily determined by monetary policy, and hence the Committee has the ability to specify a longer-run goal for inflation. The Committee reaffirms its judgment that inflation at the rate of 2 percent, as measured by the annual change in the price index for personal consumption expenditures, is most consistent over the longer run with the Federal Reserve's statutory mandate. Communicating this inflation goal clearly to the public helps keep longer-term inflation expectations firmly anchored, thereby fostering price stability and moderate long-term interest rates and enhancing the Committee's ability to promote maximum employment in the face of significant economic disturbances.

The maximum level of employment is largely determined by nonmonetary factors that affect the structure and dynamics of the labor market. These factors may change over time and may not be directly measurable. Consequently, it would not be appropriate to specify a fixed goal for employment; rather, the Committee's policy decisions must be informed by assessments of the maximum level of employment, recognizing that such assessments are necessarily uncertain and subject to revision. The Committee considers a wide range of indicators in making these assessments. Information about Committee participants' estimates of the longer-run normal rates of output growth and unemployment is published four times per year in the FOMC's Summary of Economic Projections. For example, in the most recent projections, FOMC participants' estimates of the longer-run normal rate of unemployment had a central tendency of 5.2 percent to 5.8 percent.

In setting monetary policy, the Committee seeks to mitigate deviations of inflation from its longer-run goal and deviations of employment from the Committee's assessments of its maximum level. These objectives are generally complementary. However, under circumstances in which the Committee judges that the objectives are not complementary, it follows a balanced approach in promoting them, taking into account the magnitude of the deviations and the potentially different time horizons over which employment and inflation are projected to return to levels judged consistent with its mandate.

The Committee intends to reaffirm these principles and to make adjustments as appropriate at its annual organizational meeting each January.

As a practical matter for investment strategists monitoring the Fed's outlook and future actions, inflation is the primary variable driving the monetary-policy stance over the medium term. The real economy largely sets the level of full employment. Monetary policy determines the inflation rate.

Economists generally believe that a low, stable inflation environment sets the best possible financial backdrop for the real economy and hence employment. Real wages and standards of living depend directly on the productivity of labor. Inflation is the result of wage gains beyond those justified by productivity gains. Economists learned during the 1970s stagflation period, when growth was weak and unemployment and inflation were high, that higher inflation is not associated with lower unemployment except perhaps in the short term. In the long run, it seems to undermine the efficient allocation of resources and financial stability, resulting in higher rather than lower unemployment. The difficult experience of other countries plagued by high inflation over the years has also strengthened the case for a lower and stable inflation environment in pursuit of optimal economic performance. Most developed economies have adopted this view.

In addition, 2-percent inflation creates a margin of safety over deflation, which is particularly destructive in a highly leveraged modern economy and as a result has become anathema to modern central bankers. It also creates a higher safety margin for potential errors in inflation measurement and provides some lubricant for economic frictions that would otherwise favor creditors over debtors.

Finally, we would note that 2-percent inflation combined with 2-percent or 3-percent real growth coming from labor force and productivity growth implies a 4-percent to 5-percent nominal GDP growth world. Alternatively, zero inflation with the same real growth potential implies nominal growth below 4 percent, which seems to be the lower threshold for normal US economic performance. The failure of Japan's economy since 1990 and the similar pattern seen in the Eurozone suggest that subpar nominal growth creates stagnation in modern developed economies with highly leveraged financial systems. Very low nominal growth can also sink an economy into a debt trap in which interest on debt accrues faster than nominal growth generates revenues to service debt. For example, once the market doubts a government's capacity to pay its debt, interest rates soar and the debt trap closes.

The adjustment to zero-inflation often requires too much time and deleveraging, and can be too disruptive to allow for sufficient (2-percent or better) real growth. On the other hand, nominal growth between 4 percent and 5 percent seems to be sufficient to service a more leveraged modern economy's debt and to allow for healthy growth. That seems to be the lesson from Bernanke's "Great Experiment." As we'll see in chapter 5, a low and stable inflation rate also seems to provide for the best returns on equities. It should not be too surprising that the best backdrop for the real economy is also the best backdrop for equity returns.

The financial stability role of the Fed

Traditionally, monetary policy has focused on the macro economy, interest rates, and inflation, while regulatory policy has focused more on banking and financial system oversight. More generally, the Federal Reserve describes its mission as falling into four general areas:

- conducting the nation's monetary policy by influencing the monetary and credit conditions in the economy in pursuit of maximum employment, stable prices, and moderate long-term interest rates;
- supervising and regulating banking institutions to ensure the safety and soundness of the nation's banking and financial system and to protect the credit rights of consumers;
- maintaining the stability of the financial system and containing systemic risk that may arise in financial markets; and
- providing financial services to depository institutions, the US government, and foreign official institutions, including playing a major role in operating the nation's payments system.[4]

At the Fed's inception in 1913, the focus of its mission was centered around "safety and soundness" issues because of the periodic banking runs and collapses that had characterized the preceding century. Monetary policy at the time was less important in the sense that the gold standard in international payments more or less constrained activist policy. Moreover, the notion of a deliberate 2-percent inflation target was heresy at that time.

As a result, before World War II, monetary policy was a more passive and constrained policy tool. In the words of the prominent monetary historian Barry Eichengreen, it took the disastrous Great Depression to break "the golden fetters" that had constrained monetary policy

---

[4] Federal Reserve Mission Statement from the Board of Governors' website: www.federalreserve.gov/aboutthefed/mission.htm.

activism up to that point. Since then, monetary policy has evolved as a more activist tool for managing business cycles. As a result, academic interest in monetary policy over the past half century garnered a lot of interest as economists learned how to best conduct monetary policy for optimal macroeconomic performance. To some extent, this focus came at the expense of the Fed's original primary mandate to promote the "safety and soundness" of the financial system. Traditionally, this has mainly meant oversight of the banking system.

The financial crisis in 2008–2009 exposed the Fed's overemphasis on macroeconomic monetary policy and neglect of financial stability issues. Many Fed critics have conflated this neglect of sufficient regulatory oversight with evidence that monetary policy has been "too easy" over the past two decades. For example, many observers have charged that the FOMC kept rates too low for too long during the housing boom years of 2004–2006, causing the reckless behavior that created the financial crisis. On the surface, this sounds reasonable.

It does not, however, stand up to scrutiny. If policy was "too easy" by the Fed's stated criteria, high inflation would have been a problem. Instead, as noted above, the low rates that the Fed set were necessary to keep inflation from turning into deflation. There is no evidence from the Fed's primary long-run mandate that policy has been too easy and inflation too high. On the contrary, the Fed has done a good job of controlling inflation around its 2-percent target.

The excesses that caused the financial crisis cannot be blamed on the Fed's interest rate policy. While it certainly deserves some criticism for inadequate regulatory oversight, the Fed was not responsible for *all* the regulatory lapses, political interference, and prudential lending standard breakdowns that allowed the financial crisis to develop over six decades. These will be addressed in more depth in chapter 8.

The main point is the Fed has one tool—monetary policy—dedicated to one long-run objective—inflation. To focus this tool on other objectives is inappropriate given its Congressional mandate. This means that the Federal Reserve should manage financial stability using its regulatory oversight tools rather than monetary policy per se. The Dodd-Frank legislation in response to the crisis sees to that.

Monetary policy during the business cycle

The monetary policy cycle shapes the business cycle. Likewise, the business cycle shapes the monetary policy cycle. It is an interactive process with cause and effect working both ways. Critics often blame monetary policy for just about all the excesses in the economy. Often, however, those excesses are the result of poor regulatory oversight, such as when excessive credit growth and leverage, rather than poor interest rate or monetary policy, destabilize particular sectors of the economy. The key insight here is that interest rates are ultimately set by the Federal Reserve to keep inflation at around 2 percent.

By other criteria, interest rates may seem too high or too low. For example, in recent years, savers have complained that rates are too low, forcing them into risky investments in search of yield. Of course, this complaint was notably absent in the early 1980s, when real short rates were quite high by historical standards. In that case, homebuilders barraged the Fed with complaints about overly tight monetary policy.

Still, the fact of the matter is the Fed is captive to its goal of containing inflation around 2 percent. Holding its monetary policy to other criteria is illogical as long as that's its mandate. It cannot hit two objectives with one "interest rate bullet" just as you cannot hit two birds with one shot (because of the Tinbergen rule, which states that for each and every policy target there must be at least one policy tool. If there are fewer tools than targets, then some policy goals will not be realized). The Fed is shooting at inflation, and it has been successful at hitting its target. To blame monetary policy for other shortcomings in the economy implicitly ignores the purpose of monetary policy, which is controlling inflation.

This makes inflation the ultimate driver of the monetary policy and business cycle, especially the cycles of recent decades as the Fed has moved progressively closer to an explicit inflation target of around 2 percent. This progression has been part and parcel of its move toward transparency, telling the public what it is doing and why, in stark contrast to the old days, when the Fed was deliberately vague about its operations. Yet, even in that world, inflation was ultimately a key objective of its policy. Without a specific target, however, the market was left to guess how much inflation any particular policy regime would tolerate and how well it operated to control price pressures. That was the heyday of Fed Watching, when expertise in reading the monetary policy "tea leaves" from a less transparent and deliberately obscure US central bank was particularly valuable.

Tracking inflation becomes critical in a world in which the business cycle is heavily influenced by the monetary policy response to inflation. The reason why you "don't fight the Fed" is that monetary policy restrains business activity when it is most worried about inflation. It does that by raising rates above their sustainable average to the point at which the federal funds rate usually exceeds the ten-year Treasury rate. As discussed above, this is a powerful signal that the economy will slow down to the recession point as the Federal Reserve tries to stop the cyclical uptrend in inflation. The inversion of the yield curve stops the natural uptrend in profits and usually generates a bear market in equities.

As a recession ensues and inflationary pressures subside, monetary policy begins to shift its attention toward containing the recession, and in recent low-inflation years, toward preventing inflation from declining too much and morphing into deflation (when prices begin to actually decline rather than just increase at a slowing pace, causing growing deleveraging pressures in a highly indebted economy). Stimulative policy, which reduces the federal funds rate below its sustainable average, causing the yield curve to steepen, generally reaches its cyclical extreme when the Fed is most concerned about fostering a sustainable expansion that will head off deflationary forces. At this stage of the cycle, "don't fight the Fed" means a bull market in equities is good to go.

The policy role of wage inflation

The cycle in inflation is closely tied to the cycle in wages. In turn, the cycle in wages is closely tied to the cycle in unemployment. Simply put, wage pressures are weak when unemployment is high and there is a lot of slack in the labor market. Conversely, a tight labor market with very low unemployment tends to occur toward the end of the business cycle, when wage pressures are highest and inflation moves above the Fed's target as a result.

Exhibit 3.10 illustrates the movement of the federal funds rate and wage growth over the past 25 years. The solid line shows that the federal funds rate tends to collapse during recessions (grey shaded areas) and reach a bottom early in a recovery. The recovery from the 2007–2009 recession started with the funds rate already close to zero as a result of the financial crisis. Because of this zero-bound limitation, to provide the extra stimulus that monetary policy usually provides in the first stage of an expansion, the Fed had to use QE, whereby it purchased assets, such as long-maturity Treasury and agency securities, to provide more liquidity to the banking system and to keep longer-term interest rates low.

Notice that wage pressures tend to drop throughout a recession and well into the early stage of a recovery, when labor slack is greatest.

Exhibit 3.10 Growing Wage Pressures Force Fed to Remove Stimulus (shaded areas represent recessions)

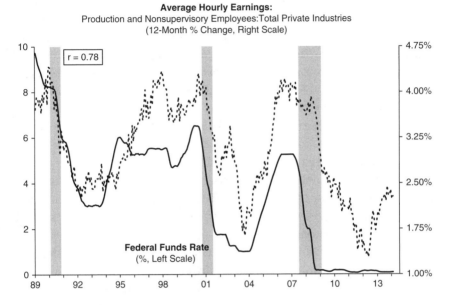

Average Hourly Earnings:
Production and Nonsupervisory Employees:Total Private Industries
(12-Month % Change, Right Scale)

Source: Haver Analytics.
Data as of August 2014.

Even though the unemployment rate starts falling in the early stage of the recovery, wage inflation tends to keep declining a while longer because the unemployment rate is still higher than normal. Eventually, the unemployment rate drops enough and the labor market tightens enough that wage pressures stop falling and start to increase again, as in 1994, 2004, and 2013. Wage inflation eventually causes price inflation. Because wages lag behind the unemployment rate, which itself is a lagging indicator, as discussed in chapter 2, price inflation has an even longer lagged response to a pickup in business activity. This makes inflation a long lagging indicator of the business cycle and explains why monetary policy must be forward looking.

In 1994 and 2004, the pickup in wage pressures was the cyclical cue for the Fed to start withdrawing monetary stimulus ("to ease off the accelerator") by raising rates from very low levels. In 2013, with policy rates essentially at zero, the first step toward normalizing policy was to start tapering the Fed's asset purchases as a precondition for the eventual rate hikes when wage pressures became even stronger.

As can also be seen in Exhibit 3.10, wage growth tends to breach the 4-percent level in the years right before recessions start. That's not a coincidence. With long-term productivity growing about 2 percent, wage growth greater than 4 percent implies inflation of over 2 percent (4 percent nominal wage gain minus 2 percent "real," or productivity-justified, wage gain). To stop inflation from rising too far above its target, the Fed clamps down on the economy when growth is generating excessive wage pressure—that is, wage growth that is too far above productivity gains. Essentially, at this stage of the business cycle the labor market has become too tight and growth needs to slow down to a more sustainable (less inflationary) pace based on the trend growth in labor supply and productivity.

These parameters that characterize recent business cycles are not written in stone. First, trend productivity growth can change. Second, the Fed could target more or less inflation. For example, some critics argue that true price stability would target an average of zero inflation over time, instead of 2 percent. In that case, the Fed would need to respond with tight policy when wage inflation breaches 2 percent (the approximate average long-term US productivity growth rate) instead of 4 percent, which allows for 2-percent productivity growth and 2-percent inflation. If productivity growth averaged 3 percent over the long haul, the Fed could tolerate 5-percent wage growth instead of 4 percent and still hit its 2-percent inflation target. The bottom line is that inflation depends on the excess of wage growth over the growth rate of labor productivity.

What's the "new normal" for interest rates?

Since World War II, US interest rates have experienced both the most extreme secular bear market in US history and the most extreme bull market. The bull market saw nominal ten-year Treasury yields fall from an all-time peak over 15 percent in 1981 to an all-time low under 2 percent in 2012. That long decline reversed a three-decade uptrend that began right after World War II, when yields increased from under 2 percent, a record low to that point in US history, to 15 percent by 1981.

Essentially, the great inflation that began in the mid-1960s and peaked in the early 1980s drove interest rates to all-time highs by 1981 as the Fed was eventually forced to push rates far enough above inflation to break its back. Then, for the next decade, interest rates remained high in real terms to keep inflation falling. By the turn of the century, rates were back in a range comparable to those of the 1950s and the early 1960s, the last time nominal rates were relatively normal by historical standards.

The historical "norm" for interest rates is likely close to the "new normal" that will shake out after their unprecedented swings since 1945. Before World War II, rates were less correlated with inflation because investors could rely on the fact that inflation averaged close to zero over long stretches of time. Indeed, the purchasing power of a dollar in the 1930s was similar to its purchasing power in the 1830s as central banks managed money to maintain its purchasing power over time.

The traditional pattern was that inflation would be high during times of war, like the Civil War and World War I, when financial discipline was sacrificed to win the wars. The quid pro quo for bondholders who helped finance the wars was an implicit commitment to restore the purchasing power of money after the war. This required a deflationary period after wars, as was seen during the last third of the 1800s after the Civil War and also during the first few years after World War I. The highest real Treasury bill interest rate in the twentieth century was registered in 1920 around 20 percent when an almost 8-percent nominal yield combined with double-digit deflation.

This historical pattern up to the 1940s was one reason most economists expected a renewed depression when World War II ended. Instead, under the influence of the Keynesian analysis of the Great Depression, there was no deflationary monetary policy to reverse the inflation of World War II. In fact, since World War II, the United States has experienced the most persistently inflationary period in its history, with only minimal short-lived bouts of deflation.

Partly this was deliberate and partly it reflected unintended consequences as central banks were learning to conduct monetary policy with a fiat standard rather than the gold standard that prevailed before the war. For example, as inflation accelerated in the 1960s and 1970s, policymakers raised rates too slowly and were always behind the curve. In addition, the notion that higher inflation could buy lower unemployment was disproven by the stagflation of the times, and in 1979 Volcker said "enough already" to the high and rising inflation. Since then, inflation has come down to its intended 2-percent target as central banks have ratcheted long-term inflation expectations back down from levels uncomfortably close to 10 percent. As discussed above, this inflation target comes from a post-World War II consensus view among economists that 2 percent is a better inflation target

Exhibit 3.11   Round-Trip Back to Normal

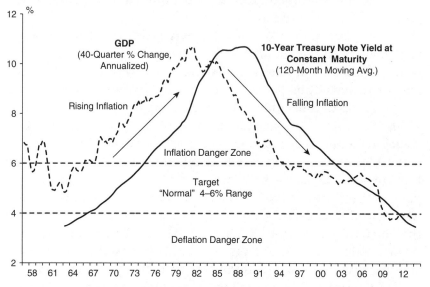

Source: Federal Reserve Board, Bureau of Economic Analysis/Haver Analytics.
Data as of April 18, 2014.

than zero. Inflation too much below 2 percent raises the risk of deflation, and inflation expectations much above 2 percent are considered destabilizing.

Exhibit 3.11 shows again this round trip from rising long-term inflation to falling long-term inflation, or disinflation. The graph shows ten-year averages for ten-year Treasury rates and nominal GDP growth, which reflect secular, or structural, moves rather than short-term fluctuations. Notice that during the rising inflation period, the ten-year yield averaged consistently below the nominal GDP growth rate, which was driven ever higher by inflation. Basically, interest rates were too low relative to inflation throughout the period up to 1981. Volcker changed that, and interest rates averaged substantially above nominal GDP growth until the early 2000s, when the disinflation trend went too far, threatening to turn into deflation.

In fact, the monetary policy experience of the new century has been dominated by the desire to stop low inflation from turning into deflation, a policy called reflation. Instead of continuing to push down on inflation, longer-term policy, on balance, has been trying to keep it up toward 2 percent. Exhibit 3.12 illustrates this long-term struggle to

Exhibit 3.12 Federal Funds above Nominal GDP: Disinflation. Funds below Nominal GDP: Reflation Force

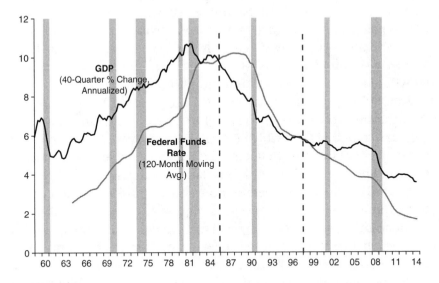

Source: FRB, BEA/Haver Analytics.

Data as of August 2014.

prevent deflation. The ten-year average of the Federal funds rate was way too low relative to inflation and nominal GDP during the late 1960s and 1970s. The gap reversed in the 1980s with Volcker's tighter policy, which worked to bring down inflation. Eventually, growing deflationary pressures forced easier monetary policy, and policy rates have fallen below the trend in nominal GDP growth to stop it from declining excessively.

Still, as shown earlier in Exhibit 3.1, the 4-year average growth rate of nominal GDP fell below its 60-year range to the lowest level since the 1930s, as the Great Recession and mild deflation combined during the financial crisis to threaten an even bigger economic collapse. The Fed responded by cutting rates to zero and adopting a quantitative easing strategy that has succeeded in pushing nominal GDP back into the bottom of its likely "new normal" range between 4 percent and 6 percent. As discussed before, 4 percent appears to be the minimum necessary to prevent debt deflation, deleveraging pressures from getting the upper hand, as was the case in the 2007–2009 period when the housing finance debacle threatened to bring down the system. Since incomes and revenues to service debt grow in proportion to nominal GDP, cash flows growing in the 4 percent to 6 percent range seem to be adequate to service the outstanding debt in the United States. Less than 4-percent nominal GDP growth seems to cause deleveraging that can cumulate in a self-reinforcing fashion like the deflationary busts that were common before World War II. Over 6-percent nominal GDP growth tends to untether inflation from the 2-percent target.

It should be apparent from Exhibits 3.11 and 3.12 that there is a strong correlation between the level of interest rates and the trend growth in nominal GDP, which is largely driven by the trend growth in inflation (since real growth potential is relatively stable, based on labor force and productivity growth). If inflation averages around 2 percent as the Fed desires, then there is no trend in inflation, only cyclical fluctuations around 2 percent. This implies that there will likely be no trend in interest rates. They will only fluctuate around stationary averages that correspond to the "new normal" range of nominal GDP growth of 4 percent to 6 percent, with a likely average of about 4.5 percent over time. This corresponds to the 2-percent inflation target plus a "new normal" real GDP growth rate of about 2.5 percent.

In their book, *Triumph of the Optimists,*[5] Elroy Dimson, Paul Marsh, and Mike Staunton looked at US Treasury bill and bond yields over the last century (1900–2000). The data show that real Treasury bill yields averaged about 0.9 percent over the period. The real return to medium- and long-term government bonds was 1.6 percent. Presumably because of higher inflation risk, the real yield on bonds averaged 1.8 percent after 1950, compared to 1.4 percent before 1950, as inflation risks were lower in the old monetary regime.

If we add 2 percentage points for inflation to a 0.9 percent real money market rate, the historical experience suggests that the nominal Fed funds rate should average a bit under 3 percent over the business cycle. Likewise, adding 2 percent to a 1.8 percent real yield for bonds gives a nominal ten-year Treasury yield average just under 4 percent over the business cycle.

These averages are likely reflective of what the "new normal" will look like if the Fed is successful in meeting its inflation objective over time, assuming a normal credit demand environment, with a caveat. Because of weak age demographics for borrowing and an already lever-aged economy, real interest rates will likely continue to average below

[5] Elroy Dimson, Paul Marsh, and Mike Staunton, *Triumph of the Optimists, 101 Years of Global Investment Returns* (Princeton University Press, 2002).

normal over the next couple of cycles. For this reason, real interest rates could average about a half point below what historical norms would suggest. This implies average nominal rates of about 2.5 percent for the short-end and 3.5 percent for the ten-year Treasury over the business cycle.

One consequence of the unusually high interest rates during the mid-1970s to mid-1990s period has been extreme sample bias in perceptions of what constitutes "normal" interest rates. Our "new normal" interest-rate structure is lower than the consensus among economists, including Federal Reserve officials. For example, in December 2012, the preponderance (17 out of 19) of FOMC members projected the longer-run average for the Federal funds rate in a range of 3.75 percent to 4.50 percent, with a majority expecting 4 percent, or more. Only one member expected that the long-run average funds rate would be as low as 3 percent. By March of 2014, the cluster of outlooks among FOMC members had moved down a bit into the 3.5-percent to 4-percent range.

There has been a consistent upward bias in forecasters' outlook for interest rates ever since inflation began its long descent in the early 1980s. The downtrend in inflation was generally underanticipated, causing interest rates to come down more than generally anticipated. The higher average interest rates of the mid-1970 to mid-1990s period have biased "normal" interest-rate forecasts higher than what seems likely, in our view.

Real interest rates were unusually high during the 1980s and 1990s compared to historical averages. This was part of the dynamic that brought inflation down over time. Basing "normal" real interest-rate expectations on these unusually high real rates is mistaken in our view given the more symmetric risks around deflation and inflation in a low inflation environment. High real rates in this environment unnecessarily raise the risk of deflation. *An interest-rate range more like that of the 1955–1965 low-inflation period seems more likely.* As a result, we expect the consensus view of "normal" interest rates to continue to decline more in line with our view based on a much broader historical sample rather than one skewed by the unusual interest-rate experience of the mid-1970s to mid-1990s period.

The "new normal" yield curve

The gap between the ten-year Treasury note rate and the overnight Fed funds rate averaged roughly 100 basis points over the past half century.

That is also the case for the 1900–2000 period, using the Treasury bill rate as a proxy for the Fed funds rate. As shown in the section above, during that period, Treasury bills averaged a 0.9 percent real yield and Treasury bonds averaged 1.6 percent. The yield premium on bonds over bills was 0.5 percent before 1950 and 0.9 percent after 1950. We attribute the difference to the increased inflation risk premium in a fiat money system.

As shown in Exhibit 3.13, the difference between the overnight and the ten-year rate can vary quite a bit over long stretches of time (ten-year spans). During the rising inflation era into the early 1980s, the difference was much smaller than normal because short rates rose faster in response to inflation than long rates rose. This reflected a persistent underanticipation of inflation embodied in long rates compared to what actually transpired.

The opposite was true during the falling inflation era, as short rates came down faster than long rates because long rates persistently embodied excessive inflation expectations compared to what actually transpired. Basically, declining interest rates and inflation were constantly surprising a market that was slow to adjust its inflation expectations lower.

What's more, the reflation effort of the past decade has required an easier-than-normal monetary policy to prevent persistent deflation

Exhibit 3.13   Yield Gap Wider to Stop Deflation

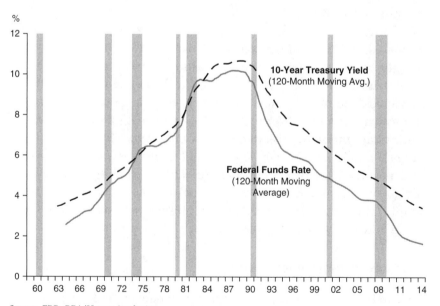

Source: FRB, BEA/Haver Analytics.

Data as of August 15, 2014.

from engulfing the economy. This is reflected in a steeper yield curve than normal, with the yield gap between overnight money and the ten-year yield over the past ten years almost double its long historical average.

Exhibit 3.9 shows the yield curve spread in contemporaneous rather than long-average terms. The historical average of the spread of about one percentage point (0.9 percentage point average in the modern fiat money period after 1950) is comprised of high-frequency deviations that are systematically related to the business cycle. As already noted, when the spread is 2 or more percentage points, monetary policy is very stimulative. When the spread turns negative, a recession is generally right around the corner, as it signals tight monetary policy. The extreme inversion of the early 1980s seems an outlier that was necessary to break the back of the worst inflation in US history.

If we allow for about 100 basis points of variance around a 3.5 percent average ten-year yield, that would imply a range of 2.5 percent to 4.5 percent in long rates in a world in which debt and GDP growth are somewhat slower for demographic and excessive leverage reasons. For money market rates, more variance, say 200 basis points, on either side of a 2.5-percent average rate, would imply a range of about 0.5 to 4.5 percent over the business cycle. With a peak Fed funds rate at about 4.5 percent when the Fed is most concerned with addressing inflation, long rates would fall in anticipation of an end to the rate hike cycle and falling rates through the ensuing recession and early recovery stage. A 4.5-percent peak in the Fed funds rate would normally go with a lower bond yield and an inverted yield curve going into a recession.

Putting it all together and assuming some residual debt-growth restraint from the debt supercycle ending in 2006, a good guess for the "new normal" is a somewhat lower than average real interest-rate structure for the foreseeable future, with the Fed funds rate averaging around 2.5 percent and the ten-year Treasury note averaging around 3.5 percent over the next couple of business cycles. As financial repression diminishes over time and debt growth normalizes, a half-point rise in real interest rates from those levels would restore historical norms.

The dollar

As we highlighted above, the Fed's 2-percent inflation target constrains it from controlling other potential targets, such as the foreign exchange value of the dollar, for example. During the period of quantitative easing it was common to hear all sorts of criticism suggesting that US monetary policy was "debasing" the dollar deliberately to gain a competitive advantage in foreign trade. Frequently, when the policy interest rate target is cut, one hears the same kind of commentary. Sometimes, the comments come from officials in other countries who like to blame their domestic economic problems on US monetary policy making the dollar exchange rate "too high" or "too low." Indeed, when the Fed was aggressively trying to stimulate the economy, foreign critics complained about the so-called dollar policy of "debasement." Then, when the Fed began to curtail its quantitative easing in 2013, the same critics complained when their currencies weakened as a result. Likewise, there has been a barrage of criticism from market participants and financial media suggesting the Fed targets a weak dollar with its easy money policy.

More generally, it is common to hear commentators on Fed policy attribute all sorts of alternative goals to monetary policy other than inflation. Some of the conspiracy theorists believe the Fed targets equity prices at particular points in time. There was a false but widespread view after the 1987 stock market crash that the crash ended because the Federal Reserve purchased equities for its own account. This misconception resurfaced during the financial crisis in late 2008.

The Fed targets inflation. Everything else is determined by the economic forces that accompany its 2-percent inflation target. For the dollar's foreign exchange value, this means "benign neglect." The dollar's foreign exchange value is left to be determined by market forces or the intervention of other countries, such as China, that have managed their exchange rate against the dollar.

Still, while the dollar's foreign exchange value is the province of the Treasury Department, and Federal Reserve officials defer to the Treasury Secretary as the official spokesperson for the dollar, the dollar's value over the long run is determined by the US inflation rate compared to that of other currencies. Arbitrage through trade and capital flows means prices of goods, services, and assets tend to reflect global forces of supply and demand. Thus, over the long run, currency values tend to reflect the differences in inflation rates that determine purchasing power parity, or fair value, exchange rates.

For example, the Japanese yen was the strongest currency in the world between 1990 and 2013, when "Abenomics" forced the Bank of Japan to finally adopt a 2-percent inflation target. Before that, Japan had averaged around zero inflation for almost a quarter century while other developed countries, like the United States, averaged about 2 percent. The Bank of Japan was out of step with the "2-percent solution." As a result, the purchasing power of the yen rose against the currencies of other developed economies. The yen went from almost 150 to the dollar in 1990 to almost 75 to the dollar in mid-2012, essentially doubling in value against most other developed market currencies where higher inflation prevailed.

The US dollar policy of "benign neglect" forces other countries to adopt a 2-percent inflation target or else see their currencies strengthen (if inflation runs below the 2-percent pace, as in Japan before "Abenomics") or weaken (if inflation exceeds that 2-percent annual average rate over the long run). Aside from Japan and the Eurozone, most other developed economies have adopted the 2-percent target, or something close to it. On the other hand, emerging markets generally run higher inflation rates. Consequently, their currencies have depreciated against the dollar over long periods of time. That is changing as more developing economies bring down inflation expectations. As a result, world inflation has declined dramatically since 2000.

Exhibit 3.14 Undervalued Dollar a Major Plus for US Growth after the Financial Crisis

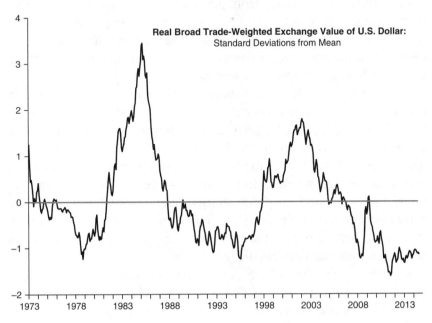

Source: Federal Reserve Board.

Data as of August 15, 2014.

Exhibit 3.14 shows the real trade-weighted value of the dollar (in standard deviations from the mean) since the Bretton Woods system broke down and the dollar's foreign exchange value began to float. The dollar's deviation from purchasing power parity or "fair value" (its mean for the period) has gone through long cycles. As seen in Exhibit 3.14, most recently, the dollar has gone from significantly over-valued (almost 2 standard deviations above "fair value" or purchasing power parity rate) in 2002 to significantly undervalued (below "fair value") in 2013. These long cycles of rising and falling values tend to reflect the varying natures of trade and capital flows in different global business cycles as a result of growth and interest-rate differentials. The dollar's premier reserve currency status and the fact that the majority of "safe-haven" assets tend to be denominated in dollars also accounts for some of the short-term fluctuations in its exchange rate. Indeed, the dollar tends to rise during "risk-off" episodes and decline with growing "risk-on" flows when global business is thriving.

To summarize exchange-rate determination, theory and empirical evidence show that the dollar's exchange rate against different currencies tends to fluctuate in the short term according to the manufacturing cycle and "flight-to-safety" considerations, and in the medium term according to *deviations* from purchasing power parity and relative differentials in growth and interest rates. In the long term, the short- and medium-term effects wash out, leaving inflation differentials and relative purchasing power parity to be the ultimate determinant of the dollar's value against other currencies.

From 1995 until 2002, the dollar went from an undervaluation extreme to an overvaluation extreme that reflected an improving US financial situation. The US fiscal deficit disappeared over that period as the budget was balanced in 2000 for the first time in decades. As seen in Exhibit 3.2, the US expansion was more equity financed than debt financed. As a result, there was less need to borrow from the rest of the world, and the dollar strengthened. As foreign-based dollar debtors scrambled to get enough US currency between 1994 and 2000, there were several non-dollar currency crises that culminated in the Asian currency crisis during the late 1990s.

In contrast, the 2002–2008 period was characterized by a declining dollar. Countries such as China depended on growing trade surpluses for growth, while other countries, such as the United States, enabled those surpluses by running ever-larger trade deficits. China recycled the dollars it earned from rising trade surpluses back to the trade-deficit countries as loans. This financed housing booms in deficit countries, like the United States, the United Kingdom, Spain, and Ireland, where home prices spiraled ever higher as current account deficits got wider and wider. In addition, China's official dollar purchases stopped its currency from appreciating against the greenback, allowing it to maintain a competitive advantage and keep its trade surplus growing. This whole dynamic helped cause, and ended with, the financial crisis. Since then, a new global dynamic has taken hold, suggesting the dollar is in the early stage of a strengthening cycle as global trade rebalances. China's surplus has fallen from almost 10 percent of GDP to about 2 percent as its economy transitions from export-led growth to domestic demand-led growth. In the United States, the current account deficit has dropped from about 6 percent of GDP to one-third that level. This rebalancing is positive for the dollar and has created a global pattern of growth more like that of the 1990s.

As noted above, while the dollar goes through long cycles of over- and undervaluation, its ultimate value varies mainly according to inflation differentials between countries. Most major developed economies, aside from Japan, have had broadly similar inflation experiences because their central banks also see 2 percent as a reasonable policy benchmark. This means that over the long run they maintain a relatively stable exchange rate with the dollar.

As more emerging markets garner investment grade status by adopting more orthodox monetary and fiscal policies, this naturally implies lower inflation targets similar to those in the developed world. The long tradition of currency debasement in the emerging countries will end for those countries that move in the direction of more price stability over time. For the rest, the barriers to development and rising standards of living will remain formidable and unfortunate. Low, stable inflation expectations that converge with those in the developed world seem to be a helpful element for raising living standards and more efficient allocation of capital. It is also a necessary ingredient for long-term stability in the exchange rate.

The Great Experiment

The gap between the US response to its long disinflation trend and those of Japan and Europe has provided a valuable social experiment in economic policymaking. Through the 1960s, 1970s and 1980s, central bankers learned the inflationary dangers of fiat money systems. Japan was the first major developed economy to escape the inflationary up-spiral when it refused to accommodate the second oil price shock in the late 1970s. In the United States, Volcker tamed the "inflation beast." As part of the process of currency unification, the countries that ultimately joined the Euro began an inflation convergence process in the early 1980s that started the inflation downtrend in Europe. Prior to this inflation convergence, which made exchange rate convergence possible, inflation rates in Europe varied widely. Aside from Japan, which went overboard in the deflationary direction by the 1990s, the rest of the developed world has successfully brought inflation down to around 2 percent, although Europe has struggled since the financial crisis to avoid a Japanese-like outcome.

The powerful economic dynamics that reduced inflation from double digits in the early 1980s to the low single digits by the 1990s had a momentum that raised the risk of deflation. This was not apparent to most central bankers, who had been inculcated with an asymmetric anti-inflation bias as a result of the 1970s inflation experience. It is not surprising that Japan, where these disinflationary forces were earliest to arrive and were strongest, was taken by surprise. An anti-inflation bias is also part of traditional central banking "folklore" because history offers numerous examples of ruinous hyperinflation episodes caused by excessive money printing. This is an especially powerful memory at the Bundesbank and in Germany more generally, where the 1920s hyperinflation remains deeply ingrained in the social psyche. What's more, deflation is mainly a pre-World War II phenomenon that most people, including economists and current central bankers, have never experienced. For all these reasons, central bankers were unprepared to varying degrees as the risk of deflation gradually increased over the past two decades.

The experience from Japan's 1990s crisis helped awaken these concerns, especially in the United States, where Bernanke had a deep understanding of the debt-deflation experience in the United States during the 1930s. The key policy takeaway from the lessons of debt-deflation dynamics is that actions that seem excessive in a normal environment are necessary in a debt-deflation environment. What would be profligacy in a normal economy—that is, big fiscal deficits and aggressively easy monetary policy—is critically important for defeating a deflationary threat, as we already discussed in earlier sections. Flooding the banking system with base money helps offset the collapse in the money multiplier when fear becomes excessive.

Fiscal "profligacy" to deal with the crisis caused enormous political controversy. Fortunately, in the United States, where the fiscal deficit swelled to 10 percent of GDP during the crisis, the highest level since World War II, this political backlash did not stop the recovery. By the time fiscal austerity was implemented in 2013, the US economy was almost four years into recovery. Most important, the Federal Reserve countered that fiscal austerity with a third round of QE to ensure that the expansion would not fizzle out.

In contrast, in Europe austerity was pursued too soon and monetary policy was hamstrung by the lack of centralized authority. What's more, the ECB made a serious policy mistake by raising its policy rate in April 2011. As a result, while the United States kept growing, Europe was back in recession by the end of that year and the euro's survival came into doubt. The divergent results of the two blocs' policy responses to the crisis is glaring. Just after the recession ended in 2009, the unemployment rate in the United States peaked at 10 percent and was about the same as in the Eurozone (Exhibit 3.15). By April 2011, when the ECB hiked rates, unemployment had slipped a bit in Europe but still remained close to

Exhibit 3.15   United States Embraces Best Economic Thinking. Politicized Monetary and Fiscal Policy in Europe Reject Appropriate Medicine

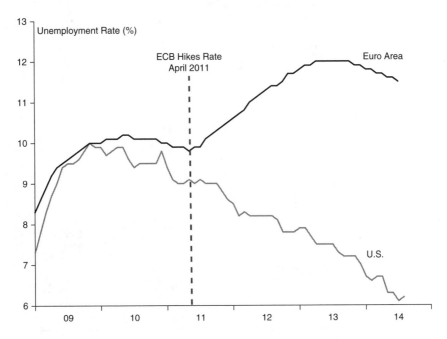

Source: BLS, EUROSTAT/Haver Analytics.
Data as of August 15, 2014.

10 percent. Thanks to more aggressive stimulus, especially on the fiscal side, it had already declined to 9 percent in the United States. By the end of 2013, Europe's unemployment rate had jumped to 12 percent, while the US rate was approaching half that level, providing clear evidence that pro-growth US policies worked, while austerity crippled Europe's recovery.

In prematurely going for budget balance without support from monetary policy and restored banking health, Europe stifled growth and ended up with depression-like unemployment. In the United States, stronger GDP growth generated much faster tax revenue growth, and the fiscal deficit was little different by 2014 from that in Europe, where austerity forced deficit contractions. Arguably, the US fiscal drag in 2013 was imposed prematurely, as most economists would agree. Nevertheless, it came after a more entrenched private-sector expansion was under way. In Europe, fiscal austerity was much more premature, and the 2011 monetary tightening a costly mistake.

Exhibit 3.16 shows the relative growth rates of the Fed and ECB balance sheets since the financial crisis. By this metric, Fed policy was more than five times as expansive as the ECB policy. In addition, while

Exhibit 3.16   There Is a Time to Be Expansive

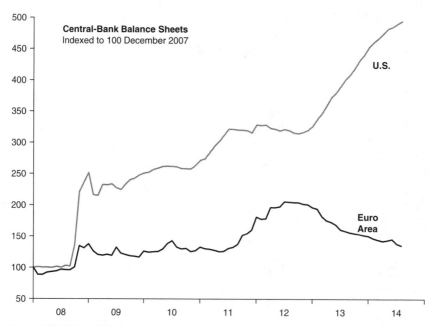

Source: FRB, ECB, BoJ/Haver Analytics.

Data as of August 2014.

the Fed's QE3 policy kept its balance sheet growing in 2013 and 2014, the ECB's balance sheet was already shrinking. It should not be surprising that the gap between US and European growth widened and deflationary risks rose in Europe by that time.

The main point cannot be overemphasized. When deflation rather than inflation is the primary risk in a highly leveraged economy, prudence dictates aggressive policy stimulus that would seem irresponsible under other conditions. Populist backlash is to be expected in this situation, and that's exactly what happened. *Time* magazine's "Man of the Year" for 2009, Bernanke, was castigated by the pitchfork wielding zealots of monetary and fiscal orthodoxy.

Most people rely on rules of thumb because there are many things they do not understand. Monetary policy is one of those things many feel qualified to judge despite inadequate insight. "Balance the budget" and "don't print money" are two rules of thumb that work under some but not all circumstances. It's fortunate that Bernanke knew the difference. It's too bad the ECB did not. Like the BOJ before it, the ECB came up with all kinds of rationalizations for ignoring the obvious. Shrinking your balance sheet as deflationary risks rise makes no sense, and the results speak for themselves.

Barry Eichengreen cited "golden fetters" as a mindset that precluded a successful policy response to the Great Depression. Indeed, the solutions required for a faster recovery from that financial collapse were not in the toolbox of the Gold Standard policy options. Only when those fetters were broken and the Gold Standard abandoned did one country after another climb out of the deflationary abyss.

Europe experienced its worst economic crisis since the 1930s, with an unemployment rate about double that in the United States five years after the recession, as a limited mindset prevented the policies necessary to reestablish normal growth. The new fetters are "inflation-phobia" fetters. At their roots, they share the same irrational dogmatic belief that proved the "golden fetters" so counterproductive. The idea that massive central bank balance sheet expansion must be avoided at all costs is one of those ingrained beliefs very closely associated with the idea that large-scale money printing should be avoided at all costs. History shows that's not always the case, and as noted above, knowing the difference is critical.

As a final bit of evidence on this point, consider the expansion of the balance sheet of the Swiss National Bank (SNB) from less than 100 percent of GDP to over 300 percent of GDP (Exhibit 3.17). Has there been

Exhibit 3.17 Switzerland Proves the Point. When Fear's Rampant, It Must Be Countered, or It Will Spread

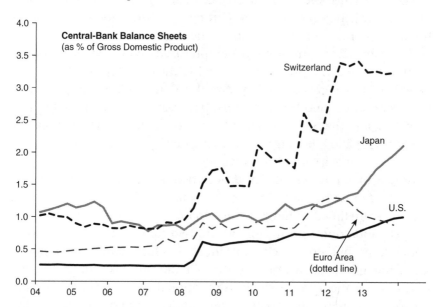

Source: Haver Analytics.
Data as of August 2014.

rampant inflation in Switzerland? Has its currency been debased? The answer to both questions is a resounding no. Deflationary pressures on the Swiss franc have been more intense than those on the dollar. Because Switzerland has the longest history of political and currency stability in the world, the euro crisis caused a huge "flight-to-safety" demand for the Swiss currency relative to the size of the Swiss economy and financial system. To prevent a destabilizing surge in the franc's foreign exchange value, the SNB sterilized the inflows by providing more of its own currency to the market. It offset the surge in demand with a surge in supply that maintained price stability. Nobody is accused the Swiss of policy profligacy.

Some investment implications of the euro crisis

Before we move on to put the various asset classes—bonds, stocks, and tangible assets—into the business cycle framework, let's summarize some of the investment implications of the differing monetary policy approaches discussed in this chapter.

Exchange rates are largely determined over the very long run by inflation differentials, which in turn are determined by monetary policy, whether deliberately or as a side effect of targeting another objective. For example, a small country may find it useful to peg its exchange rate to that of a major economy trading partner rather than targeting an inflation rate. In that case, inflation in the small economy will generally track that of the large economy over very long periods of time assuming it can maintain the peg without too much trouble. Indeed, in the short term, maintaining the peg may require withstanding a lot of volatility through other adjustment mechanisms, like trade and capital flows, rather than inflation.

The experience of Japan and Europe, two major developed regions that have chosen a different monetary policy course than the United States, offers a clear lesson: lower relative trend inflation means a stronger currency. First, Japan has been the main outlier from the 2-percent inflation trend in other developed economies, with inflation consistently running close to zero since 1990. As a result, from over 300 yen to the dollar before the Breton Woods system broke down in 1971, its currency appreciated to the point at which it only took 75 yen to buy a dollar in 2012. Conventional wisdom identifies currency strength with a strong economy, and the yen was the strongest currency in the world until "Abenomics" changed Japan's deflationary monetary policy. Unfortunately, while Japan had the strongest currency in the world since 1990, it also had the weakest economic performance of any major economy, with nominal GDP flat during this period accompanied by mounting government debt. The argument for zero inflation as a policy target is not bolstered by Japan's experience. Japanese equities were the worst performing of any developed economy for over 20 years.

Second, until the financial crisis, Europe's monetary policy was more in sync with that of the United States. After the crisis, the two diverged, as discussed above. With inflation close to zero and growth averaging only around 1 percent, Europe was at risk of a prolonged Japanese-style stagnation with zero to 1-percent nominal growth compared to 4 to 5 percent in the United States. If this situation persists, the euro could take the place of the yen as the world's strongest currency. This assumes Japan can successfully hit its new policy target of 2-percent inflation and Europe continues to miss the 2-percent mark. If Japan lapses back into deflation, it would join the Eurozone as a strong-currency, stagnant economy.

Ostensibly, the ECB would like to avoid a Japanese-style stagnation, and it talks about moving inflation up toward 2 percent. Yet, letting money and credit aggregates contract and shrinking its balance sheet are inconsistent with its professions to boost inflation and curb currency appreciation. Like Japan before it, Europe seems to only move to avoid tail risks, such as the breakup of the euro. Unfortunately, it has not recognized the need for the proactive "profligacy" that is necessary to escape the deflationary vortex. Japan seems to have recognized this point after seeing Bernanke's success, albeit almost 25 years too late. Europe seems to have put much-needed political and institutional reforms ahead of needed policy stimulus and economic growth. The risk is that prolonged economic stagnation will undermine political cohesion and create both political and economic instability.

On balance, these considerations, along with much more favorable demographics, suggest that the US economy has considerable comparative advantage for economic growth going forward. Partly, this reflects advantages from developing its natural resource endowments. Partly, it reflects a culture that tolerates failure and risk-taking in an ever faster changing world driven by technologies that were incomprehensible just a decade ago. Still, the role of proactive, well-understood monetary policy also deserves some of the credit. Without it, the United States could have found itself in much worse shape following the Great Recession.

Whether Europe ends up like Japan in the 1990–2012 period, or more like the United States will help determine whether European risk assets, such as equities, end up in a Japanese-style secular bear market or move more in sync with a better-performing US market. In the meantime, tight monetary policy made European fixed-income markets more attractive and the Euro exchange rate the strongest of the major currencies until the ECB's belated adoption of quantitative easing. The difference between zero and 5-percent nominal GDP growth is significant in its impact on asset returns. The bottom line is deflation risk favors high-quality fixed income over equities, something we'll see when we discuss asset performance in different economic environments.

4
Bonds and Credit

The two main cyclical determinants of fixed-income returns arise from duration risk and credit risk. Duration risk reflects the sensitivity of bond values to fluctuations in interest rates and depends on the distribution of payment through time. The longer the duration of a bond with a fixed payments stream, the more sensitive its price is to interest-rate changes. Credit risk premia refer to the extra interest rate that lower-quality credits have to pay above the "risk-free rate" to borrow in the markets. In good times, these premia tend to be much lower than in crises.

Both sources of fluctuations in fixed-income valuations have a predictable cyclical pattern. The monetary policy cycle tends to drive the interest-rate cycle, which in turn determines when in the business cycle it is best to embrace, or to avoid, duration risk. Likewise, there is a cycle in credit risk associated with the stages of the business cycle. There are times when "fear and loathing" dominate credit valuations, and times when complacency rules and investors are willing to take much more risk for very little incremental return. We will address the cyclical behavior in duration and credit risk in turn. First, however, it is helpful to discuss the anchors of longer-term valuation around which these cyclical fluctuations occur.

Valuation anchors

As we saw earlier, in the foreign exchange markets we find that the primary long-term relative-value determinant is the difference between countries' domestic inflation rates because of purchasing-power-parity forces. Deviations from this basic anchor tend to be self-correcting over very long stretches of time as shorter-term influences get washed out.

For equities, as we will discuss in the next chapter, the valuation anchor tends to be the present value of the earnings capacity of companies. However, just as currencies can deviate substantially from their valuation anchors, so too can equities. In fact, secular bull and bear markets tend to be associated with correcting excessive deviations from valuation anchors. In 2000, for example, the US equity market was the most overvalued relative to its earnings capacity since at least 1929. It took about a decade of a secular bear market and two business cycles before those valuation excesses were corrected and a new secular bull market began. Essentially, earnings had to grow into the valuations before normal returns could be expected to resume.

For corporate bonds, the fundamental valuation anchor depends on the "normal" structure of the yield curve for Treasuries and the "normal" credit-risk premia that are paid over and above the like-duration Treasury rate, which is used to benchmark credit risk. US Treasury credit is treated as if it has close to zero risk of default because the government borrows in the same currency that it issues and the debt is backed by the full faith and credit of the US government.

The view on inflation is essential for bond valuations and that is why part of the underlying interest-rate outlook embodied in our "new normal" yield curve for Treasury securities includes a view about inflation. Specifically, the "new normal" yield curve that we discussed in chapter 3 is based on a 2-percent inflation rate over the long haul, with a relatively low risk that this inflation anchor will be disrupted by political interference with the Federal Reserve's long-run goals for monetary policy.

An upward-sloping yield-curve anchor assumes a slightly positive long-term inflation rate. In contrast, a long-run expectation of sufficiently high deflation would create a persistently negatively sloped or inverted curve, as in the United States during the post–Civil War era of the late nineteenth century. The main point is that a valuation anchor for the fixed-income market, or any US asset market for that matter, usually requires a view about the macroeconomic growth and monetary policy environment over a longer-term horizon of a decade, or more. A lot of the economic instability in the 1970s arose from the disruption of underlying valuation anchors as inflation accelerated.

The credit-risk premia anchor also seems to have been affected in the mid-1960s as corporate America embraced increasing leverage. Corporate BAA credit spreads over Treasuries fluctuated fairly tightly around 100 basis points between 1945 and 1965. Then, they took a quantum leap higher that has persisted ever since, with spreads averaging about twice that level. This appears to be related to the downshift in profit margins at about the same time. Profit margins are a cushion for debt repayment. Higher margins imply more cash available to make debt payments. Lower margins, on the other hand, increase credit risk. Increased leverage and rising interest rates seem to explain much of the shift to lower margins after 1965.

The credit-spread "anchor" also appears to have increased at about the same time with higher interest rates and increased interest-rate volatility, raising the question whether the "new-normal" interest environment we are projecting creates forces that will reduce the credit-spread anchor over time. Such a decline would be consistent with our view that profit margins have broken out to a new higher secular range as a direct result of the declining labor share of income, lower interest rates, and a more efficient allocation of resources in a low-inflation environment. Demographics and increased automation are powerful forces for this secular shift, which will be discussed in our more detailed look at profit margins and equity valuation.

To summarize, valuation anchors are the first step toward establishing fundamental asset values, whether for currencies, bonds, or stocks. Some asset values are more easily estimated than others. There are several ways to value real estate that establish useful anchors (for example, the capitalization rate simply discounts the net rental streams at a required rate of return to estimate the present value of the property). On the other hand, other assets, such as gold, which doesn't generate an income stream, seem much less amenable to an anchor valuation based on financial characteristics.

One characteristic of a useful anchor is that it provides a fundamental force for mean reversion. As a result, anchors are the basis for strategic allocation over longer time horizons. Good models of anchor valuation generally imply the risk and return characteristics that can be expected from an asset class over the long term. To deduce these returns, capital-market assumptions about inflation, interest rates, real economic growth, and regional differences in these parameters are among the model inputs that are generally necessary. Together with correlations across asset classes, these anchor valuations form the basis for strategic portfolio construction.

The conventional approach of asset allocators is to use historical averages for many of the required parameters. Accurately understanding structural changes in the fundamental macroeconomics behind the capital-market assumptions that go into valuation anchors is one of the most valuable insights an investment manager can have. Indeed, most of the crowd operates as if reversion to the historical mean is always the appropriate approach for strategic allocation. However, when fundamentals change, a new mean can result. Two examples of fundamental changes highlighted in this book are (1) likely lower-than-historical-average future interest rates and (2) higher-than-historical-average profit margins. Both have the effect of raising anchor valuations on equities and lowering the credit-spread "anchor."

Our focus in this book is on cyclical fluctuations in asset values. These are generally short-term deviations from anchor valuations caused by business cycle pressures on average valuation. This is the basis for a lot of tactical allocation decision-making. Nevertheless, insights about fundamental structural shifts can also add to returns and should be on the radar screen of a good strategist. They can be part of "what's different this time" in each business cycle.

Cyclical duration risk and tactical fixed-income allocation

Over the course of a business cycle, Treasury bond yields have a high and a low point. Since yields are inversely related to prices, the best time to buy (at the lowest price) comes when the long-term yield makes its cycle high. Conversely, the best time to sell (at the highest price) is when the cyclical low point in long yields is reached. From a tactical viewpoint, this is the simple message from the business cycle: as yields rise from their cycle low point, it is advantageous to be underweight Treasury bonds. As yields peak and begin to fall, it is advantageous to be overweight from the "normal" strategic allocation assigned to fixed income in general, and Treasuries in particular. By doing this, a portfolio achieves a higher return over the cycle than that of a static strategic allocation.

Since longer-duration portfolios lose more when interest rates rise and gain more when interest rates fall, a higher tactical allocation to fixed income and maximum extension of duration within benchmark limitations makes most sense when rates have peaked and are set to decline. This generally occurs when monetary policy is tight and the yield curve is inverted. When long rates are lower than short rates, it's generally a signal that the tightening cycle is near its end and that prices for Treasuries are set to increase.

Usually, this is when the transition from a "bear-flattening" phase of the cycle to a "bull-flattening" phase takes place. In the "bear-flattening" phase (when the Fed is tightening policy), it is a "bear" market in bonds because bond prices are falling (long-term interest rates are rising). While the whole yield curve shifts up, short rates rise more than long rates (hence the flattening of the curve). This is the early phase of the monetary tightening process when the yield curve is moving from maximum steepness to more-than-normal flatness.

The end phase of the tightening process is signaled by the reluctance of long-term interest rates to move higher even as the Federal Reserve continues to boost short-term interest rates. When the terminal boosts in short-term interest rates are followed by declining long rates, the cycle has moved into the "bull-flattening" phase, when the yield curve can transition from completely flat to inverted. At this point, it usually means that the market is judging incoming economic information as starting to suggest a recessionary slowdown on the horizon and/or waning inflation pressures. Remember that the last tightening phase usually takes place in an environment of excessive wage pressure, low unemployment, tight capacity utilization rates, and rising inflation. These factors tend to keep the Fed tightening until it is convinced that it has turned the tide from rising inflation pressures to declining inflation pressures. Anticipation of this tide turn is first seen in longer-term bond yields, in which the incentive to catch the yield peak is greatest from a tactical business cycle timing point of view.

For example, between June 2005 and July 2006, the Federal Reserve raised its funds rate target about 225 basis points from 3.0 percent to 5.25 percent. The ten-year Treasury note yield rose from about 4 percent to 5.1 percent over the same period. This was a "bear-flattening" phase with interest rates rising across the maturity spectrum ("bear" phase), but with the overnight rate increase exceeding the ten-year rate increase by about 110 basis points ("flattening").

During the subsequent year (July 2006-July 2007), the Fed held policy steady at a 5.25-percent funds rate level, while 10-year and 30-year bond yields averaged slightly lower. The curve was slightly inverted for a year as investors guessed that the Fed had finished tightening. This was a good time to overweight Treasuries. Indeed, by December 2007, the recession had begun. The Fed quickly cut the funds rate by a full percentage point during the six months leading up to the recession. A new bond bull market had begun. Those who bought the ten-year

Treasury note around a 5-percent yield in late 2006 and early 2007, when the funds rate was at 5.25 percent, saw big gains by December 2008, when yields plummeted to 2.42 percent.

Timing the cycle is not always easy. As already noted, there are often idiosyncratic risks associated with business cycles. The financial crisis of 2008–2009 again provides a good example. In the summer of 2008, many traditional cyclical indicators were behaving as if the recession would be over by early 2009. The Fed had cut the funds rate to 2 percent by then, from 5.25 percent at the peak, and the ten-year Treasury yield was averaging around 4 percent. The positive 200-basis point yield-curve spread was above normal, suggesting an impending recovery.

All this changed, however, when financial markets began to roil anew in August and September, culminating in the collapse of Lehman Brothers. When Bear Stearns had failed in the spring of 2008, its resolution left the impression that creditors would always be protected when the government resolved financial failures. That perception changed when, to their big surprise, creditors lost everything along with equity holders when Lehman failed.

It's fair to say that these developments were not well anticipated by the bond market. They did, however, dramatically extend the bull market in Treasury bonds. As a result, investors who were overweight Treasuries based on cyclical timing turned out to be doubly blessed by the ensuing financial crisis. Corporate credit, on the other hand, experienced one of the worst bear markets in credit spreads since the Great Depression as the rules of the game were seen to have changed dramatically between the demise of Bear Stearns and that of Lehman. Uncertainty spiraled. Fears of depression and default skyrocketed. Risk appetite plunged. It was the perfect set of circumstances for Treasuries to outperform and a perfect storm for corporate credit to underperform. The financial crisis exacerbated the "bull steepening" that was already under way well before Lehman Brothers collapsed almost a year into the recession. The fallout from its collapse forced an extraordinary fiscal and monetary policy response and delayed the start of the recovery until mid-2009.

With the Fed funds rate pinned near zero and three successive rounds of quantitative easing, the yield curve went through an unusual early-cycle phase of "bull flattening" starting in early 2010 as Federal Reserve bond purchases dragged down interest rates across the maturity spectrum. Promises of zero rates for an extended period added to the downward pressure on longer maturities. This unusual early-cycle "bull-flattening" phase ended in the spring of 2013 when Fed Chairman Ben Bernanke signaled that quantitative easing (QE) needed to be gradually withdrawn. During the year before that, ten-year Treasury yields averaged less than 2 percent, testing the lowest levels since World War II, the last time when the Federal Reserve had engaged in such a massive asset-purchase program.

Bernanke's signal that asset purchases would be curtailed marked the cyclical turning point for a "bear steepening" to begin. Because this meant lower Treasury prices ahead and bigger price declines for longer-dated Treasuries than shorter-maturity Treasuries, it was the time to underweight fixed income below benchmark strategic allocations and tactically decrease duration. It probably also marked the end of the secular bull market in bonds that began in 1981 during Paul Volcker's tenure, when the benchmark ten-year Treasury note yielded over 15 percent.

As the market moved from pricing-in the end of the Fed's long-maturity asset purchases in 2014 to pricing in the beginning of Fed rate hikes in 2015, upward pressure on interest rates began to shift from the back of the curve in 2013 to the front in 2014, as shorter maturities are most affected by an anticipated rise in the near-term federal funds rate trajectory. This marked a shift from a "bear-steepening" phase of the cycle to a more normal "bear-flattening" phase, which always occurs when the Fed moves from maximum accommodation toward a more normal monetary policy that moves the yield curve from extremely steep toward its normal ("average") shape before the actual tightening phase of policy begins to flatten further its normal upward tilt.

While the cycle that culminated in the financial crisis had its idiosyncratic deviations from the typical business cycle pattern, it also conformed fairly well to the breakdown outlined in Exhibit 4.1, which summarizes the business cycle pattern of duration risk and the optimal tactical fixed-income allocation based on this pattern. In particular, if we treat quantitative easing and extended forward rate guidance as a substitute for further rate cuts when the zero-bound precludes additional interest-rate reductions, then that exceptional monetary policy fits nicely into the framework laid out in the exhibit, with the notable exception that it added a brief period of "bull flattening" because of quantitative easing that is unusual for that stage of the cycle.

Exhibit 4.1 shows that more generally, starting with the early-recovery phase of the business cycle, there is a period of maximum monetary accommodation. This is the phase in which monetary policy is trying to cement the recovery and avoid a relapse into recession. The lowest bond yields of the cycle usually occur early in this phase as additional rate cuts from the Fed are anticipated and doubts about the sustainability of the recovery dominate market sentiment. Since the shape of the yield curve reflects the degree of monetary accommodation over the cycle, the yield curve is usually in its steepest position in this phase of the cycle.

As outlined in our discussion of business cycle patterns, at some point in this phase of the cycle markets start sensing that the Fed's next move will be a rate hike rather than another rate cut. By that time, the bond yield will have normally bottomed and started to build in the rising interest-rate trajectory for the coming expansion. As that

Exhibit 4.1 Fixed-Income Tactical Response to Duration-Risk Cycle

Business Cycle Phase	Fed-Policy Driving Analogy	Tactical Duration Position	Yield-Curve Move	Tactical Deviation From Benchmark
Early Recovery	Maximum Monetary Acceleration	Start to Reduce Duration to Neutral	From Bull to Bear Steepening (QE Bull Flattens the Curve)	Overweight to Neutral
Early to Mid-cycle Expansion	Easing Off Accelerator	Reduce Portfolio Duration to Underweight	Bear Flattening	Neutral to Underweight
Mid-cycle to Late-Stage Expansion	Tapping on Brakes	Increase to Neutral	Bear Flattening	Underweight to Neutral
Imminent Recession	Brakes On	Increase Portfolio Duration to Maximum	Inversion and Shift to Bull Steepening	Neutral to Overweight
Recession	Easing Off Brakes Tapping on Accelerator	Stay Overweight Duration	Rapid Bull Steepening	Overweight

happens, it's usually a good time to scale back a tactical overweight position in duration to a more neutral weighting.

It is not unusual for the market to swing back and forth at this stage of the cycle, going from thinking that the Fed is through easing to expecting it to ease again, since the information flow tends to be mixed before the expansion is solidified, causing bouts of confidence and doubt. The recovery out of the 2008–2009 financial crisis was even more uneven than usual in this regard. Indeed, both the second and third rounds of quantitative easing came after markets had already made moves suggesting that further Fed action was unnecessary. Instead, subsequent events intervened to cause the Fed to buy more insurance for the recovery. As noted above, 10-year yields only bottomed when the Fed was ready to end its last round of quantitative easing.

As Exhibit 4.1 shows, in the next phase of early-to-mid-cycle expansion the Fed moves from maximum accommodation to a more neutral policy. By definition, we regard a neutral policy as one in which the yield curve approaches its "normal" slope (about a 100 basis-points spread between long and short rates). Essentially, that is the indication that the Fed "has taken its foot off the accelerator and shifted into cruise control." This means that interest rates rise off their lows as the Fed normalizes short-term rates for an economy that is in its mid-cycle "not too hot, not too cold" phase, and the yield curve flattens. The transition from an early to a mid-cycle expansion can create the biggest losses from duration risks in the fixed-income market. Being underweight duration can be most worthwhile in this phase in which the Fed normalizes rates as confidence in the recovery solidifies.

As interest rates normalize, preparing for the next phase of rising rates adds to the pressure to maintain an underweight in bonds. Eventually, the yield curve moves from "normal steepness" to "flatter than normal," signaling that Fed policy is becoming "tight" relative to economic conditions. The flatter the yield curve, the tighter the policy stance. With a tight monetary policy, the risk of recession becomes greater than the risk of inflation. The yield curve inverts if the market senses that the Fed has gone too far and a recession is imminent. Usually this is the signal to increase duration. Ultimately, the optimal phase for maximum fixed-income exposure is right before a recession. Indeed, aside from benefitting from the cyclical peak in rates, this is also the time of the cycle when bonds outperform equities by the biggest margin, as we'll discuss later.

Fine-tuning exceptions

It should be noted that while the Fed prefers to conduct policy as smoothly and predictably as possible, interest-rate policy can veer from the cyclical pattern illustrated in Exhibit 4.1. During the 1990s expansion, for example, the Fed raised rates 300 basis points between early 1994 and mid-1998, from 3 percent to 6 percent. This turned out to be too much, and the Fed ended up backtracking by about 125 basis points in response to several external crises, as well as the epic failure of Long-Term Capital Management in September 1998, related to the Russian and Asian financial crises. Despite such mid-course corrections, the yield-curve pattern over the cycle remained fairly normal. Eventually, the Fed raised rates to 6.5 percent in 2000, the yield curve inverted, and the economy finally went into recession after one of the longest expansions on record. Inflation expectations were still coming down toward "new-normal" levels in the 1990s, making appropriate policy rates lower than the Fed thought in 1995.

Cyclical spread trades in long maturities

While non-callable long-duration bonds are more sensitive to fluctuations in interest rates than shorter duration bonds, some clarification is useful as to what we mean by "fluctuations in interest rates." There are potentially different rates for every maturity of bonds across the Treasury yield curve. Monetary policy primarily affects the shortest maturities by fixing the overnight rate and providing an outlook for its level with its forward guidance. In particular, the outlook for monetary policy becomes more uncertain as the time horizon lengthens, say from three or six months to eighteen or twenty-four months. The cloud of uncertainty, or confidence interval, around the policy rate necessarily increases the further out in time the forecast moves.

The particular interest rate that influences the price of a long bond is its own coupon rate relative to the coupon rate on a new issue at par. It is the change in this relationship that causes fluctuations in the market price of a long bond. For example, the market price of a 4-percent coupon 30-year Treasury bond is much more sensitive to a rise in the new-issue coupon rate to 5 percent than a 10-year Treasury note under the same coupon assumptions.

Nevertheless, there is a sense in which a 30-year bond is less sensitive to the interest-rate cycle than a 10-year issue. Over the life of a 30-year bond, the next one or two years of monetary policy rate setting are less significant than for a 10-year note. In the extreme case of a perpetuity (an infinite-lived coupon stream), short-term rate fluctuations are insignificant influences on valuation with one condition. That condition is whether or not the monetary policy in a business cycle changes the long-term outlook for interest rates and inflation beyond the current cycle. To the extent that a "a new-normal" interest-rate structure of the sort described in chapter 3 is an accurate representation of an anchored long-horizon interest-rate outlook, with the yield curve fluctuating cyclically around a " new normal" yield curve that is stationary, long-term bond yields will move in a narrower range than shorter-term rates compared to a regime in which yields are affected by unanchored inflation expectations.

As the markets have maintained inflation expectations close to the Fed's 2-percent anchor over the past three business cycles, this cyclical relationship has become more pronounced. That is, the 30-year bond yield has exhibited much less cyclical variability than the 10-year note

Exhibit 4.2 Spread between Bond and Ten-Year Note Follows the Business Cycle

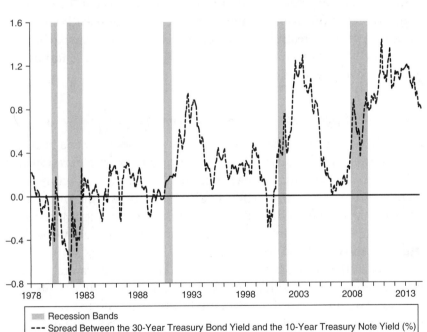

Recession Bands
--- Spread Between the 30-Year Treasury Bond Yield and the 10-Year Treasury Note Yield (%)

Source: Federal Reserve Board/Haver Analytics.
Data as of August 2014.

yield, giving rise to the cyclical pattern in the spread illustrated in Exhibit 4.2.

The 10-year Treasury yield reacts more to changes in the Fed funds rate or the monetary policy cycle in a world with well-anchored inflation expectations because the current business cycle is a much bigger proportion of the time horizon for a 10-year issue compared to a 30-year Treasury security. Since the average of short rates over the life of the issue is a big determinant of yield to maturity, shorter instruments respond more to near-term policy. As a result, when interest rates bottom during the recovery phase of the business cycle, the spread between the 30-year bond and the 10-year note tends to reach its cyclical peak. Then, as monetary policy moves from maximum accommodation to "normalized" rates, the 10-year yield tends to rise more than the 30-year yield, compressing the spread. Finally, in the last stage of a monetary policy tightening cycle and yield-curve inversion, the 10-year yield can actually rise above the 30-year yield, as seen in the late 1980s, late 1990s, and 2006. This roughly 120 basis-point range in the spread provides a popular fixed-income strategy over the business cycle, in which a duration-weighted tactical short position in the 10-year note against a long position in the 30-year bond takes advantage of the spread compression over the course of an expansion. Obviously, the position can be reversed when recession is imminent until a recovery seems assured.

Keep in mind potential structural trend changes

Tactically structuring a fixed-income portfolio based on the business cycle is thus fairly straightforward. For example, from a duration-risk point of view, assuming a "new normal" interest rate structure with average ten-year Treasury yields somewhere around the low to mid 3-percent level, buying that duration above the average interest rate and selling it below can help ladder a portfolio with above-normal returns compared to the benchmark.

Greater difficulty tends to arise from making correct capital-market assumptions, such as estimating what the "normal" interest rate and inflation rate might be, given structural shifts that tend to prevail over the longer horizon. As discussed earlier, making correct capital-market assumptions is critical. Indeed, many prominent institutional fixed-income managers were destroyed by the unanticipated rise in inflation and interest rates during the late 1970s and early 1980s. After all, the highest interest rates in US history (at least up to that point) looked quite enticing to anyone operating with the old mean-reversion "anchor." The problem was that interest rates kept moving ever higher for several years in the worst bond bear market in US history to the dismay of investors who got in years too early in anticipation of an imminent mean reversion.

The mean-reversion anchor requires two kinds of knowledge in order to be useful. *First*, the mean can shift with underlying changes in the structure of the economy. When that happens, basing a strategy on reversion to the old mean can be fruitless, and often outright dangerous. Knowing there's a new mean improves the strategy. Also, mean changes can take time. For example, interest rates now are back to "normal," but it took about 50 years to get there. The market can stay undervalued longer than one can stay solvent is a common Wall Street axiom for a reason. *Second*, and related, there can be extended periods of nonstationarity, when the mean is trending. A fixed mean requires a stationary phenomenon. Valuation anchors lose their anchoring ability if their determinants are trending in one direction or another, causing the mean to trend as well.

The credit-risk cycle and tactical fixed-income allocation

Market perceptions of credit risk fluctuate in a roughly systematic way over the business cycle. Fear of default is generally greatest during a recession. As a result, the markets build in the biggest credit-risk premia during downturns. A sign that a recession may be nearing its end is often flashed when credit spreads come off their peaks, suggesting the worst of the fear is over.

Over the course of the recovery and expansion, credit spreads narrow to the point that they eventually fall below their cycle average as they reflect an excessive confidence that defaults will be lower than they ultimately turn out to be. Between the extremes of excessive fear of default during recession and the excessive complacency of late-cycle optimism, there lies an actual cyclical default experience that will determine the realized returns to corporate fixed-income investments. Buying when fear is excessive and selling when it's absent is the basic way to take advantage of the cyclical fluctuations in credit spreads.

The underlying valuation anchor that prices credit over the cycle is the cash flow generated by corporations that is available to pay back debt and interest expense. In recessions, the information flow is the most negative of the cycle, raising the most doubt about payback ability. At the peak of the cycle, the gestalt created by the information flow is most positive, and default risks seem most remote. However, by definition, it is at the peak that the gestalt begins to shift in the negative direction as the first cracks begin to appear from those who have gotten themselves overextended. Most bad loans are created in good times, when overconfidence causes lending standards to deteriorate.

The extra cushion of cash beyond what is required to pay back interest and principal due on debt is the profit margin. When profit margins are high, corporations have extra cash flow available to make debt payments. Since interest expense is tax deductible, it's the pretax profit margin that is most closely associated with corporate capacity to make good on debt obligations. For this reason, there is a close association between credit spreads and profit margins.

If we look over the history of profit margins, we do see that major downturns in profit margins are always associated with widening credit spreads. The two biggest spread-widening episodes in US corporate bonds since the 1920s occurred in the early 1930s and during the 2008–20009 financial crisis. These are the only two times in which the spread between BAA corporate credit and comparable-duration Treasuries rose above 5 percentage points on a monthly average basis. Following the Depression episode, it took over a decade for spreads to finally normalize (during World War II). In contrast, thanks to the more enlightened policy response following the Great Recession, spreads returned to their precrisis normal range much more quickly. Still, the self-inflicted European crisis in 2011 created a significant degree of relapse in the credit recovery process there. This is another of many data points contrasting the results of the Great Experiment in economic policy that differentiates the relative effectiveness of the US and European policy responses to the financial crisis in 2008–2009.

Exhibit 4.3 shows the BAA credit spread to the ten-year Treasury yield since the end of World War II. Between 1945 and 1965 it fluctuated around a mean of 100 basis points, rising above that level in recessions and falling below it during expansions. Note that the trough in the spread tended to occur roughly in the *mid-cycle* period and that during the *late-cycle* period it was generally reverting to the mean.

The same pattern is evident in the profit-margin measure (shown inverted in Exhibit 4.3), which fluctuated between about 15 percent and 20 percent during the 1945–1965 period. In each of the three

Exhibit 4.3 Cyclical Variation in Credit Spreads Jumped to a Higher Range after 1965 as Profit Margins Shifted Lower (inverted right scale)

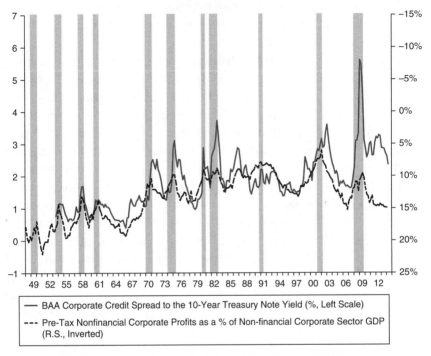

— BAA Corporate Credit Spread to the 10-Year Treasury Note Yield (%, Left Scale)
--- Pre-Tax Nonfinancial Corporate Profits as a % of Non-financial Corporate Sector GDP (R.S., Inverted)

Source: Bureau of Economic Analysis, Federal Reserve Board/Haver Analytics.
Data as of April 2014.

recessions between 1952 and 1962 it briefly went under 15 percent at the same time that the credit spread jumped over 100 basis points. The profit margin measure used in the illustration is pretax nonfinancial corporate profits divided by nonfinancial corporate output, with both measures coming from the National Income Product Accounts (NIPA).

There are various measures of profits besides the NIPA account profits, including measures of reported and operating profits from companies each quarter. However, these often involve window dressing and special-item exceptions. In contrast, the NIPA profits come off the tax returns filed with the Internal Revenue Service (IRS), where there is no incentive for exaggeration. In any event, for macroeconomic business cycle research, the NIPA measure seems to be preferable for various reasons, not least because the overall accounting system is consistent with the profits measure.

In any case, after 1965 there is a noticeable shift in the range for both the profit-margin measure and the spread. This reflects the structural shift that we referred to in our discussion of valuation anchors. The structural shift to lower profit margins and higher credit spreads after 1965 coincided with a sharp uptick in interest expense due to rising interest rates and increased leverage. Adding net interest expense to after-tax corporate profits gives a "total return" measure to both equity and debt holders relative to output produced. As can be seen in Exhibit 4.4, this ratio has been in the same range over the past 60 years, fluctuating mainly between 7.5 percent and 12.5 percent. Since the financial crisis, it has broken above that range for reasons we will discuss in the next chapter. The key point for now is that unlike the profit margin, the "total-return to capital" measure has been relatively stable or stationary over the postwar period up until 2010. The equity share of output has diminished as the interest-rate share increased with leverage. For bond holders, more leverage and interest expense means more risk for any given level

Exhibit 4.4   Profit Margin Shifted Down as More Revenue Went to Debt Payments

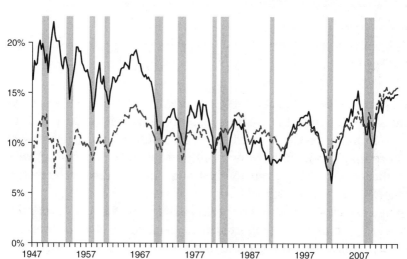

Recession Bands

—— Pre-Tax Nonfinancial Corporate Profits as a % of Non-financial Corporate Sector GDP

- - After-Tax Nonfinancial Corporate Profits plus Net Interest as a % of Non-financial Corporate Sector GDP

Source: Bureau of Economic Analysis/Haver Analytics.

Data as of April 2014.

of profit margins. As a result, spreads have been higher on average since 1965.

Since 1965, the credit spread measure has fluctuated around 200 basis points, with bigger deviations topping 300 basis points during recessions but seldom falling below 150 basis points. Likewise, the profit margin measure shifted out of the 15 percent to 20 percent range into a lower 10 percent to 15 percent range.

Note that the post–World War II low point for profit margins occurred in the aftermath of the tech bubble's bursting in the 2001 recession. There was also a cyclical peaking in the credit spread shortly after that recession. When that combination (credit spread just over 300 basis points and the profit margin close to 500 basis points) is contrasted with the next recession between 2007 and 2009 (when credit spreads approached 600 basis points and profit margins bottomed around 1000 basis points), the critical distinction between the two expansions preceding those recessions is clearly evident. The earlier expansion and recession were less of a credit event and more of an equity valuation bubble event. The subsequent cycle was less of an equity event and more of a credit bubble. Indeed, the 1990s expansion was less reliant on leverage and more reliant on equity value appreciation. The 2000s expansion reversed those roles during the secular bear market in equities. That's why the spread widening was twice as great and the profit-margin hit only half as bad in 2009 compared to the 2001 recession.

Basically, the profit-margin change dwarfed the credit-spread change in the 2001 recession, while the opposite was true in the 2008–2009 period. The overreaction in credit-spread widening during the 2008–2009 recession compared to what was "justified" by the relatively lesser deterioration in profit margins created the greatest opportunity for a spread-compression trade of the past 60 years. Indeed, in early 2009, people were buying into the idea of a 1930s-style depression and, as a result, credit was priced for massive defaults. Profit margins did not justify that pricing of credit, however, as companies were quick to cut costs and liquidate inventory, while aggregate demand stabilized at a higher-than-expected level as a result of the aggressive government response that restored confidence in the banking system. In this environment, inventories and production levels soon turned out to be too low. The recovery began at that point.

Obviously, it was a once-in-a-lifetime opportunity to take credit risk and get a big payoff. Normally, the opportunities in credit are much

Exhibit 4.5 Fixed-Income Tactical Response to Credit-Risk Cycle

Business-Cycle Phase	Credit-Spread Direction	Profit-Margin Dynamics	Credit Positioning	Treasury Position
Early Recovery	Rapid to Modest Declines	Rising	Neutral to Overweight	Overweight to Neutral
Early to Mid-cycle Expansion	Decline	Rising	Overweight	Neutral to Underweight
Mid-cycle to Late-Stage Expansion	Cycle Lows Eventually Transition to Rising	Transition to Declining	Overweight to Underweight	Underweight to Neutral
Imminent Recession	Rising	Declining	Underweight	Neutral to Overweight
Recession	Rising to Peak	Falling to Cycle Low	Underweight to Neutral	Overweight

more muted. Tactical opportunities over the cycle arise as laid out in Exhibit 4.5.

The best cyclical opportunity to profit from spread contraction is usually right before a recovery begins, as was the case in early 2009. The most rapid decline in spreads is usually at this early recovery stage of the cycle. Spread compression usually continues through the midcycle stage of the expansion. At this point it is not unusual for spreads to fall below a justifiable mean, with the cycle low point usually occurring well before a recession begins. In fact, one of the signs that recession risk is rising is usually a reversal of spread contraction and the beginning of a new widening cycle. By the time a recession is imminent, spread widening has usually anticipated a deterioration in the economy, which has to build up to a critical mass before output begins to decline with business cutbacks. Once a recession is underway, problems in credit proliferate rapidly. Spread widening becomes most pronounced at this stage.

The biggest gains in profit margins tend to come in the early stage of the recovery to the midcycle expansion phase. The midcycle is marked by a transition from (1) above-average unemployment, (2) below-average wage gains and inflation, and (3) above-average slack in production capacity to the next phase of (1) below-average unemployment, (2) above-average wage gains and inflation, and (3) below-average excess capacity for growth. The midcycle is the point at which, to varying degrees, the various indicators of economic health start to move above their average levels for the cycle.

Rising wages and interest rates cut into profit margins as do rising nonlabor costs of energy and materials. As these costs rise and eat into corporate revenues, they reduce profit margins and spreads start to rise because lower margins increase credit risk. It is not a coincidence that Fed tightening to slow inflation pressures, profit-margin pressures, and rising credit spreads tend to be late-cycle indications that the expansion is getting long in the tooth. Usually, monetary policy is catching up to an economy with substantial "animal spirits" at this stage. Often, investment in business equipment and nonresidential structures is at a peak. (Rising investment spending also starts to cut into margins, but it's necessary to expand capacity at the stage of the cycle at which supply bottlenecks are also creating inflation pressures.)

As profit margins fall going into a recession, businesses have to adjust. These adjustments tend toward cost-cutting efficiencies, and the mood becomes more defensive and less expansive. These adjustments become self-reinforcing as cutbacks beget cutbacks. Only when things have overadjusted to the downside and some catalysts for expansion start to emerge does the recession end. Generally credit spreads are widest right before that point.

Tactically positioning for corporate bonds over the cycle basically involves taking advantage of these cyclical movements in credit spreads. Just as there are fine-tuning exceptions to smooth interest-rate cycles, there are idiosyncratic phases of credit risk-on and risk-off not entirely related to the cycle. However, these tend to be more short lived and provide trading opportunities rather than having enough staying power for tactical reallocation of portfolios.

Tactical strategies blending the interest-rate and credit-risk cycles

As Exhibit 4.5 illustrates, the cyclical fixed-income strategies for credit risk and interest-rate risks are complementary. The optimal time to load up on long-duration Treasuries is usually the same time at which a portfolio manager would want to minimize credit risk, namely in the run-up to a recession. While both kinds of bonds share interest-rate risk characteristics, Treasuries are a purer instrument for playing duration risk. They lack credit risk. They are generally not callable before maturity. They shine in a risk-off environment.

On the other hand, corporate bonds benefit from an improving economy, which occurs when credit spreads generally contract as interest rates on Treasuries rise more than corporate bond yields, and Treasury prices decline more as a result. Basically, the credit improvement hedges against some of the interest rate rise. For this reason, a tactical tilt away from Treasuries and toward corporate credit usually makes the most sense beginning in the main recovery phase until credit conditions begin to deteriorate (which is usually signaled by spreads widening late in the cycle). At that point it's usually a good idea to transition back toward Treasuries and away from corporate bonds in preparation for a tougher credit environment going into the recession and the bigger bang for the buck that Treasuries enjoy when rates start to fall most dramatically. Spread widening can more than offset a declining interest-rate structure when a flight-to-quality panic is in full swing, as many investors learned in late 2008 and early 2009.

The credit spectrum

Just as interest-rate risks increase as the duration of a bond lengthens, credit risk rises as credit quality declines. This means that just as the duration mix of the portfolio can be adjusted to take advantage of the business cycle pattern, so can the credit-quality mix of the portfolio. High-yield ("junk") credit spreads are more volatile generally than spreads on investment-grade credits.

Exhibit 4.3 used yields on Moody's BAA-rated corporate bonds minus the yields on comparable-duration Treasury instruments as a measure of credit risk. Partly, that's because there is a long history of yield data for that credit rating. Partly, it's because it represents an issue that is of medium or moderate credit risk. BAA credits are a notch above a speculative, "junk" or high-yield credit. As such, it's a good representation of the basic credit situation in corporate America.

High-yield debt generally sees its best returns when bought during "the depths of despair" in a recession. In fact, many investors consider high-yield bonds as an equity substitute. Whether you bought a stock index or a portfolio of speculative-grade bonds on March 9, 2009, when the bull market in equities began, returns were spectacular a year later in either case. Conversely, at the late stage of an expansion, when recession storm clouds are gathering, spread widening and the associated bond-price declines are generally more pronounced for lower-grade credits. Improving the quality of credit in the portfolio makes the most sense at that stage of the cycle.

Finally, it should be noted that there is a cycle in bank lending to businesses that tends to reinforce the credit-risk cycle. This cycle is still significant in the United States and even more so in the rest of the developed world. Over the years, US corporate borrowing has shifted to market instruments and away from bank lending. During the 1980s, the high-yield bond market took off in a big way, exacerbating the disintermediation of bank lending. Other regions of the world have much bigger banking systems relative to their corporate bond markets and overall economies. Europe and Japan, for example, are much more reliant on bank finance, making the size of their banks much bigger compared to gross domestic product (GDP) than is the case in the United States. This makes bank credit an even bigger driver of the business cycle in Europe and Japan.

Market risks, volatility, and the yield curve

While different kinds of risks influence prices of different asset classes according to their financial characteristics, there are also elements in the risk environment that create general market risk. For example, geopolitical conflict that disrupts the world's oil supply and sends energy prices soaring can cause a global recession that is not predictable from the stage of the business cycle. During the 2010–2012 period, fiscal policy battles raised fears of default on US government debt. During that period, measures of policy uncertainty spiked, volatility surged, and risk assets suffered because of fears of renewed economic weakness. The European financial crisis in 2011–2012 reignited fears of a Lehman-like collapse in global finance. In all such cases, elevated market volatility is to be expected. Shocks to the economic environment that are pervasive in their effects raise market risk and increase the volatility of returns. Aside from idiosyncratic market risks such as oil price shocks, policy conflicts, and financial crises, there is also a systematic pattern of market risk that follows the business cycle, and which is evident in the cyclical pattern of market volatility.

It is not surprising that the underlying riskiness to returns varies across the business cycle. This is suggested by our documentation of how credit risk rises and falls at different stages of the business cycle. More generally, as business conditions improve over the cycle, the odds of systemic or market-wide risk subside. Conversely, after the midcycle, excesses tend to build in leverage and enthusiasm for projects that may not pan out. Then, as the business environment deteriorates across the board and recessionary forces cumulate, market risk increases. This pattern is evident in measures of market volatility, such as the VIX, which is the ticker symbol for the Chicago Board Options Exchange Market Volatility Index, a popular measure of the implied volatility of the Standard & Poor's (S&P) 500 index. A commonly cited gauge of market fear, it is a measure of the market's expectations for stock market volatility over the next 30 days.

Exhibit 4.6 shows monthly VIX averages since 1985. The VIX shows a general cyclicality, with low levels when economic conditions are best and complacency is widespread, and rising levels when people get nervous about the economic outlook and equity prices become more volatile as a result. Over the past two decades, the VIX has ranged between about 10 and 20 during the early-recovery phase of

Exhibit 4.6   VIX Has a Cyclical Pattern

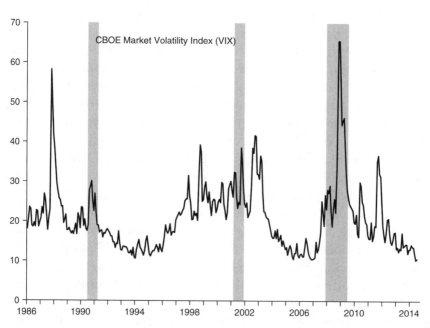

Source: Chicago Board Options Exchange/Haver Analytics.
Data as of August 2014.

the business cycle. This was true in the 1992–1994 period and the 2004–2006 period. As observed in the exhibit, the volatility, or "fear," index tends to jump into the 20 to 30 range in the late cycle, with spikes above 30 associated with extreme market nervousness going into recessions, or short-lived bouts of anxiety due to specific events that tend to end up having only temporary effects on the markets. The peaks over 50 coincide with the 1987 stock market crash and the late-2008 financial crisis. The big spike in the aftermath of the Lehman Brothers failure was followed by a lesser one in late 2011 during the worst days of the European financial crisis. During the 1987 stock market crash, the VIX briefly reached over 140. Then, again, beginning with the Thai currency crisis in the summer of 1997, a more general Asian currency crisis developed, causing a spike into the high 30s on a monthly average basis by 1998 as the Russian debt crisis sank Long-Term Capital Management. Although the US recession was nearing its end, a similar spike occurred around the 9/11 attacks when the US stock market was shut down for several days.

Volatility spikes associated with credit-market events such as the Lehman crisis often take place during recessions. Still, while recessions tend to make credit events more likely, "volatility" events can happen at any point in the cycle, as the examples above make clear. The 1987 stock market crash and the 1998 Asian currency crisis, for example, were mid- to late-cycle events. Often the Fed responds to these events to avoid a recessionary impact from them. For example, there was a short-lived reversal of the Fed's rate hiking trajectory after the 1987 crash. Similarly, the Fed cut rates a bit in response to the 1998 events (although within a year it was hiking them again). In the 2011 European crisis case, inappropriately tight monetary and fiscal policies had pushed the Eurozone back into recession after a very short recovery from the initial financial crisis in 2008–2009. Because of the magnitude of the problem, the risk to the rest of the world, including the United States, was another Lehman-like collapse in global finance. Reflecting this risk, the VIX surged. In this case, constrained by the zero-bound on overnight interest rates, the Fed expanded its QE program in order to fight headwinds to growth from Europe's double-dip recession.

While volatility events sparked by external crises, such as the Thai currency crisis in 1997 and the European banking crisis in 2011, are often independent of the US business cycle, higher volatility in the late-cycle and recession phase of the business cycle reflects the fact

Exhibit 4.7   Volatility Cycles Follow the Signals Coming from the Yield Curve Spread

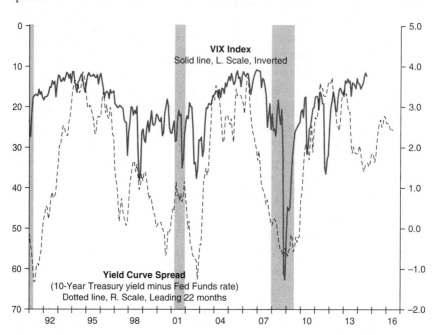

Source: Chicago Board Options Exchange/Haver Analytics.
Data as of August 2014.

that more things go wrong at that stage compared to the early-recovery phase when the risk dynamic is improving. For example, credit downgrades to corporate and state and local government borrowers tend to increase and upgrades decrease, compared to a reverse dynamic after a year or two of recovery, when the rising tide improves the financial metrics on which borrowers are judged.

Exhibit 4.7 shows the history of monthly volatility against the yield curve (as measured by the gap between the ten-year Treasury yield and the federal funds rate). The yield curve measure leads volatility by about two years. When the Fed is truly tightening policy and the yield curve inverts, it tends to predict increased market volatility two years ahead. This should not be surprising since the inverted yield curve tends to portend a recession, and maximum equity market risk and volatility generally occur around recession periods.

Conversely, at some point during the recession, the Fed becomes engaged in its most aggressive rate cutting, which, as discussed, tends to coincide with the maximum steepening phase of the yield curve.

In the three most recent business cycles, the yield curve steepened to more than a 300-basis-point gap. As seen in the Exhibit 4.7, these periods of extreme steepness eventually were followed by extended periods of low volatility as the Fed's support calmed the markets to cycle lows usually around 10 to 12 as measured by the VIX.

Thus, market risk tends to be the highest following Fed tightening and the lowest when the Federal Reserve is most accommodative. This accommodation is aimed initially at ending a recession and ultimately at facilitating a sustainable expansion in order to avert the risk that the economy will stagnate in a deflationary morass, in which the incentives are to cut costs, lay off workers, and hoard cash, rather than spend, hire, and invest. As those downside risks recede with increased liquidity, market risk and volatility decline. The steep yield curve early in the recovery is the most powerful single indicator that a positive economic dynamic is starting to develop and volatility will eventually subside as market risk declines. These periods of maximum steepness in the yield curve coincide with periods when the Fed "has the market's back." At this stage, "don't fight the Fed" means buy equities.

Conversely, a negative risk dynamic is developing when the yield curve turns against expansionary forces by becoming inverted. "Don't fight the Fed" means "look out below" when the yield curve is inverted. Maximum market risk and volatility tend to accompany the recessions that inevitably follow inverted yield curves. The credit cycle is one of the manifestations of this cyclical dynamic in market risk. A strengthening aggregate economy reduces downside risks, including credit risks. A weakening aggregate economy raises a whole array of risks. As usual, Warren Buffett said it best: "only when the tide goes out do you discover who's been swimming naked." Leverage amplifies risk and volatility. It makes the tide go out faster.

The leverage cycle

Excesses tend to accumulate over a business cycle until they reach "the straw that breaks the camel's back" stage, at which point a recession begins. The tendency for profit margins to shrink, credit risk to rise, and market risk and volatility to pick up late in the cycle is not especially surprising given human nature. Since "animal spirits" rise as economic conditions strengthen, it is not surprising to see a cyclical pattern of leveraging within the business cycle. Indeed, leverage

Exhibit 4.8 Leverage Cycle Most Extreme during the Housing Bubble Period (2004–2007)

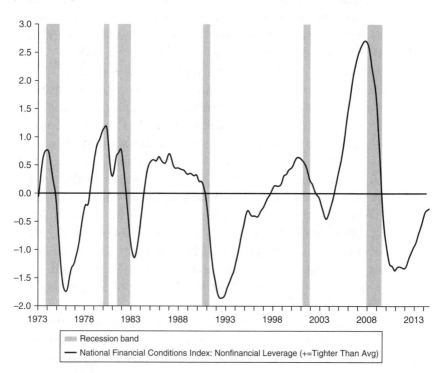

Recession band

— National Financial Conditions Index: Nonfinancial Leverage (+=Tighter Than Avg)

Source: Federal Reserve Board/Haver Analytics.

growth tends to peak late in the cycle when "animal spirits" are high and credit is easily available. Eventually, rising interest rates to address inflation pressures start the process of tightening credit. As the economic growth momentum weakens, overextended borrowers start to have problems paying off loans and defaults rise. The gestalt shifts toward generally tighter financial conditions that turn the cycle from rising leverage growth to declining leverage growth.

As shown in Exhibit 4.8, the leverage cycle during the lead up to and aftermath of the financial crisis was the most extreme in the past several decades. The leverage cycle in the 1990s was quite mild by comparison. In part, this reflected the long unwinding of the extreme 1980s leverage cycle associated with the junk-bonds and savings-and-loan (S&L) crisis. The contrast between the respective leverage cycles is another example of the "what's different this time" element between the 1990s cycle and the early-2000s cycle. Equity valuation excesses drove the former, and home-lending excesses drove the latter. As a result, there were significant differences in the patterns of these two recent business cycles that arose directly from the difference in where the excesses had accumulated. In particular, consumers were hit much harder by the housing-leverage-driven banking and economic crisis that was worse than anything in recent memory.

The magnitude of overleveraging during the 2000s expansion is illustrated in Exhibit 4.8. The measure of non-financial sector leverage shown here is a normalized blend of household and non-financial business sector leverage created by the Federal Reserve Bank of Chicago research staff. The household measure is the growth in the ratio of household mortgage and consumer debt to the underlying assets being financed, namely residential investment and personal consumption expenditures on durable goods, such as autos. A rise in this ratio means a more highly leveraged household sector. In other words, a high ratio means that any given dollar of spending on household assets uses more borrowed funds. As households stretch their finances over the business cycle, perhaps because they feel more secure in their jobs or because credit just becomes easier to access, or both, they become more vulnerable to economic reversals.

The business-leverage component is computed from the growth rate in the ratio of non-financial business debt outstanding to GDP. This measure rises when a given amount of GDP growth is associated with more business borrowing. When combined, the household-leverage component and the business-leverage component provide an aggregate look at the private sector's changing financial vulnerability over the course of the business cycle.

The exhibit shows that in the early recovery stage, the growth in leverage tends to fall well below trend (into the –1 to –2 standard deviation range), as seen around 1976, 1983, 1992, and 2010 as poor economic conditions, low confidence, and tight credit hurt credit growth coming out of a recession. This typically marks the turning point at which deleveraging pressures start to turn toward releveraging back to normal (where normal equals 0 in the exhibit). During this stage of moving from below-normal leverage growth to normal, the economy is usually in the first half of the business cycle, with several years of growth ahead before the next recession. During this phase of the leverage cycle, credit conditions tend to turn increasingly easy from the tougher standards of the "rapid-deleveraging" phase during the recession and early recovery phase. Difficulties obtaining loans ease. As economic conditions improve, banks become more willing to make commercial-and-industrial (C&I) loans to small and large businesses. As the labor market improves and home prices recover, mortgage and consumer lending become more attractive. The cycle following the Great Recession provides a good example. When house prices were declining between 2007 and 2010, mortgage collateral values became suspect and lending terms tightened dramatically. As prices started to rise in 2011, worries about home price deflation began to diminish and credit accessibility started to rise again.

On the demand side, the need and willingness to borrow rise with the growing economy. Also, assessments of future business and consumer confidence are highly procyclical, rising with profits, income, employment, and production. The capacity to borrow is also higher at the beginning of a releveraging cycle after balance sheets have been repaired, and it grows with the economy. Indeed, in the early stage of a recovery, a base is formed of optimal balance sheet health for that cycle, a starting point that improves with economic conditions. At the same time, the pressure on banks and other credit providers to expand their business becomes more intense in a recovery, competition heats up, and borrowers begin to be courted anew after having received the cold shoulder during the recession, and a new credit and leverage cycle begins.

Countless indicators support this pattern. For example, the share of nonperforming loans on bank balance sheets tends to peak early in the recovery stage of the business cycle after shooting sharply higher during the recession. As lending is still cautious and nonperforming loans decline with improving economic conditions when the new cycle begins, banks' ratio of loans to deposits falls and their capacity to lend increases. Appetite for increased lending starts to pick up. Similarly, credit conditions in the capital markets tend to be best as the recovery transitions to expansion. At this stage of the cycle, a rising tide lifts all boats, helping both defaults on bonds across the credit spectrum and nonperforming loans as a share of aggregate loans to continue to decline, bolstering confidence that further leverage can be handled. This improving credit picture usually continues until late in the expansion.

To encourage more borrowing in this environment of good times, banks begin to ease lending standards, and bonds are underwritten with increasingly loose covenants. As credit becomes increasingly available, merger and acquisition activity heats up, the degree of leverage in deal financing, commercial-and-industrial loans, and mortgage lending tends to rise, loan covenants loosen, and payment-in-kind issuance picks up. To get more deals done, collateral requirements and subordination terms shift from favoring the lenders to favoring the borrowers.

As this process continues and leverage rises, there eventually comes a point in the business cycle at which the gestalt shifts from improving credit quality to deteriorating credit quality. "Too much of a good thing" starts to become apparent late in the cycle. Changes by credit-rating agencies shift from favoring upgrades toward more downgrades as the economic outlook worsens. Bond defaults and problem loans begin to increase.

The deterioration in financial conditions that accompanies a recession takes time to build up. Inevitably, as seen in Exhibit 4.8, excessive growth in leverage spurred by overheated "animal spirits" creates vulnerabilities that turn lethal when the monetary policy stance becomes focused on slowing the economy to contain inflation. Credit conditions tighten, loans are harder to roll over, and bonds are more difficult to refinance and must be repaid instead.

Recessions and financial crises tend to be proportional to excessive indebtedness. Exhibit 4.8 shows that since 1973, most recessions began with leverage growth above average but within one standard deviation from normal. The 2002–2007 expansion was exceptional in this regard, with the leverage indicator increasing well over two standard deviations above normal. The late-1980s show a long, drawn-out period of above-normal leveraging associated with the birth of the "junk-bond" market and its interplay with the newly deregulated S&L industry. The deleveraging following that period was a major drag on the economy in the early 1990s. The period from the early 1990s until about 2007 was an even more extended leveraging cycle that was only slightly interrupted during the 2001 recession. That recession was relatively mild by historical standards and didn't include a major washout of leverage. This, combined with the breakdown in lending standards during the subsequent cycle, created an even larger accumulation of debt relative to income. One reason the financial crisis in 2008–2009 was so severe was the extraordinary leverage built up during the two expansions leading up to it.

Credit spreads anticipate loan losses

The financial markets tend to anticipate the deterioration in credit quality well before bank loan charge-offs materialize. Exhibit 4.9 shows the spread between the yield on an index of high yield ("junk") bonds and the yield on the ten-year Treasury note plotted against the charge-off rate on C&I bank loans. Spread widening leads the rise in charge-offs by about three quarters as bond markets tend to respond immediately to new information, while loan charge-offs take time. There is usually some negotiation involved, and perhaps wishful thinking, before lenders decide to classify a bad loan as such. In any case, the anticipated default rate implied in high-yield bonds provides a good leading indicator of where credit conditions are headed. This warning sign from the credit markets is a valuable leading indicator of a rising risk of recession. As can be seen, both charge-offs and spreads tend to bottom during the midcycle phase of the business

Exhibit 4.9 Credit Spreads Lead Loan Losses

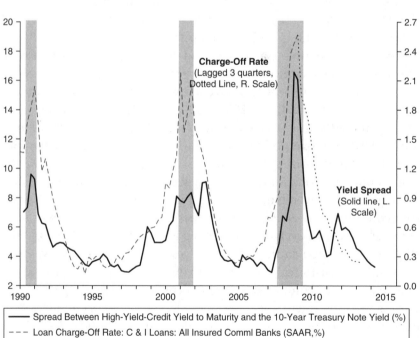

Source: Bank of America Merrill Lynch, Federal Reserve Board/Haver Analytics.
Data as of August 2014.

expansion and start to rise during the last couple of years before a recession.

Watch the financial stress indicators

Credit spreads and market volatility (VIX) are examples of stress indicators emanating from specific markets. Aggregate indicators of financial stress use different statistical procedures to create a composite measure of overall stress. For example, the St. Louis Federal Reserve Bank uses principal components analysis to extract financial stress information out of 18 weekly series of data. These include US interest rates, yield spreads, and other indicators. The individual credit spreads already mentioned in this chapter, the BAA bonds index yield minus the ten-year Treasury yield, and the High Yield Bond index yield minus the ten-Year Treasury yield are among the various spread indicators that signal financial stress in this measure.

Exhibit 4.10   Financial Stress Rises Going into Recessions

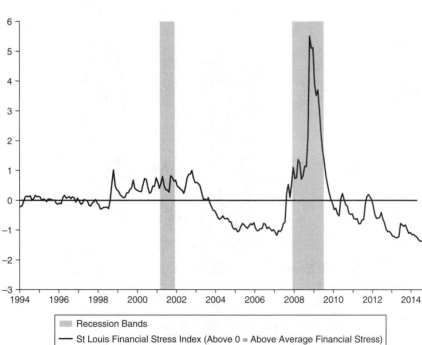

Source: St. Louis Federal Reserve Bank/Haver Analytics.

Data as of August 15, 2014.

Financial stress comes from different sources at different times. During the 2008–2009 period, the greatest stress was coming out of US financial markets and banks. Since the St. Louis Fed measure is comprised purely of US market metrics, it shows particularly pronounced stress around that financial crisis compared to other periods when cyclical stress fluctuations were one-sixth the magnitude of what happened in late 2008 and early 2009 (Exhibit 4.10)

As seen in the exhibit, general financial stress tends to run above average from the late stage of expansions through the early-stage of the recovery. Sometime late in the recovery, toward the midcycle, it transitions to below-normal levels until excesses build to the point at which stress rises above normal again. This tends to coincide with the tight phase of monetary policy. In fact, because the slope of the Treasury yield curve is one of the best cyclical indicators of the

Exhibit 4.11   United States Was Primary Source of Stress in 2008–2009. Europe Was the Culprit in 2011–2012

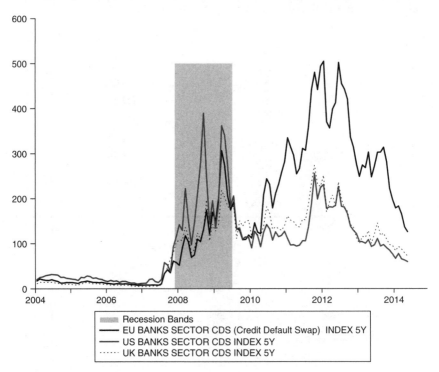

Source: DataStream.

Data as of May 6, 2014

monetary policy stance, it is one of the components of the St. Louis Fed's stress measure.

Since each business cycle is different, the sources of stress vary according to where the excesses develop in financial markets. Are they in equities, mortgage derivatives, or are they outside the United States, say in the European banking system? US bank spreads were the widest among US, UK, and European banks during the immediate aftermath of Lehman's collapse. By 2010, they were back to normal, while Europe's banks saw spreads blow out to new highs in 2011, after the ECB prematurely tightened monetary policy (Exhibit 4.11). Europe's banks were encouraged to buy sovereign debt during the first wave of the financial crisis when Lehman failed, as there was a widespread market and regulatory view that one European sovereign debt was almost as good as another. They were denominated in the same currency, and the individual government default risks were deemed to be quite low. Country-default risk measures were tightly clustered around low levels as a result.

That all changed in the second wave of crisis during the double-dip phase of Europe's recession. Spreads between peripheral sovereign bonds and the "core" countries widened dramatically as the euro's very existence came into doubt. This severely weakened bank balance sheets that were overladen with bad sovereign credits that had plummeted in value. What had seemed like low risk assets became "junk" quality as fiscal crises spread throughout the periphery, raising default risk assessments dramatically. Note that the St. Louis Fed domestic stress measure shows relatively muted stress spikes in 2011 and 2012 during the second wave of European financial crisis. A more European-focused measure would show much greater stress there during that time. Indeed, credit default swap spreads for European banks blew out in 2011 and 2012 to wider levels than in 2008 and 2009.

The cyclical pattern in financial stress evident in Exhibit 4.10 is a key factor in determining tactical allocations of "risk-on" and "risk-off" assets. Often just as important, however, are the idiosyncratic sources of stress that vary from cycle to cycle. As usual, knowing "what's different this time" is an important source of investment insight.

5
Equities and Profits

Equity prices depend primarily on the underlying earnings of companies. More specifically, they depend on how the market currently values the expected future earnings stream of a company. Because most of the earnings of most companies are further out in the future and less certain than bond payments, returns on equities are generally much more volatile than those on investment-grade bonds.

Structural or long-run risk and uncertainty

The degree of perceived uncertainty about the future can oscillate quite a bit depending on the policy outlook, geopolitical relationships, and the pace of disruptive technological changes, among other things. While heightened uncertainty about the future generally implies a bigger risk premium for equities over bonds, the source of uncertainty can sometimes be more of a detriment for bond returns than equity returns. For example, inflation uncertainty is *more problematic* for bond values, assuming the payments streams are not adjusted to compensate for it, as is the case for most fixed-income assets. Also helping stocks relatively, there are areas within the equity market that provide reasonable protection against inflation. In fact, the rise of inflation-adjusted bonds in the 1980s was largely a response to the high-inflation experience of the time. On the other hand, deflation is positive for bonds, as their fixed payments actually gain real value when the general price level falls. In contrast, the impact of deflation on most equities is negative, especially for highly leveraged companies. That's because deflation raises the real burden of debt.

A case in point of the relatively bigger impact of inflation uncertainty on bonds is the secular bear market in bonds from 1965 to 1982, a period characterized by persistently unanticipated inflation that outstripped returns on financial assets. However, the negative real returns on bonds during the period lagged the negative returns on equities by several percentage points. Conversely, when inflation began to trend lower after 1982, the usual excess return on equities compared to government bonds narrowed, as both asset classes experienced over a quarter century of catch-up following secular bear markets in the 1970s. By about 2010, the average 30-year return on bonds (1980–2010) was about the same as the 30-year return on equities for the first time in 80 years.

On average, over time, stocks have yielded more than 4 percentage points of extra return compared to government bonds to compensate for their greater average risk. However, over the past 200 years, there have been some rare examples of long periods, such as the 1980–2010 period mentioned above, when the gap largely disappeared, or even became negative, and periods when the gap exploded out to about 10 percentage points in favor of equities, such as between 1935 and 1965. There are important structural differences in the macroeconomic backdrop that help account for these significant differences in long-term (30-year) returns of stocks and bonds. Understanding the fundamental reasons for these structural shifts yields useful insights for strategic asset allocation.

Cyclical sources of risk and uncertainty

As with bonds, there are also important systematic differences in how equities perform over shorter time horizons (i.e., a business cycle). Corporate profits are highly cyclical, and stock prices fluctuate constantly trying to discount them. Mispriced cyclical profit fluctuations often cause significant deviations from long-term fundamental valuation levels. Buying stocks when sentiment about profits and the economy is at a cycle low point and selling them when the profits outlook is overly optimistic is a worthwhile approach to tactical allocation.

Uncertainty about the profits outlook swings over the business cycle along with uncertainty about other relevant determinants of valuations, such as interest rates and economic growth. Risk, fear, uncertainty, and volatility are highly cyclical, as we saw in the last chapter. All of these ingredients work together in a predictable cyclical fashion to provide tactical asset allocation opportunities for astute investment managers.

In addition, equities vary quite a bit in their cyclical sensitivities. Basic necessities such as food, medical care, and utilities are less sensitive to the business cycle than more discretionary spending, such as purchases of automobiles and other consumer durable goods, vacations, or investment in business equipment. As we have seen, housing investment is also highly cyclical. Generally speaking, purchases of big-ticket items that are infrequent and can be postponed are most sensitive to business conditions and, as a result, discretionary-sector profits are more leveraged to the business cycle. This makes the relative performance of the consumer-staples sector compared to the consumer-discretionary sector a useful indicator of how investors judge the economic outlook.

Utilities and telecommunications sector performance also exhibit defensive characteristics. In addition, as higher-than-normal dividend payers, these sectors also exhibit more-than-average sensitivity to the interest-rate cycle, generally outperforming when rates fall and underperforming when rates rise. On the other hand, health-care and technology sector companies include some of the businesses most affected by disruptive accelerating progress in information technology and science. This means that they include many rapidly growing companies as new applications are brought to market.

Pervasive information technology applications are increasingly transformative across most of the economy. On the one hand, this disrupts the franchises of many businesses and forces rapid adjustment to the new possibilities. There's a greater risk of failure in this environment. On the other hand, the scale of application of new technology has created unprecedented wealth and opportunity. These considerations imply that there are growth and value differences within sectors depending on the nature of the enterprise. Some health-care businesses, for example, are mainly technology businesses. Others are less so. Some are more defensive, others are more discretionary, so their cyclical relative performance may diverge.

Industrial, materials, and energy companies tend to be more geared to economic activity than staples, utilities, and health-care businesses. As a result, they tend to follow the manufacturing cycle more closely than the more defensive sectors. For example, late in the cycle, when activity is approaching its peak, strains on natural resource supplies and industrial capacity tend to give them increasing price power, helping the revenues and profits of these companies. As a result, they tend to be relative outperformers in the second half of an expansion.

Financial stocks also have a cyclical pattern that is tied into the interest rate, credit, and leverage cycles that we discussed in chapter 4. Their earnings fluctuate with interest-rate margins, lending growth, and capital-market activity, which are all highly cyclical. In addition, asset-value fluctuations over the cycle can have big effects on the massive and highly leveraged balance sheets of big financial institutions, influencing their equity values along with earnings growth.

Thus, just as there are many dimensions to asset management within the fixed-income universe, there are perhaps even more in the equity world. These additional dimensions reflect factors that typically generate uncertainty that impacts valuations. Also, because fixed income has a preferential place in the capital structure of corporations, it generally receives a lower return than equity. By its very nature, equity investment is a risky business. Like all risk, however, equity risk can be managed. This is true from both a strategic and tactical point of view.

The long-run valuation anchor for equities

Traditionally, stocks have been judged by various valuation methods. Dividend yield, price-to-value-of-underlying assets, and price-earnings ratios are some of the typical approaches. All of these methods require some refinement for useful application, and all are related in some way. The connection between the various methods is implicit in the following two relationships that define the real return on equities:

Actual real return = Dividend yield + Real share-price appreciation

(1)　　　　　　　　　　　　　　　　　　or

Required real return = Risk-free real bond yield + Equity risk premium.

Equity risk premium

The equity risk premium is defined as the additional yield investors demand to take the extra risk associated with equities compared to government bonds. As we have discussed in earlier chapters, unlike the classical period when inflation averaged zero over long periods, the Keynesian period has been characterized by persistent and variable inflation, as well as deliberate policy activism to dampen the business

Exhibit 5.1 Lower Volatility Differential Suggests Lower Equity Risk Premium

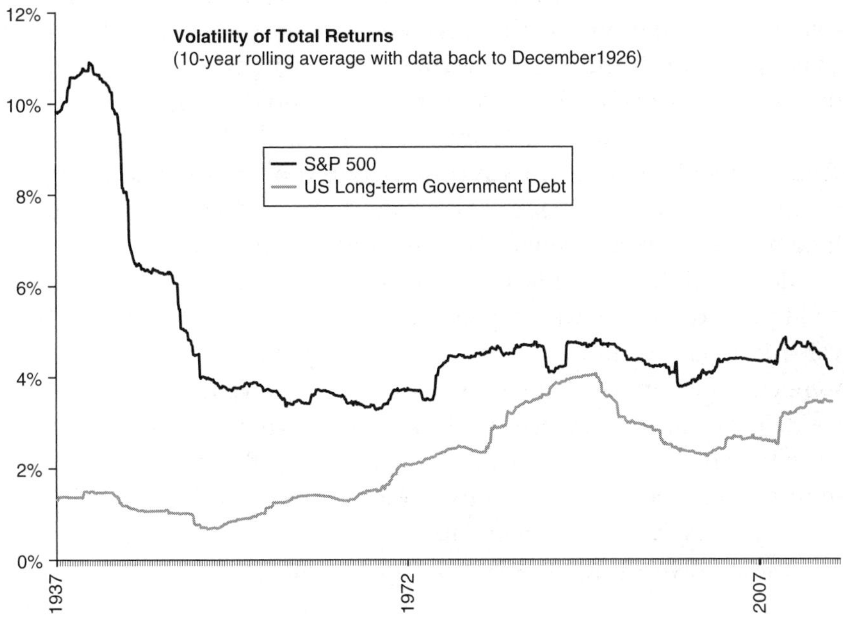

Source: Ibbotson Associates.
Data as of March 31, 2014

cycle. Increased inflation uncertainty, which hurts bonds more, the absence of offsetting deflation, and reduced gross domestic product (GDP) variability have all worked to reduce the equity risk premium compared to the pre-Keynesian period. This is evident in Exhibit 5.1, which shows the shrinking differential between the volatility of returns on bonds and equities in the post–World War II fiat money period.

The narrowed gap between the volatility of returns on stocks and bonds implies a reduced equity risk premium. Indeed, including the volatility differential between stocks and bonds returns in an equation predicting price-earnings ratios (PEs) from Treasury-yield levels greatly improves the model and boosts the PE, consistent with a much lower equity risk premium in the current environment.

Dividend yield

Ultimately, the value of a stock lies in the stream of dividend income it generates over time. The present value of that dividend stream is one way to assign value. The dividend discount model attempts to measure this.

The dividend yield-Treasury yield relationship has also been used to measure stock valuation. However, it should be obvious from the total return equations (1) that dividends are only a *partial determinant* of equity returns and therefore their value. Changes in other return determinants can shift the relationship between dividend yield, actual return, and fair value. Such shifts explain why the dividend yield-Treasury yield relationship was disrupted in the late 1950s as the inflation environment changed, and show that the dividend yield is an incomplete valuation gauge for comparisons across time.

Indeed, Exhibit 5.2 indicates that up until the late 1950s, the dividend yield on stocks was higher than the yield on Treasury bonds. A valuation rule of thumb up to that point in history held that stocks were cheap when the dividend yield was well above the Treasury bond yield. That made sense before World War II, when inflation averaged close to zero over long periods of time, keeping the volatility of bond returns low, especially relative to those of equities, as Exhibit 5.1 illustrates. However, in the Keynesian world of fiat money, bond volatility rose relative to equities because of the larger impact of inflation

Exhibit 5.2 Low Inflation Associated with Higher Dividend Yields Compared to Bond Yields

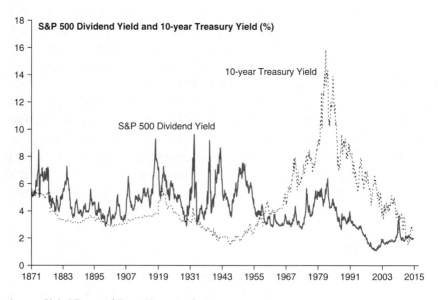

Source: Global Financial Data, Haver Analytics.

Data as of August 2014

uncertainty on real bond returns. Investors who relied on the old dividends-bonds yield rule of thumb sold stocks in the late 1950s when Treasury yields rose above dividend yields, as they perceived stocks as overvalued relative to bonds and not worth buying until the dividend yield exceeded the Treasury yield again. Those who stuck to that old rule of thumb missed one of the biggest equity bull markets in history because the dividend yield did not rise above the ten-year yield for the next 50 years. Clearly something fundamental had changed, providing another example in which traditional "mean reversion" strategies failed because of a structural shift in the economy. So what went wrong?

In the pre-Keynesian world of frequent bouts of deflation, as shown in Exhibit 5.7, the dividend yield had to exceed the Treasury yield in order for investors to be enticed to keep investing in stocks because they couldn't count on stock price appreciation in that environment. For example, during the 54-year period between 1871 and 1925, the stock market index only increased from four to ten, an average annual pace of less than 2 percent. In the persistently positive inflation, post–World War II world, more of the return came from price appreciation as earnings tend to grow roughly in line with nominal GDP. Also important, since the terminal principal repayment on bonds is fixed, it will lose considerable real value in a high inflation world, proportional to the term to maturity and the level of inflation over that time. The bond yield has to adjust to this loss of value to compensate for inflation effects.

In contrast, dividends are not fixed, so they can increase with inflation. As a result, dividend yields require less of an adjustment than bond yields to a higher inflation trend. Each year, the dividend can rise by the inflation rate as can the earnings and price of the stock. If dividends, earnings, and stock prices rise with the inflation rate, the yield can stay the same and the investor is still compensated for inflation losses. The net result in this scenario is a more constant dividend yield compared to bond yields.

Thus, a steady 2- or 3-percent dividend yield can remain attractive in a high inflation world, while bond yields need to increase relatively more to compensate investors. This difference in the way equity and bond values respond to inflation helps explain the shift in the dividend yield-Treasury yield relationship that occurred in the late 1950s as financial assets adjusted to the new Keynesian world of higher, persistent inflation. That also explains why, as inflation has come back down to much lower levels and the Fed has earned credibility for its commitment to low inflation, the dividend yield-Treasury yield relationship has moved back closer to its long-run historical relationship. Indeed, reflecting rising deflation risks, the dividend yield has recently exceeded the ten-year Treasury yield for the first time in over half a century.

Thus, one implication of the "new normal," low-inflation world is this restored relationship between dividend and sovereign yields. In addition to the United States, this is evident in Japan, the United Kingdom, and Germany, among other countries, where the dividend yield is now generally much closer to, or even above, the yield on long-term government debt for the first time since the 1950s. Not surprisingly, the relationship was first restored, and is strongest and most obvious, in Japan, which was the first major economy to see persistent deflation in the fiat money era.

Another consequence of the "new normal is the old normal" paradigm is an increased role for dividends in the overall returns on equities. Traditionally, roughly half of the return from equities has come from dividends and the reinvestment of dividends.

Market value to replacement cost

Another approach to valuation looks at the ratio of the equity market value of a company to the replacement cost of its underlying assets. This ratio is called Tobin's Q, after the late Yale professor James Tobin, who related this ratio to incentives for investment in physical capital. More elementary versions, such as price-to-book value, are also used. Basically, if the equity market value of a company is lower than its replacement cost, a profit can be made by buying the equity and selling the company's assets, or disinvesting. If the equity market value is greater than the replacement cost, equities are deemed expensive or overvalued, as it pays to sell shares and invest in assets to expand the company.

This approach links a strong stock market to strong investment growth, and it makes the most sense for tangible assets that have very liquid markets. However, as modern postindustrial economies have grown increasingly knowledge based, with a higher share of value created from intangible, intellectual property, this valuation method has become harder to apply. Generally speaking, the market appears persistently overvalued by this metric if intangible assets are not given their due. The difficulty of valuing human capital and other knowledge-based assets makes this measure an increasingly questionable way to judge the value of the equity market.

Earnings yield or price-earnings multiple

Ultimately, the earnings paid out to stockholders in the form of dividends or share buybacks are the basis for equity value. If we rewrite the relationships in (1) to show the fair value or equilibrium relationship, then

Actual real return on equities = k (E/P) + g = r + b = Required real return on equities,

where "**k**" is the payout ratio from earnings, "**E**", and "**P**" is the price per share.

In addition to the share of earnings paid as dividends, "**k**" includes the share of earnings used to buy back stock. The part of earnings not paid as either dividends or to buy stock is reinvested to grow per-share value at an annual rate "**g**." Alternatively, the total real return is the risk-free real rate "**r**" on government bonds (for example, the TIPS yield) plus the equity risk premium "**b**."

This relationship determines the fair market price-earnings multiple P/E = k/(r+b-g), where the actual return on equity matches the return investors require given the risk-free rate "**r**." Given the limitations of the other approaches and the feasibility of estimating these parameters, this method is more practical for estimating valuation levels.

Valuation in a reflationary monetary setting

Taking the valuation parameters one by one, we can estimate the fair market value PE ratio. First, as noted above, the difference between the total returns on stocks and government bonds has averaged a bit more than 4 percent since 1926. However, this measure of the equity risk premium "**b**" has been quite volatile over subperiods of time and has shown a tendency to decline over time. As discussed above, we attribute this longer-term downtrend to the shrinking volatility differential between stocks and bonds returns since World War II. The proactive management of fiscal and monetary policy has dampened economic fluctuations and reduced equity-return volatility compared to the 1920–1940 period, as shown in Exhibit 5.1. For example, the speed and aggressiveness of the fiscal and monetary policy response to the 2008 financial crisis dwarfs the 1930s policy response, illustrating how much more proactive policy is today compared to the past. At the same time, the increased volatility of inflation expectations that resulted from activist fiscal and monetary policy has boosted the vola-tility of bond returns compared to the relatively more stable-money period before World War II. The net result is a narrower risk premium "**b**" for equities.

Second, the average real rate of government bonds has varied sub-stantially over long periods of time. As we noted earlier, the authors of *Triumph of the Optimists* found that the real return on US government bonds averaged about 1.6 percent from 1900 to 2000. The *Barclays Equity Gilt Study* 2014 finds a 2.4 percent real return average for the 1925–2013 period.

As shown in Exhibit 5.3, the decades since 1982 have been charac-terized by above-normal rates of return on government bonds as infla-tion was wrung out. This creates a sample bias that has caused market participants, including some Fed officials, to expect excessively high interest rates going forward, in our view, and is the basis for our lower-than-consensus outlook for the "new normal" interest-rate structure in the coming decades.

Our view seems to be consistent with the signal coming from the Treasury Inflation Protected Securities (TIPS) market. Since it began in 2004, the 20-year maturity TIPS yield has averaged 1.6 percent. This is a superior measure of the real yield compared to actual ex-post bond returns, which include unexpected capital gains and losses. Since 1983, these have generally included gains during the biggest bond bull market in US history. Basically, the end of disinflation suggests a structural shift to more "normal" bond yields, which also seems to be the message from the TIPS market since 1.6 percent happens to be

Exhibit 5.3   Real Investment Returns by Decade (% pa)

	Equities	Government Bond	Corporate Bond	Cash
1933–43	4.8	1.7		−2.6
1943–53	8.8	−2.3		−3.3
1953–63	13.8	0.6		0.9
1963–73	1.7	−1.6		0.8
1973–83	3.6	−2.0		0.6
1983–93	9.9	10.0	9.9	2.5
1993–2003	7.9	5.5	5.5	1.7
2003–2013	5.5	3.4	3.9	−0.8

Source: Center for Research in Security Prices (CRSP).

the average real return on government bonds during the 1900–2000 period. The "new normal" is apparently the "old normal" restored after a round trip from 1965 to about 2000, when inflation first got out of control and was then reined back in.

Third, the dividend payout ratio "**k**" (which takes account of stocks buybacks) and the growth rate "**g**" of dividends and earnings have varied over time as well. Exhibit 5.4 shows some historical values for these parameters computed by Professor Jeremy Siegel in *Stocks for the Long Run.*

Two features of the results stand out. Dividend yields and payout ratios were higher in the pre–World War II period and, as a result, the earnings growth component was lower. In line with our earlier discussion, the reverse is true in the post–World War II period. This trend of declining dividend yields reached its extreme during the tech bubble period (when payout ratios reached their lowest level in at least 60 years and stock prices surged ahead of earnings) and has been correcting since. Estimates for "**k**" are getting closer to the historical average of about 0.6, with a likely rising tendency given the more favorable tax treatment of dividends relative to ordinary income in recent years. Averaging the growth rates in dividends and per-share earnings growth shown in Exhibit 5.4 for the recent period gives a value of about 1.75 percent for *real* dividend and earnings growth "**g**." This is more consistent with the somewhat higher growth rate we expect in dividends and the somewhat lower rate we should expect in per-share earnings as a result of higher payout ratios. Putting these factors together results in a PE ratio of between 15 and 21 on current earnings in a reflationary, low real risk-free rate environment, with a reduced equity premium (of between 3 percent and 4 percent) reflecting the

Exhibit 5.4   Dividend Yields and Payout Ratios Higher in the Prewar Period (%)

	Dividend Yield*	Payout Ratio*	Real GDP growth rate	Real growth rate of Earnings per share	Growth rate of Dividends per share
1871–2001	4.5	58.8	3.9	1.25	1.09
1871–1945	5.1	66.8	4.5	0.66	0.74
1946–2001	3.5	51.9	3.1	2.05	1.56

*Median Value

Source: Jeremy Siegel, *Stocks for the Long Run*

impact of proactive monetary and fiscal policy on the relative volatilities of stocks versus bonds. This compares with a historical average PE of about 15 based on the total-return average over history that generated "Siegel's constant," real returns of 6.75 percent. A lower average equity risk premium suggests future real returns between about 5 percent and 6 percent.

Long-term equity performance in different inflation environments

History (and recent experience) shows that equities go through long cycles of sustained over- or undervaluation. History also shows that the macro-monetary environment influences the level of key determinants of equity returns, such as the risk-free real interest rate and the equity risk premium. In particular, real interest rates vary according to the underlying long-term inflation environment and the monetary policy response to it. Furthermore, as we discussed in chapter 2, history shows that activist policy has considerably dampened the volatility of economic growth and presumably, as a result, the equity risk premium.

In the post-2000 environment, monetary policy has been aimed at preventing persistent deflation, an effort called reflation. As a result, real interest rates have been unusually low since 2000, especially compared to the prior two decades when they were unusually high in order to bring inflation down from historic highs. Here we discuss the implications of a prolonged reflationary macro-monetary environment for future equity returns and show that long periods of near-equal returns on stocks and bonds tend to be followed by long periods of greater-than-average equity outperformance. This is what we expect in the years ahead as reflationary efforts persist.

Low valuations have preceded above-normal returns

Valuations are a useful guide to long-term equity returns. As noted above, over long time frames, say more than 50 years, US equities have tended to yield around 6.75 percent adjusted for inflation and the reinvestment of dividend payments (real total return). Buying stocks when they were below the trend line implied by this long-term return eventually resulted in above-average returns, while buying stocks when they were above it inevitably resulted in subpar returns.

For example, in March 2009, with the Standard & Poor's (S&P) 500 index below 700, the market's valuation was roughly 40 percent below its trend line value of about 1050. During the 140 years up to that point, there were only *26 months* when the market was that cheap relative to its trend (Exhibit 5.5). Aside from wartime, there were several months in 1920, 1932, and 1982 when stocks were as cheap as they got in March 2009. By this valuation metric, stocks were at a once-in-a-generation buying point in March 2009.

This extreme undervaluation was the culmination of a secular bear market that began in 2000 from one of the most extreme overvaluation points in stock market history. Many valuation metrics show the stock market was more overvalued in 2000 than at any time in history, as can be seen in Exhibit 5.5. The secular bull market between 1982 and 2000 accounts for almost all of the highest rolling 20-year price-return averages for equities in US history. As with all other long periods of above-normal returns, that long period of above-average returns began from a historically low valuation starting point.

Exhibit 5.6 shows that 20-year returns tend to be highest when the beginning PE is lowest (starting from a PE of just 10). The top decile

Exhibit 5.5   A 6.75% Trend Line

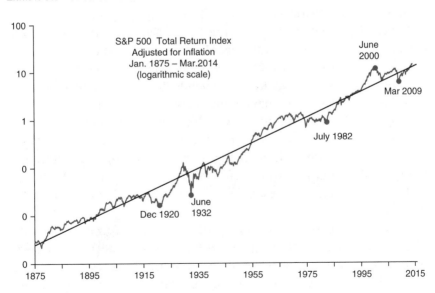

Source: Global Financial Data, Bureau of Labor Statistics.

Data through March 2014.

Exhibit 5.6   Rolling 20-Year Period Returns

		1881–2013		
	Cyclically-Adjusted Price Earnings Ratio P/E10 or Shiller CAPE for the S&P500			
Decile of Return	Beginning PE	Ending PE	20-Year Average Return (price only)	20-Year Average Total Return (includes reinvested dividends)
1	10	29	11.3%	15.3%
2	12	23	9.3%	13.2%
3	14	18	7.8%	12.2%
4	17	18	6.4%	10.3%
5	17	17	5.1%	9.9%
6	18	11	3.7%	7.8%
7	16	13	3.1%	7.6%
8	14	14	2.1%	7.2%
9	13	12	1.5%	6.9%
10	17	11	–0.1%	5.4%

Source: Shiller data.

of returns (with dividends reinvested) averaged over 15 percent, with just over 11 percentage points of price appreciation. Notice that in the bottom half of the total-return distribution, dividends account for the majority of returns. In fact, in the bottom decile, price returns averaged slightly negative, but thanks to dividends, total returns still averaged over 5 percent. Also, note that by the end of the 20-year periods yielding the top two deciles of returns, PE multiples were extremely high. The strong conclusion from this historical experience is that equity valuations and returns are mean reverting, anchored by long-term macroeconomic fundamentals. However, a full cycle from under- to overvaluation and back can take more than 25 years, as the 1982–2009 experience illustrates.

As should be expected following a long period of unprecedentedly high returns such as that up to the massive overvaluation in 2000, performance over the next decade was among the worst for any decade in history. The Great Recession exacerbated the disappointing equity market performance during the decade, with the S&P 500 still a third below its 2000 peak and the NASDAQ only about 40 percent of its March 10, 2000 high almost a decade later. The sharp compression from record overvaluation to near-record undervaluation in such a short span is something Americans had not experienced since the 1930s. Extreme risk aversion was a natural result. This extreme risk aversion and massive undervaluation created big investment opportunities for those investors who kept their emotions in check and their eyes on the market's long-term earnings potential.

The role of inflation, deflation, and monetary policy trends in valuation extremes

The valuation low points in Exhibit 5.5—that is, December 1920, June 1932, July 1982, and March 2009—happen to represent extreme episodes in the history of the financial system and monetary policy. For example, the July 1982 market low coincided with the highest real interest rates in a nondeflationary environment in US history as a result of Paul Volcker's tight policy to break the back of the worst peacetime inflation in US history. The other three lows occurred at the opposite extreme, with the economy and banking system in the throes of the worst debt-deflation cycles of the past 90 years.

Although the nominal short-term risk-free rate may have been low near zero in these deflationary episodes, the real rate was higher than normal because of deflation. For example, with price declines averaging over 10 percent a year in the early 1930s, the then near-zero Treasury bill yield translated into a double-digit real risk-free rate rivaling the rates on bills in 1982 even after they were adjusted for inflation. In all these cases, real risk-free yields rose well above their long-term averages. While deflation was more severe in the 1920 and 1932 episodes, the recent milder deflation threat has also been extremely disruptive because leverage today is much more pervasive in the US household and financial sectors. In addition, in all these episodes, credit spreads widened to record highs. For example, in early 2009, corporate credit spreads widened to levels last seen in the 1930s as the markets temporarily doubted policymakers' ability to avert a depression.

The required return on equity is the sum of the risk-free government bond rate and the equity risk premium (ERP) that investors demand as compensation for the risk associated with equity investment. Since equity stands further down the corporate capital-structure hierarchy than bonds, it's a given that a record rise in corporate credit spreads implies a big rise in the equity risk premium. Since they're closest in the capital-structure hierarchy to equity, the massive widening of high-yield debt spreads probably gives the best indication of the impact of these panics on the equity risk premium.

The reason deflationary panics tend to be associated with historically low PEs is that they raise both the real risk-free yield because of the zero bound on nominal interest rates *and* the equity risk premium because of their ballooning impact on credit spreads. A PE of 8 or 9 implies a required real rate of return on equity of more than 10 percent. The preference for safety and liquidity is highest in these panic periods. Hence the flight to Treasury bills.

The 1982 experience was the odd man out in this respect. Rather than *deflation*, it was Volcker's *fight against inflation* that kept money market rates up around 20 percent. With inflation around 10 percent, that still represented an extraordinarily high real yield, and meant stocks had to yield even more to be worthy of consideration (i.e., low PEs were required). The point is that extreme lows in valuation are associated with very high *real* interest rates, whether because of deflation or the need to fight inflation.

The foregoing makes clear that the best equity-buying opportunities in history have occurred when stocks were most undervalued because of the kind of panic that sets in during financial crises, whether inflationary or deflationary. More generally, those episodes point out the critical role that monetary policy and inflation/deflation trends play in influencing the risk-free return and the equity risk premium.

Inflation trends key

When correlating equity returns with inflation, most strategists tend to sort returns by calendar-year inflation rates. The results show that the best returns generally occur when inflation is "neither too hot nor too cold." Periods of very high inflation or deflation tend to correlate with poor returns because they are associated with periods of poor economic performance and financial instability. This is one of the many reasons why modern central banks aim for low and stable inflation. The nineteenth century was an exception to the rule that deflation is bad for equities and economic growth. This was a period of so-called deflationary boom in the sense that trend growth was relatively strong as the United States industrialized, while inflation was generally negative, as post–Civil War monetary policy was aimed at restoring the prewar gold value of the dollar by shrinking the money supply, a classic prescription for deflation.

Exhibit 5.7 Is the Great Moderation Over? Not Likely

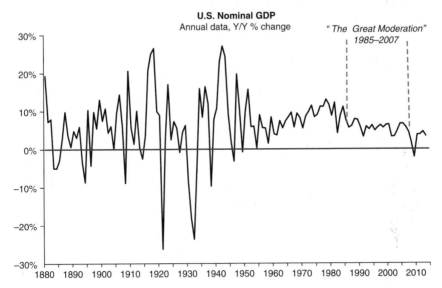

U.S. Nominal GDP
Annual data, Y/Y % change

" The Great Moderation"
1985–2007

Source: Global Financial Data.

Data as of May 6, 2014.

As discussed, deflation, recessions, and depressions were much more frequent prior to World War II. Exhibit 5.7 shows the year-over-year growth rate of nominal GDP back to the 1880s. Even the so-called 1950s golden age shows high GDP volatility compared to the post-1980 period. The extremely muted GDP cycles from the mid-1980s to the mid-2000s, when nominal GDP variation was compressed in a roughly 3 percent to 8 percent range, is referred to as the Great Moderation. This period saw the most sustained growth with the least frequent interruptions by recessions in US history: roughly 12 months of recession in just over two decades. This falling inflation period also coincides with the strongest bull market in financial assets in US history and, on the downside, a growing complacency about risk that was rudely disrupted by subsequent volatility. Investors came to believe that the Great Moderation would last forever, and the equity risk premium plunged as a result. The massive equity overvaluation that culminated in the Y2K tech bubble set the stage for underperformance during the next decade. The underpricing of risk caused by the complacency engendered by the Great Moderation also contributed to the credit excesses of the 1980–2008 period.

Volatility, valuation, and the risk-free real rate have been strongly affected by the variations in the patterns of macroeconomic history. Prior to World War II, orthodox monetary and fiscal policy aimed for zero inflation and balanced budgets. These firm policy anchors were associated with the much greater volatility in economic cycles apparent in Exhibit 5.7. The post–World War II Keynesian world, sparked by the backlash against this policy orthodoxy because of the Great Depression, has been much less volatile as measured by swings in nominal GDP.

This stability in GDP growth has come at the expense of persistent inflation and fiscal deficits as policy buffered tougher adjustments. The latest financial crisis proves the point. Markets were briefly priced for protracted deflation and economic depression. However, the unprecedented monetary and fiscal response to the crisis, which far exceeded the response to the 1930s crisis both in terms of the Fed's increase in the monetary base and the size of the fiscal deficit, precluded a much worse outcome. The downshift in volatility after World War II, shown in Exhibit 5.7, reflects this fundamental shift in policy regimes.

The point of this diversion into macroeconomic history is that there is more to the relationship between equity returns, inflation, and relative yields than can be captured in simple year-to-year correlations. There are effects that depend on the momentum, trends, and the higher-order derivatives that are missed in simple correlations but are implicit in expectations about the future that shape returns. For this reason, understanding the broader macro patterns can give more insight into valuation than is typically possible using simple correlations. In fact, most correlations are unstable over time, often because of changing macro environments. Changing correlations tend to have fundamental economic reasons that are ignored when blindly plugging long-term averages into quantitative models. Insightful gleaning of this information requires historical knowledge and economic understanding that is hard to discern from mechanical statistical techniques.

Exhibit 5.8 looks at the 1926–2013 period and several subperiods within it. The subperiods were chosen to distinguish fundamentally different macromonetary environments. First, looking at the entire period, which averages out the quite distinctive subperiods, we notice that the annual average total return on equities was 10.1 percent in nominal terms (with reinvested dividends). Subtracting inflation leaves a 7.3 percent real return average. Because of the strong bull

Exhibit 5.8   The Trend in Inflation Shapes Asset Returns

	Zero Inflation	Low Stable Inflation	Rising Inflation	Falling Inflation	Reflation	Low, Stable Inflation	Entire Period
	1926–1945	1954–1965	1972–1981	1982–2000	2001–2008	2009–2013	1926–2013
				Annualized Returns			
Treasury Bills	1.06%	2.55%	7.79%	6.22%	2.70%	0.06%	3.50%
U.S. LT Government Bonds	4.71%	2.05%	2.80%	12.55%	9.25%	1.94%	5.47%
S&P 500 Index	7.13%	15.67%	6.47%	16.88%	−2.89%	17.93%	10.08%
Return from Reinvested Dividends	5.46%	3.70%	4.52%	3.16%	1.82%	2.22%	4.03%
Price Appreciation Per Year	1.56%	11.58%	1.85%	13.33%	−4.63%	15.40%	5.82%
Inflation Rate	0.10%	1.80%	7.70%	2.60%	2.50%	1.60%	2.70%
Risk-free Real Rate	0.96%	0.75%	0.09%	3.62%	0.20%	−1.54%	0.80%
GDP (nominal)	4.60%	6.00%	10.70%	6.40%	4.80%	3.90%	6.10%
Profits* (nominal)	4.10%	7.70%	8.70%	7.00%	7.90%	10.80%	6.50%
Equity Market Valuation at beginning of period	Over	Under	Over	Under	Over	Under	

*Profits data start in 1929. GDP profits before tax with IVA and CCAdj

The inflation measure used is the GDP Implicit Price Deflator

Source: Haver Analytics, BEA, Ibbotson

market since 2009, this is a bit above the longer-term trend return in Exhibit 5.5, which is based on a 6.75 percent real return. This 6.75 percent is known as Siegel's constant after Jeremy Siegel.

Why real returns average around this level is a major question since it lies beneath the mean reversion of equity values over very long time spans. The answer is found in the long-term earnings growth trend, real risk-free yields, and the premium that investors demand for riskier equity investments compared to bonds. Obviously, these determinants of long-term returns can, and do, change as the macro-policy environment changes. Siegel's constant just reflects the average outcome from these varying factors.

The entire period shows that the normal *short-term real* risk-free rate is usually around 1 percent or less (averaging about 0.8 percent), which helps explain why the huge positive deviations from this level created undervaluation extremes when real rates on corporate and even "risk-free" credit soared to the double-digit levels discussed earlier. The *real long-term* risk-free rate has averaged about 2.8 percent, the difference between the average yield for long-term government bonds and inflation during this time (5.5 percent minus 2.7 percent). Notice that the period of rising inflation during the 1970s and the period of falling inflation since 1982 were characterized by substantial deviations in the average risk-free rate, both the short-term and long-term rates. Monetary policy kept real interest rates too low in the 1970s, causing inflation to accelerate, and much above "normal" after 1982, causing inflation to keep declining, culminating in the deflation threats of the post-2000 period.

The transition from the *rising* inflation to the *falling* inflation regimes also marked the transition out of the equity bear market from the mid-1960s when the Dow struggled for more than 15 years to break free of the 1,000 level. With falling inflation and interest rates from 1982, the Dow rose to eventually become stuck around the 10,000 level starting in 1998, not breaking free from it sustainably until 2010. Negative real equity returns during the rising inflation period 1972–1981 were followed by some of the best returns ever from the 1982 market low to the 2000 peak. As noted above, after that, returns rivaled the worst outcomes for any ten-year period. This very erratic performance makes it clear why equities are a risky asset. Between 1971 and 2008, for example, the total annualized return on the S&P 500 index was in the 5 percent to 10 percent range in only *five* out of 37 years.

Outlook for a reflationary environment

Given the important role that the monetary policy and inflation environment play in determining the risk-free real interest rate and in influencing the equity risk premium, a view about the likely policy regime ahead is critical to the assessment of the required return on equities. More specifically, the question that arises from these observations is how can we best characterize the attempted transition that is now underway from a falling inflation environment to a low, stable inflation environment, and what does it imply for asset returns? Obviously, this transition is not assured, as the unanticipated brush with deflation over the 2007–2009 period made clear. Indeed, there are strong deflationary undertows in the global economy and that is why the Federal Reserve has had to maintain a lower-than-normal risk-free rate since 2000. To avoid deflation and rising real interest rates, the short-term real risk-free interest rate had to average close to zero between 2001 and 2008, and less than zero between 2009 and 2014, as shown in Exhibit 5.8. On balance, it has been a decade requiring that monetary policy fight deflation, an effort economists call "reflation," and which requires "abnormally" low interest rates and abundant liquidity. These conditions generally bolster equity values.

Before we get into the implications of successful reflation for equity valuation, some justification for the view that deflation has been the main threat in recent years is probably warranted since the conventional wisdom was very slow to accept this. The facts, however, speak for themselves. *First*, around the world, inflation has fallen to levels not seen in more than a half century. This is not a one-off event due to the latest financial crisis, but rather the result of an entrenched trend. Nominal GDP decelerated for over a quarter century, and during the past 15 years has averaged below the 4.9 percent pace that characterized the zero-inflation period 1926–1945 shown in Exhibit 5.8. Zero inflation implies some years of deflation to offset the inflation that occurs during cyclical peaks.

Second, there is a global savings glut that has driven down returns on financial assets around the world. In the last business expansion (2001–2007), this excess saving from large trade surplus countries like China was recycled to finance housing booms, fiscal deficits, and growing current-account deficits in countries such as the United States, the United Kingdom, Ireland, Spain, Greece, and some Eastern European countries. The global recovery taking shape since 2009 is more balanced as the low savers are in the process of transitioning to higher saving rates and slower domestic demand growth. This is already evident in the collapse of the US trade deficit from almost 7 percent to only about 2 percent of GDP by 2014 and the rise in the household saving rate from zero to 4 or 5 percent. The excesses that absorbed the global savings glut in the 2001–2007 cycle were still being corrected and remained a headwind for the global expansion five years after the Great Recession.

The offset to this additional demand deficiency will have to come from increased domestic demand and lower saving in the high-saving countries. The transition takes time, however, and is especially difficult in Europe and China. In the United States, fiscal stimulus helped sustain aggregate demand for a while as the economy reeled under the stress of the Great Recession and its aftermath. Without a global rebalancing, however, a chronic savings glut implies an aggregate demand deficiency that would keep downward pressure on wages and prices. Successful reflation would stabilize the downward trend in US nominal GDP and inflation. A global rebalancing of savings would help reduce the deflationary undertow in the global economy and lead to more balanced world growth, lower overall economic volatility, and better returns.

Implications of successful reflation and of a low nominal GDP growth, stable inflation environment for equity valuations

The "new normal" is the old normal

From a long-term perspective, the pre–World War II orthodoxy implied zero inflation over long periods. A dollar in the 1930s had the same purchasing power as a dollar in the 1830s. After World War II, the world began an experiment with fiat money and countercyclical fiscal policy that has been hugely successful when judged by the collapse of GDP volatility shown in Exhibit 5.7. Nevertheless, it took time to learn how to manage this new fiat-based monetary policy and fiscal deficits. Inflation threatened to get out of control in the late 1970s and early 1980s. Since then, it has progressively gotten lower to the point where deflation has become the main threat. That is why extraordinary measures such as zero interest rates and quantitative easing were put in place.

In essence, the United States is attempting a transition to a low, trendless inflation environment. The "new normal" of low and stable inflation is the "old normal" that prevailed before the mid-1960s. This outlook for low and stable, trendless inflation shapes the valuation parameters for the US equity market going forward.

A glance at Exhibit 5.8 shows two subperiods of relatively low, trendless inflation: the period before and just after World War II. Inflation was a bit higher in the latter period (1.8 percent versus 0.1 percent). The short-term risk-free real rate was about 1 percent in both cases. The real cost of long-term credit was much higher in the prewar period, making bonds relatively more attractive compared to the 1954–1964 period, when equities show their greatest relative outperformance compared to long-term government bonds. Equity returns were about twice as high in the latter period (15.7 percent vs. 7.1 percent) because of the extreme initial undervaluation coming out of World War II (Exhibit 5.5). Also, despite comparable real growth in both periods, profits growth was almost twice as high in the latter period.

One of the insights from these low-inflation periods is the changing importance of dividends in the overall return. Because of poor stock-price appreciation, dividends accounted for about three quarters of the return in the first period. Despite very strong price gains in the latter period, dividends still accounted for about a quarter of returns. Dividends also made up the bulk of the returns in the 1970s bear market, although inflation was high enough to swamp total returns and leave *real returns* negative.

It is the 1982–2000 period that stands out as a protracted period with the lowest contribution from dividends to total returns, in large part as a reflection of the unusually strong effect of PE multiple expansion on total return. Since 2000, dividend yields have generally been rising from all-time lows, and dividends provided the only return to equities while prices declined between 2000 and 2009. A consequence of a low-inflation world is a bigger role for dividends in total returns compared to the unusual 1982–2000 world of rising PE multiples.

As Exhibit 5.8 shows, a long-term period of accelerating inflation, such as 1972–1981, is bad for both stocks and bonds. However, as noted above, because the interest and principal are fixed, unexpected inflation is worse for bonds. This is evident in Exhibit 5.8, which shows that long-term government bonds averaged just 2.8 percent in total return compared to 6.5 percent for equities during that time. Still, since inflation averaged 9 percent, both asset classes had negative *real* returns, with bonds just hit harder. Stocks have much better hedging features against inflation, such as the rise in product prices that offsets to some extent inflation-driven cost increases. Companies with real assets and fixed financial obligations also benefit. On the other hand, taxes tend to undermine the inflation-hedging features of equities since capital gains are taxed without adjustment for the real losses caused by inflation.

The role of the monetary-macro environment and the valuation starting point provide two important reference points for strategic asset allocation. A reflationary environment is relatively more favorable for stocks than bonds. In contrast, unsuccessful reflation that turns into deflation, as almost happened in 2008–2009, favors government bonds over stocks. As that deflationary scare dissipates, relative equity outperformance should continue given the relatively low level of interest rates.

Exhibit 5.9   US Companies Are Earning a Bigger Share of Profits Abroad

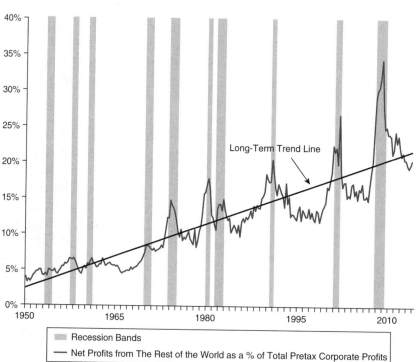

Source: Bureau of Economic Analysis/Haver Analytics.
Data as of May 2014.

The profits cycle and margins

Profits make the world go round

Over the very long run, profits have tended to grow roughly in line with nominal GDP. For example, as shown in Exhibit 5.8, between 1926 and 2013, profits and nominal GDP averaged just over 6 percent annual growth rates. Clearly, there can be substantial periods when profits grow significantly faster (2001–2013) or slower (1972–1981) than nominal GDP. In particular, lower but positive inflation periods seem to be better for profits growth relative to GDP than high inflation periods.

Since GDP growth measures domestically based production, it excludes the foreign-based production growth that creates an increasing share of US companies' profits (Exhibit 5.9). Assuming globalization continues and US corporations maintain their strong position in global commerce, it seems reasonable to expect that corporate profits growth will exceed domestic output growth for the foreseeable future. Leading-edge technology and highly efficient corporate organization make many US companies among the most productive in the world. This gives them an edge in global competition, and is helping the majority of the world's population move out of subsistence poverty at the fastest rate in human history.

To the extent that US nominal GDP growth is likely to run at just around 4 percent to 5 percent in coming years, based on slower growth demographics and low inflation, we would expect a rising share of foreign-sourced earnings to keep the underlying profits trend at least as strong as the historical average (growth of 6 percent to 7 percent per year). The United States has a large amount of capital invested around the world, which generally earns a much higher rate of return than the debt it owes to the rest of the world yields. Given the US experience since 2001—slower-than-historical-average nominal GDP growth and faster-than-historical-average profits growth—there is a good case for better-than-normal profits growth while the rest of the world keeps chasing US living standards.

Aside from this long-term trend, there is a significant cyclical component to profits growth. In fact, there is much more cyclical variation in profits than there is in GDP. Profits rise much faster earlier in the recovery and during the expansion than GDP, and begin to slow down late in the business cycle before falling more than GDP during recessions. The profits cycle is a key factor behind the cyclical performance of equity prices and provides the basis for tactical asset allocation. In addition, within the equity market, different sectors perform better or worse relative to other sectors and the overall market according to the comparative advantages and disadvantages reflected in relative earnings growth during the various phases of the business cycle.

Profits growth is the result of revenue growth and/or margin expansion, where the margin is the share of revenues left over after a company covers its expenses. While corporate revenues tend to grow in line with GDP over the long term, they are very cyclical and particularly sensitive to the cycles in big-ticket spending on consumer durables and business equipment. These items are more cyclical than GDP, and so are corporate revenues. Other cyclical areas such as housing and commercial construction also drive the revenue cycle.

The profit margin is cyclical as well, and depends on the cyclical variation in expenses relative to revenues. Labor costs are the biggest

Exhibit 5.10 Labor Costs Share of Corporate Revenues Is Highly Cyclical. Demographics Have Likely Caused Structural Shift Down

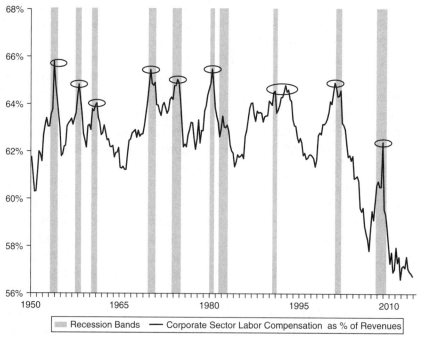

Source: Bureau of Economic Analysis/Haver Analytics.

Data as of May 2014.

expense for corporations (Exhibit 5.10), typically accounting for 60 percent to 66 percent of US corporate value added between 1950 and 2004. Since then, however, the labor share of compensation has fallen to historical lows. As we shall discuss below, this drop appears to be structural, implying a structural rise in the average profit margin.

For now, note that the first half of an expansion tends to be characterized by a falling labor-cost share, while the second half tends to be characterized by a rising labor share of costs. As a result, profit margins tend to rise toward a peak in the midcycle and then decline, generally bottoming in, or around, the recession, when the labor-cost share of revenues peaks.

Other nonlabor expenses are also somewhat cyclical, but generally less significant than labor costs given their smaller share of total costs. For example, interest expense rises with growing business investment in equipment and structures to meet rising demand as the expansion progresses, as well as with interest rates. This means that they are lower early in the cycle and higher later in the cycle. However, they are easier to hedge than labor costs. In fact, chief financial officers (CFOs) take advantage of the interest-rate cycle to lock in low interest rates and avoid the margin drag when rates rise. The long downtrend in interest rates since 1982 and the Fed's zero-rate policy have allowed companies to lock in low long-term rates and minimize interest-rate expense relative to the 1970s and 1980s, when interest rates were extraordinarily high by historical standards. This is another factor behind the rising trend in margins of recent years.

Energy and materials costs also tend to heat up later in the cycle, adding to growing margin pressures from labor and interest costs. In addition, geopolitical shocks to oil prices can shift the balance of profits from oil users to oil producers, squeezing the margins of the former. What is more, when unemployment is near its cycle low and inflation starts heating up, the Fed starts addressing it with rate hikes. Its effort to slow down growth in order to limit inflation pressures puts additional downward pressure on margins by slowing revenue growth, causing businesses to start cutting back and reinforcing a loss of macroeconomic momentum that slows revenue growth further. The various feedback loops that drove expansion start going into reverse at that stage of the cycle, eventually causing a recession.

By affecting how fast or slow business hiring and capital investment occur, profit growth is a leading indicator of the economy, a characteristic confirmed by its strong correlation with the Conference Board

Leading indicator of economic activity. In addition, as we saw in chapter 4, profit margins are also key to the cycle in credit spreads because they are one of the best financial metrics indicating how much extra cash cushion corporations have to make good on debt payments. Low profit margins in recessions increase risks of default, and as a result are associated with bigger credit-risk premia on corporate bonds. Conversely, peak margins in the midcycle expansion reflect high confidence in the financial health of corporations. This tends to create complacency about the ability of lower-grade credits to make good on debt repayments. Thus, in essence, the profits cycle drives the credit cycle.

For all these reasons, the profits cycle also drives the cyclical swings in equity prices. In a recession, the economy goes through a process that reflects businesses' response to falling profits. With weak revenues and a high labor share of costs, the squeeze is on profits. Survival depends on making tough choices, and these include layoffs when sales fall to levels that require less production. Still, while layoffs accelerate, there are risks to *excessive* cyclical layoffs because there are many frictions in the labor market that don't exist for other inputs. The cost of finding and training workers for the next cycle creates an incentive to lay off prudently and hang on to good workers even as revenues dwindle. This, combined with the fact that changes in employment occur with a lag to changes in profits growth of about two quarters, helps explain why the wage share of revenues is cyclically highest in a recession.

Inventories are much easier to adjust than the number of employees. All across the economy, inventories are drawn down from the excessive levels that piled up at the end of the expansion. New orders decline, the backlog of unfilled orders shrinks, production growth slows, and goods from inventories meet demand that previously required new production. This adjustment process eventually reaches a point at which inventories are too low and the orders backlog starts to build up again. Partly, this happens because pessimism about sales starts to exceed reality. Partly, it happens because stimulative policies start to turn aggregate demand higher.

In a self-reinforcing downturn, revenues decline, credit defaults increase, and layoffs accelerate, reducing consumer demand and causing sales to decline further. The process repeats until something stops it. Self-reinforcing cutbacks in labor demand, inventories, orders, and production vary according to confidence. In a panic, there is no downside limit to the cutbacks, absent some catalyst to stop the panic. If policymakers sit back and let it happen, the liquidation cycle can go far enough to ruin most businesses, cause mass unemployment and wipe out much wealth before running its course. The 2008–2009 financial crisis raised the specter of such a ruinous liquidation cycle in the absence of unprecedented government intervention.

In any case, profits growth and profit margins shrink in a recession and cost-cutting is the natural response. Eventually, cost-cutting and revenue growth become sufficient to stabilize margins, and profit growth begins anew. The best time in the business cycle to buy stocks is late in a recession when the dynamics for recovery are falling into place. This catches the earliest stage of a profits recovery, when the acceleration in profits growth is generally the strongest. With equity prices most depressed during the recession relative to long-term earnings growth potential and the strongest profits rebound of the cycle usually taking place when the recovery begins, the strongest cyclical gains in equities prices usually occur in the first year or two of recovery. The cyclical bottom in equity prices usually takes place a few months before the recession ends, as smart forward-looking buyers begin to anticipate the turn toward recovery.

One interesting exception to this cyclical pattern is the 2001 recession, which ended in November 2001, according to the National Bureau of Economic Research (NBER) cycle-dating committee, but was not preceded by a turn in equities. In fact, that cyclical bear market in equities did not end until about *a year after* the recession was over. The overvaluation of the market in 2000 reached a historical extreme by many measures, and the role of the equity market in fueling the prior expansion had been greater than normal. This meant there were more valuation excesses to correct than usual. In addition, fraud and extreme lapses in corporate governance in many massively overvalued companies, such as Enron and WorldCom, were only discovered after the recession ended, keeping investors nervous about equities as the recovery began. The special role of the stock market in the late 1990s boom and excesses associated with it are another example of "what's different" in particular cycles. Aside from this notable exception, equity prices have generally been a very reliable leading indicator of recoveries.

As the economy approaches midcycle and margins peak, equities tend to exhibit more "normal" returns in line with GDP and earnings growth. The fastest earnings growth is typically the first year or two of the recovery. Margins rise rapidly as operating leverage is greatest coming off the bottom of a recession, when capacity utilization is lowest. As firms increase production and sales when a recovery gets underway, they are able to cover more of their fixed costs as employees and the capital stock become more fully utilized. Recall that the average length of the workweek is a leading indicator, as existing workers put in more hours before new workers are hired. Salaried workers are paid regardless of how fast output grows; therefore, as their output increases, so do margins.

As a result of this operational leverage, it is not unusual for corporate profits to grow many multiples of GDP growth in the early recovery phase of the business cycle. Gains from 30 percent to 60 percent are not unusual in the first year of a profits recovery. That is why stock prices often see their biggest gains at that stage of the cycle as well. For example, peak year-over-year profits growth topped 55 percent in the fourth quarter of 2009, six months after the 2007–2009 recession ended. On a calendar-year basis, profits averaged over a 20-percent gain in 2010, the first full year after the recession. The S&P 500 index bottomed at 676 on March 9, 2009, about four months before the

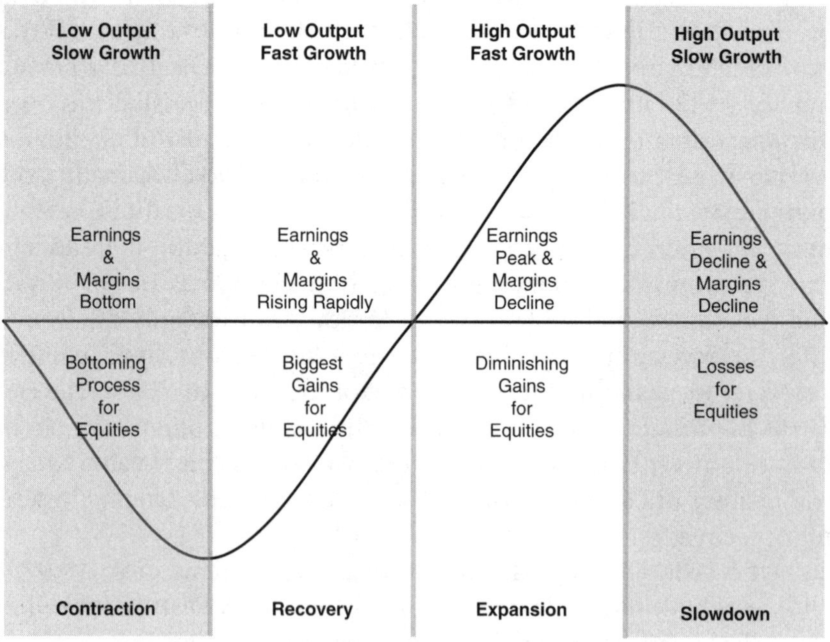

Exhibit 5.11 Tactical Strategies for Equity Investment during the Business Cycle

recession ended. By the third quarter of 2010, it had risen to 1141, a gain of about 70 percent.

Earnings growth tends to moderate from that initial cyclical surge and so do stock prices. Exhibit 5.11 shows how earnings and stock prices tend to follow the business cycle. A cyclical bull market in stocks tends to continue until a recession threatens the growth of profits. As this point approaches, the market usually is losing momentum as strong hands are selling to weak hands, in a distributive process that indicates that the market is tired and topping. This is the optimal time to lighten up on equities, overweight high-quality credit such as Treasuries, and avoid weak credits like high-yield bonds.

Lower quality (i.e., higher leverage, lower credit rating, high-risk) company stocks tend to lead the market out of a recession. They get hit the hardest in a recession and reach valuation levels that put a lower probability on their survival. The same is true about low-quality bonds. A recovery gives junk bonds a new lease on life. Companies are able to roll them over for the next cycle. Stocks of highly cyclical (high beta) companies leveraged to the business cycle generally outperform when the recovery begins as well.

As the cycle progresses and the late-cycle expansion turns into recession, this dynamic transitions to the other extreme. Low-beta, defensive stocks with less earnings vulnerability to the recession, such as utilities, health care, and telecom companies, are preferred in this environment, along with consumer staples stocks. People still need to eat and drink in a recession, but they don't need to drive a new car. Instead, they get the old car fixed.

Generally, the profit cycle is not as smooth as Exhibit 5.11 suggests. Year-over-year profit growth hits occasional bumps in the road due to temporary disruptions to demand caused by weather or temporary shocks to confidence. In addition, the mini cycles within the business cycle can keep doubts about the sustainability of the profits expansion alive. A good example is the 1980s expansion. During the first five years of that new cyclical and secular bull market, stocks and profits did quite well. By 1987, however, the profit cycle had turned sharply negative, while equity prices kept rising by an additional 40 percent in just seven months. The stock market crash on October 19, 1987, saw the Dow Jones Average drop over 20 percent in one day, its biggest one-day decline ever. The crash was taken to be a leading indicator that a recession was imminent. Instead, lacking a fundamental basis for recession, the economy recovered, including a new profit up-cycle after what turned out to be a midcycle pause in the expansion and a valuation correction for equities.

A more modest interruption of the US profits cycle occurred after two years of recovery from the 2007–2009 recession. The global slowdown in 2011–2012 precipitated by tight monetary and fiscal policies in Europe adversely affected US earnings abroad. Europe is the biggest source of external earnings for US companies, and it went back into recession after its policies were tightened prematurely. This hurt emerging markets and confidence in the global growth outlook as well. As a result, US corporate earnings growth, especially foreign-sourced earnings, slowed to a standstill by late 2012 before reaccelerating with global growth as Europe crawled out of its double-dip recession.

In sum, hiccups in earnings inevitably occur over a business cycle. Generally, however, the main pattern is a surge in profits growth in the first year or two after a recession, followed by a moderation that eventually turns negative by the end of the cycle. Strong economic growth at high capacity utilization and low unemployment rates are the death knell for profit margins. Declining profit margins after the midcycle eventually drive a deteriorating credit situation in an economy that is also typically more highly leveraged after several years of expansion and rising confidence.

The case for higher margins

As we saw in Exhibit 5.10, the labor share of income generated by corporations has plunged below the 60-percent to 66-percent range that had prevailed since World War II. There are at least two obvious reasons for the reduced role of labor in economic output.

First, technological change is proceeding at an accelerating pace as information processing capacities and speeds surge. A cell phone today has much more processing power than the room-sized computers that helped send the first man to the moon. Initially, technology replaced millions of people in clerk-like jobs at large institutions, such as insurance companies. As artificial intelligence approaches and surpasses the natural intelligence of people, machines are increasingly doing jobs that people used to do. This has significant implications for the labor share of income in the economy. Generally speaking, it means higher profit margins and a lower labor share of income.

Second, throughout the developed world, including the United States, the population is aging. There is an unprecedented share of

Exhibit 5.12 Higher Profit Margins Pay for the Retirement of an Aging Population

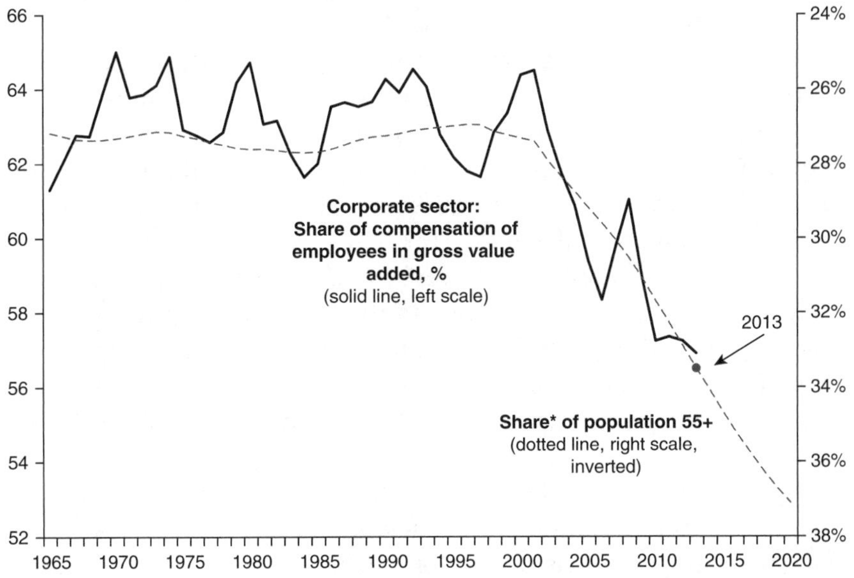

Source: Bureau of Labor Statistics, *Census Bureau Actual and Predicted Shares/ Haver Analytics.

Data as of 2013.

the population living past 65 years of age, when people tend to leave the workforce. When the US social security system was created in the 1930s, most people barely made it to retirement age. The duration of retirement was just a few years on average. Today, it's not unusual for people to spend 20 years or more in retirement.

This means that a growing fraction of the population will spend a lot more time outside the labor force than before. The collapse in the share of labor compensation into a new lower range since about 2001 when the first US baby boomers turned 55, coincide with the new downtrend in the labor force participation rate as these baby boomers retire. With lower labor force participation and advancing technology, profits growth has outstripped GDP growth by a wide margin and more than can be accounted for by the typical cyclical pattern. Not coincidentally, up until 2001, the older population's share of the total population was fairly steady at about 28 percent. By 2014, it had jumped by about 6 percentage points to 34 percent, about the same as the fall in the labor share of income (Exhibit 5.12). Labor force participation drops sharply after age 55 to about half the participation rate of the prime-age working force (25–54 years old), from about 80 percent to 40 percent, so the rising share of the 55+ cohort is significantly depressing the overall labor force participation rate.

These two forces for a lower labor force share of income raise a host of questions that are better addressed in chapter 7, in which we talk about globalization and technological change, as well as demographic factors as forces driving long-term investment themes. Here, suffice it to say that the capital share of income is naturally rising as the labor share declines. This rising capital share is necessary because as more people live in retirement, it is the capital income from their savings and investments that pays for their retirement. Automation makes possible replacing people with more capital. As a result, the compensation from this production shifts from workers to capital owners, that is, the bondholders and shareholders in the company.

Disproportionately, older people with a lifetime of savings are the shareholder and bondholder beneficiaries of this trend. In fact, this aging of the population is also one of the main factors behind the rising inequality in the distribution of wealth and income. In an advanced economy, older people are wealthier than younger ones who are just starting careers, businesses, and are saving for old age. Thanks to the marvels of technology, the economy is transitioning to return more of the income it generates to fund the incomes of the growing share of the population that is out of the workforce. These very strong forces for a reduced share of labor income create the rising profit margins seen in recent years. This is a structural shift.

The huge concentration of global wealth in the hands of retirees in the developed economies represents the capital that will help the younger developing world population raise its productivity and standards of living. Millionaires represent less than 1 percent of the world's population. In 2013, 80 percent of them lived in the United States and Europe. While less than 20 percent of the world's people live in the wealthy developed economies, they own the majority of the world's capital. Aging populations in these regions will increasingly depend on returns to this wealth for their retirement income. Younger populations in the developing world, where the other 80 percent of the world's people live, can raise their living standards more rapidly by working with the capital provided by the rich world. This capital is the basis for more rapid increases in their labor productivity, which is the key to rising living standards. The trend of US corporate profits

Exhibit 5.13 Monetary Policy and the Dollar Affect Oil Price Trends

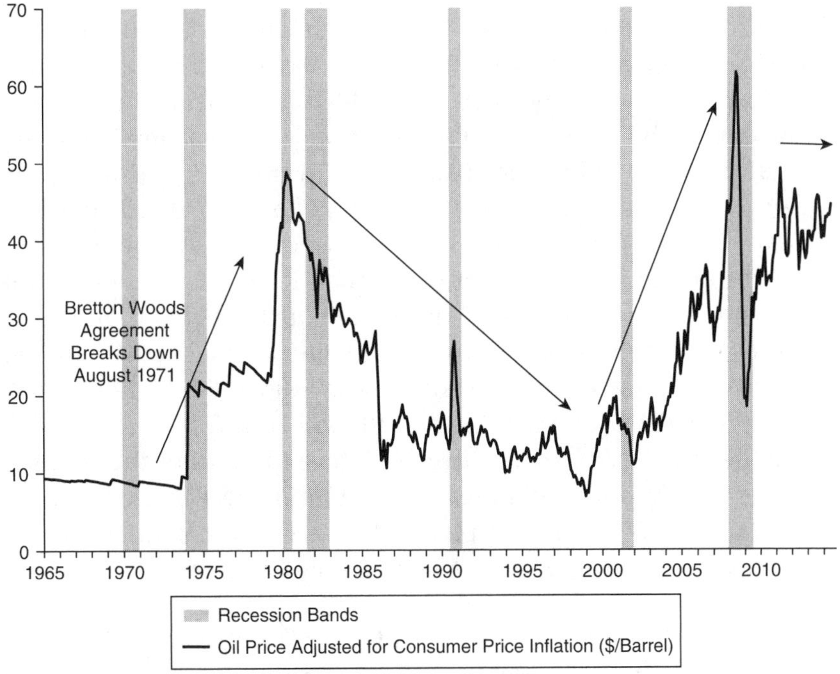

Source: Haver Analytics.
Data as of August 2014.

increasingly coming from abroad (Exhibit 5.9) is likely to continue given the high concentration of global wealth held by US companies, their high productivity, and cutting-edge technologies. In addition, a disproportionately high share of the top global brands is concentrated in US multinational companies.

Sectors and cycles

Macroeconomic trends and cycles influence not only the relative performance of asset classes but also the relative performance of sectors within the stock market. Before discussing the usual pattern of relative performance over the typical business cycle, it's useful to illustrate some of the longer-term, macroeconomic influences that have driven relative sector returns over the past half century. This is important because deviations from the usual cyclical pattern can be overwhelmed, or considerably diminished, by these longer-term trends.

Long-term trends

A good starting point is the energy sector, which was relatively stable until the early 1970s, when the dollar became a fiat currency for international transactions after the Bretton Woods system broke down in August 1971, when President Richard Nixon suspended the greenback's convertibility to gold. Organization of Petroleum Exporting Countries (OPEC), which got paid for oil in dollars, quadrupled the price of a barrel shortly thereafter from $3 to $12. As illustrated in Exhibit 5.13, the inflation-adjusted price of oil rose sharply through the 1970s, peaking shortly after the Iranian Revolution in 1979. Not coincidentally, this was a period that culminated in high inflation and a weak dollar, trends that sharply reversed once Volcker's anti-inflation policies began to work in the early 1980s. From 1980 to about 2000, real oil prices declined, reaching an inflation-adjusted value last seen before the first oil price shock in 1973. Since the turn of the century, oil prices have quadrupled in real terms, trading near their 1980 peak since 2008 except for a brief period during the recession and early-recovery period and again after the summer of 2014.

The observed trends in oil prices are also associated with trends in commodity prices more generally, which we'll address in more detail in the next chapter on tangible assets and commodity investing. The performance of the energy and materials sectors of the equity market is highly correlated with the prices of their underlying commodity outputs relative to production costs. As a result, the relative performance of the energy and materials sectors over the past 50 years has been heavily influenced by the macroeconomic trends driving the real values of their underlying commodity output.

This can be seen in Exhibit 5.14, which illustrates the relative underperformance of the energy sector during the declining oil price period until the real oil price bottom in 1999 and the subsequent relative outperformance during the 2001–2008 quadrupling of real oil prices. As global rebalancing ensued after the financial crisis and China downshifted to slower growth, questions arose about the staying power of the global commodity super cycle that dominated the 2002–2008 world expansion and investment landscape. On balance, the real price of oil was relatively weaker after 2010 and energy stocks underperformed.

The trends in energy and commodity prices over the past 50 years reflect an assortment of longer-term macroeconomic influences. Trends

Exhibit 5.14   Energy-Sector Relative Performance Follows Oil Price Trend

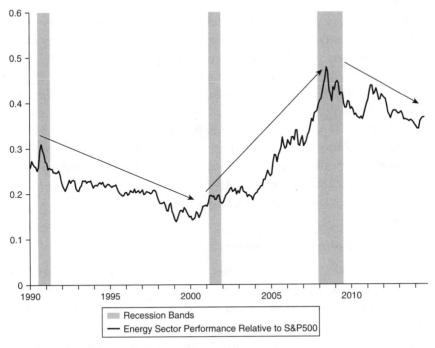

Source: Standard and Poor's/Haver Analytics.
Data as of August 2014.

in the dollar's foreign exchange value have been associated with relative commodity price changes. For example, a weak dollar was associated with the strong energy and commodity price trend of the 1970s,
while a strong dollar was associated with the reversal of this trend during the first Reagan administration. An exception, or counterexample,
is the 1985–1995 period, when the dollar was generally weak against
the other major currencies, yet commodities, including energy prices,
were also weak. The explanation for that apparent anomaly seems to
lie in falling inflation expectations and the relatively high real interest rates that characterized US policies until about 2000, when reflation became necessary to stave off cumulating deflation forces, and
policy shifted from the high real rates that drove disinflation to lower
real rates. As discussed in the next chapter, low real interest rates are
favorable for stronger tangible asset prices, while high real rates create
headwinds associated with commodity bear markets, such as the secular bear from 1980 to 2000, when oil and gold prices fell by 80 percent

in real terms through two of the longest business expansions in US history.

The flip side of these trends in commodity prices is the relative performance of the net *users* of energy and materials as inputs as opposed to the *producers*, who benefit from higher prices. For example, low energy prices are positive for the profits of transportation companies, which did relatively well during the 2010–2014 period of stable and falling energy prices. Consumer spending also suffers or benefits according to the vicissitudes of energy markets. These simple examples illustrate the constant relative value churning that takes place within the various sectors of the equity market in response to both long- and short-term forces, many of which arise from the underlying macroeconomic trends affecting the global economy.

Anatomy of a secular bear market

Often, the response to macroeconomic trends will cause overshoots that leave the sectors benefiting from a soon-to-end trend extremely overvalued relative to its neglected, disfavored brethren. For example, in the early 1980s, energy, gold, and bonds were priced as if the 1970s inflation trend and double-digit interest rates would last indefinitely. Instead, the next two decades of disinflation reversed the trends in all three asset class values, making energy and gold underperform, while bonds and other beneficiaries of nominal interest-rate declines outperformed.

In fact, the steady decline in nominal interest rates from 1981 helped drive the most powerful secular bull market in equities in US history, with P/E multiples expanding from around 10 to over 30 by the time the bubble eventually popped in 2000 after the Y2K tech frenzy. During that bull market, technology, media, and telecom (TMT) companies were all the rage as the first round of internet buildout created a multitude of new companies with plans to monetize the information highway. Inflows by retail investors to equity funds consistently exceeded flows into bond funds, growing to more than $500 billion at the peak in 2000. This exuberance for equities grew more pronounced throughout the 1990s, and was most extreme at the top. By 2000, many tech companies were absurdly overvalued when the bubble burst. On the other hand, energy, materials, and "old industrial" companies were priced as "has-beens" without a future. This set the stage for the relative performance shift that began with the new cyclical bull market in 2002 (a cyclical bull market in a secular bear market that saw the S&P

500 index first top 1500 in 1999 and then languish below that level for most of the next decade).

When the market crashed in 2001, investment preferences began a *structural* shift, as pessimism about stocks became more and more entrenched. Indeed, the bias toward bonds grew and persisted even as a strong new equity bull market began in 2009, with flows into fixed-income funds surging to $600 billion by 2011 and equity outflows remaining the order of the day.

Pessimism about equity investing tends to be greatest just when optimism is most rewarding, however. For example, a Conference Board survey of households conducted monthly since 1988 illustrates the contrarian value of excessive optimism and pessimism about equities at turning points. The survey asks respondents whether they expect stock prices to be higher or lower over the next 12 months. Interestingly, optimists generally prevail by the widest margin late in the cycle going into recessions when bear markets begin, while negativity is most pronounced at the end of recessions and early in the recovery, when stocks are about to see their best gains. The gap between optimists (higher prices expected over the next year) and pessimists (lower prices expected over the next year) has proven to be a good contrarian indicator. For example, at the end of the first quarter of 2009, when the stock market bottomed, the average gap between optimists and pessimists registered its lowest reading in the history of the series, with pessimists far outnumbering optimists. A year later, the S&P 500 index was up by more than 50 percent, the biggest 12-month gain during the entire history of that particular sentiment measure. This entrenched pessimism about equities lingered until 2014, and retail money flows continued to favor bonds over equities as a result.

During this decade of *persistent* pessimism about equity investing, the cyclical bull market of 2002–2007 included an important rotation away from the overvalued TMT stocks of the 1990s "irrational exuberance" period into the laggard sectors like energy, materials, and industrial stocks that were neglected during the internet bubble period. As a result, while the S&P 500 index worked its way back to the nominal peak levels of 1999 by 2007, the sector mix of market value had shifted dramatically. Many "new economy" large-cap technology stocks that had soared in the late 1990s were still at a fraction of their peak 2000 valuations. In fact, when the S&P 500 index briefly topped 1500 again in 2007, the technology-stock-laden NASDAQ composite was still only about half of the peak price it had reached in March 2000. On the other hand, "old economy" companies such as banks, coal, steel, and energy producers led the bull market and gained a larger share of equity market capitalization. Energy and materials companies particularly benefitted from the boom in China, where three decades of double-digit growth had created an economic critical mass that was increasingly important for the world's expansion. Its rapid industrial development essentially created a replay of the 1950s-type winners during the post–World War II rebuilding and industrialization of the developed and successfully developing economies of that time.

Nevertheless, while these "old economy" companies outperformed during the 2002–2007 cyclical bull market, the "new economy" companies that shined in the previous bull market in the 1990s slowly but surely increased their earnings even as their stock prices languished. As a result, by the time a new secular bull market began after the financial crisis, these stocks had gone from extremely overvalued in 2000 to extremely undervalued in 2009, which positioned them well to lead a new bull market based on their strong earnings power and relatively attractive valuations. Furthermore, the fact that they increasingly provided the dividend growth in a market that once again respected the major role of dividends in total long-term returns enhanced their investment appeal.

During the general remixing of performance between 2000 and 2007, with overvalued TMT stocks lagging and undervalued old economy (energy, materials, and industrials) outperforming, the financial sector marched to its own drum. As we have discussed in other places, the 1990s expansion was driven more by equity market valuation excesses and less by credit-fueled excesses. As a result, consumers barely flinched in the 2001 recession. Also, while housing stalled a bit, it was a very mild interruption in what turned out to be a strong 15-year rise in building activity that culminated in the credit and housing bubbles of 2004–2006.

The valuation of the financial sector grew with the mortgage lending it provided based on rising home prices. Thus, financial sector stocks participated in both the 1990s and early 2000s cyclical bull markets, showing relative outperformance through both expansions as well as the 2001 recession. From about 8 percent of the total S&P 500 market capitalization in 1991, the market capitalization of the financial sector grew to about 22 percent of the total market value by the time the housing market began to roll over in 2006. The 2007–2009 financial crisis corrected a very long run of financial sector outperformance that

was strongly associated with its financing of an unusually long housing boom that stretched over two business cycles. From its peak of
22 percent of the overall market capitalization in 2006, the financial
sector fell by half to just under 11 percent in the first half of 2009.

The relative performance of financial sector stocks in the 2001 and
2007–2009 recessions is a consequence of the fundamentally different
business cycles that led up to those recessions. Generally speaking, financial stocks should underperform in a recession. However, they did not
underperform in 2001. In turn, they underperformed with a vengeance
in 2007–2009 because of the largely debt-based nature of the excesses in
the 2002–2007 expansion and the massive accumulation of imbalances
in the economic and financial system that needed to be corrected.

These examples show how the differences in relative sector performance over a business cycle cannot be judged purely in the context
of business-cycle patterns. Energy and commodity price cycles can
stretch over multiple cycles, helping or hurting the affected sectors.
Also, excesses can accumulate in various sectors during more than
one cycle, as seen in the housing and financial sector valuation cycles
that went on for about 15 years without the benefit of a significant
adjustment in the intervening recession. With falling interest rates,
the long disinflation cycle from the early 1980s played a prominent
role in many of the trends and cycles in asset values. The "new normal" world of lower inflation and interest rates is different, and many
of the pre-1965 relationships that were disrupted after inflation took
off are being restored as a result. This new source of relative stability
should make tactical asset allocation based on business-cycle patterns
relatively more important as a source of excess return going forward.

Summary of tactical asset allocation by sector

The differences in sector performance over the business cycle are
largely the result of the strength and timing of the various subcycles
that make up the overall business cycle. For example, although this
was not the case after the 2008–2009 financial crisis, the housing
cycle usually leads recoveries. Companies with businesses related to
homebuilding, housing finance, and housing-related spending tend
to perform with the housing cycle. Investment in business equipment follows a cycle that is key for producers of equipment, like some
industrial and technology companies. Also, the interest-rate cycle is a
more powerful influence for some companies (Utilities) than others
(Energy). Consumer durables spending, like business equipment

spending, has a disproportionate impact on some companies (Autos) compared to other companies that also rely on consumer spending (Staples and Health Care). The cycle in credit and credit spreads influences the performance of companies dependent on borrowing, like real estate investment trusts (REITS), housing, and autos. The profits cycle influences real investment and financial activities. Tactical sector strategies take account of these considerations.

Given the crosscurrents that influence relative sector performance, it can be difficult to isolate pure business cycle effects from other fundamental factors influencing returns. As a result, sector allocation needs to incorporate more than just business-cycle considerations. That said, there are some relationships that have proven reliable over the years.

Defensive sectors

Health care, consumer staples, and utility companies tend to be less cyclical than other sectors that depend more on discretionary spending. Defensive company revenues tend to hold up relatively better in recessions, and as a result they outperform in weak economic environments. All three sectors' prices performed better in the recessions of 1991, 2001, and 2007–2009 than the overall S&P 500 composite index.

Prices of utility companies are also more sensitive to interest-rate fluctuations. They are often considered bond proxies as they tend to deliver more of their returns in the form of dividends rather than price appreciation. The return of inflation and interest rates to a lower "new normal" range has caused valuations of utility companies to shift back to the higher PE multiples that prevailed in the 1950s and early 1960s. This one-off structural shift caused a temporary bout of relative out performance as they revalued. From a cyclical standpoint, their relative performance follows the interest-rate cycle discussed in chapter 4.

Cyclical sectors

Consumer discretionary, financials, materials, energy, and industrial companies (MEI) tend to have more volatile revenues than the defensive sectors, causing their stock prices to fluctuate more than the overall market average (i.e., they have higher-than-average beta). The consumer discretionary and financial sectors tend to be *early-cycle* equity market leaders compared to the MEI sectors, which are *late-cycle* leaders. Partly, this reflects the higher proportion of international revenues in the late-cycle sectors and the fact that the United States tends to lead the global business cycle in and out of recessions. For example, the financial and consumer-discretionary sectors peaked in the first half of 2007, well before the recession started in December of that year. Industrial sector prices peaked at about the same time as the overall S&P 500 index in the fall of 2007. While the United States was well into recession in the first half of 2008, the rest of the world was still growing, and upward pressure on energy and materials prices grew through the early summer of that year, when they eventually peaked. The rest of the world went into recession shortly thereafter.

Telecom and information technology

The telecom services sector has consolidated and become a very small part of the overall market, shrinking from about 10 percent of total market capitalization in the early 1990s to only about 2 percent in 2014. While margins in most sectors have been trending higher in recent years for reasons discussed earlier, the telecom sector is an exception. Compared to their historical average, its margins dropped more than 50 percent and are now the lowest on average of any other sector.

On the other hand, the information technology sector soared from about 5 percent of stock market capitalization in the early 1990s to over 30 percent at the peak of the Y2K bubble. After the bubble popped, it

Exhibit 5.15 Cyclical Timing of Sector Overweights

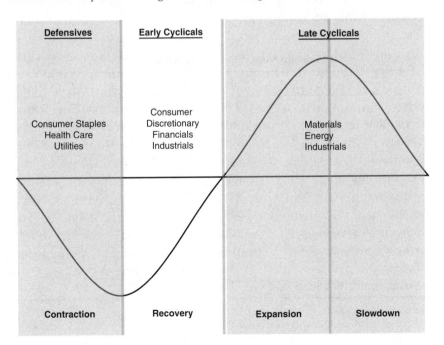

settled into a 15 percent to 20 percent range. Information technology is transforming the world (telecom services are the backbone of this transformation). This is a long-term growth story with less of an apparent cyclical component. Since the late-1990s bubble, the information technology sector has mainly been in a long-term correction and consolidation phase from which it is finally breaking out to the upside. Perhaps more cyclical behavior will eventually emerge. For now, this younger part of the economy is dominated by rapid growth and development. Exhibit 5.15 summarizes the typical relative performance pattern of the sectors over the business cycle.

Domestic versus foreign-sourced sector earnings

As noted earlier, one reason the value of the US equity market has grown larger relative to GDP is the increasing share of profits that companies are earning abroad (i.e., from economic activity not included in US GDP, Exhibit 5.9). The share of earnings coming from overseas operations varies dramatically across sectors. For example, heavily regulated and domestic service-oriented sectors tend to have much lower than average foreign-sourced revenues and profits. These include the telecom, utility, and financial sectors. The first two get minimal revenues from abroad, while the financial sector receives less than 20 percent of its revenues from abroad compared to roughly a third for the S&P 500 aggregate (Exhibit 5.16).

Exhibit 5.16   Average Foreign Sales as % of Total Sales

	2009	2010	2011	2012	2013
Energy	31%	30%	31%	33%	35%
Information Technology	58%	58%	58%	58%	56%
Materials	43%	45%	47%	48%	47%
Industrials	35%	36%	38%	37%	37%
Consumer Staples	32%	35%	36%	36%	36%
Health Care	33%	33%	33%	34%	35%
S&P 500	**32%**	**32%**	**33%**	**33%**	**33%**
Consumer Discretionary	26%	25%	28%	28%	30%
Financials	17%	17%	18%	18%	18%
Utilities	4%	4%	5%	5%	4%
Telecommunication Services	2%	3%	5%	1%	1%

Source: Standard & Poor's.

At the other extreme are the information technology and materials sectors, in which close to half or more of revenues come from outside the United States. The United States' comparative advantage in science and technology makes it a global leader in technological innovation and the application of new technology to economic activity. In addition, vast US natural resource endowments and state-of-the-art technology allow it also to sell large volumes of materials to the rest of the world. For example, the United States has long been the largest exporter of agricultural products in the world. In addition, this combination has recently also turned it into the largest exporter of refined oil products.

As a result of this widespread variation in sensitivity to external economic growth, relative sector performance depends not just on the US business cycle but also on the business cycles in other regions of the world. When global growth is highly synchronized, this regional dispersion in revenue sources is less significant. However, it can make a big difference when the United States is out of sync with the rest of the global economy, as happened in 2011 and 2012. The United States continued to recover during those years, while Europe went back into recession. In addition, China and the emerging world slowed down dramatically. During that period, companies that relied primarily on US domestic demand did relatively better than those more dependent on sales in Europe and emerging markets. This turned out to be a significant factor for relative sector performance.

Changes in the foreign exchange value of the dollar can also cause disproportionate effects on the revenues of companies that sell a lot outside the United States. Because of the impact of the dollar on commodity prices, the relative performance of the energy and materials sectors is particularly sensitive to the value of the dollar.

It should also be pointed out that within sectors there are companies and industries that depend to differing degrees on foreign versus domestic demand. For example, within the health-care sector, hospitals are more reliant on domestic conditions, while medical device and pharmaceutical companies are global players.

The asynchronous global growth pattern also worked to differentiate the US equity market from those of other countries in the first five years of the recovery that began in 2009. US stocks outperformed the general global average partly because of better policy support for the recovery compared to other countries and partly because of the changed nature of the new growth cycle, which required a rebalancing of global trade flows. For example, China shrank its trade surplus from 10 percent of GDP to a third of that level between 2008 and 2013. This was a substantial drag on its overall growth rate, which fell from over 10 percent to around 7.5 percent as a result. In the United States, in contrast, the complementary adjustment required shrinking the trade deficit from 6 percent of GDP to about 3 percent by 2013. Fortunately, this adjustment was facilitated by a dramatic increase in US domestic energy production. The boom in US energy output simultaneously added to GDP growth *and* reduced the biggest single category of imports. The United States went from the world's biggest *energy importer* to the world's biggest *energy producer* and biggest *refined oil products exporter* in less than a decade. The benefit of much lower energy prices than in the rest of the world as a result of the energy boom offered the United States an additional relative stimulus to growth.

6
Commodities and Tangible Assets

Unlike bonds with fixed coupons, tangible assets generally offer much more protection against unexpected inflation. On the other hand, high-quality noncallable bonds, such as Treasury coupon securities, offer much better protection against unanticipated deflation, which enhances their real returns. Since deflation has been rare and inflation prevalent in the new world of fiat money since World War II, commodities and other tangible assets, like real estate and collectibles, have become important asset classes for a broadly diversified portfolio.

While most tangible assets are usually held for periods longer than a business cycle and depend on more idiosyncratic influences—such as "location, location, location" in the case of real estate—commodities have proven to be a useful asset class for tactical allocations over the business cycle. More specifically, a portfolio that invests in a broad index of commodity futures that is rolled over in successive periods when the futures contracts expire has proven to be an excellent diversifier in a broader portfolio.

Empirical research finds that a long commodities futures portfolio at least matches equity returns over long periods of time with superior skewness properties and no extra risk. In addition, its return correlates negatively with both stock and bond returns. When using Treasury bills as the margin collateral for the futures position without leverage, fully collateralized commodity futures have essentially the same returns and Sharpe ratio as equities.[1]

Direct investment in commodities is less effective for diversification than the futures-based approach. Commodity prices have gone

[1] See, for example, Gary B. Gorton and K. Geert Rouwenhorst, *Facts and Fantasies about Commodity Futures*, Yale I.C.F. Working Paper No. 04–20, February 28, 2005.

through long secular bull and bear markets based on various trends in macroeconomic variables like inflation and the strength and mix of global growth relative to long-term commodity supply conditions. Over the very long run, periods of strong commodity prices have increased the incentive to search for cheaper alternatives and to develop new technologies that reduce production costs.

The energy price surge over the 2002–2008 period is a good example. It sparked the development of, and made practical, a host of new products like electric cars and solar power to reduce energy use. In fact, the energy content of developed economies' GDP began to fall in the early 1980s in response to the energy price surge of the 1970s. This trend got extra impetus when oil prices quadrupled during the 2000–2008 period. In addition, high prices stimulated investment in new supply. Fracking technology made natural gas relatively abundant in the United States, causing its price to collapse following alarmingly high levels in the decade prior to the Great Recession. It also contributed to an unexpected oil boom in the United States that saved the world from a crude-oil supply crunch given worsening production conditions in Organization of Petroleum Exporting Countries (OPEC) and many other oil-producing countries, and turned the country into the world's largest energy producer. All of these considerations mean that commodity investing, particularly direct investment in commodities, is fraught with risk, just like equities.

On the other hand, direct commodity investment has proven to be a good hedge against inflation, as have most other tangible assets. Equities are more of a mixed bag in this regard because company assets can be a blend of good or bad inflation hedges, depending on the business. As we discussed in the previous chapter, stocks of commodity producers, like energy and materials companies, have proven to be better inflation hedges than those of companies with inflation-sensitive input costs and an inability to pass on the rising costs. For example, a mortgage REIT that holds a portfolio of fixed-rate loans that is financed with short-term funds would be an extreme example of a company that would be hurt by rising inflation and its impact on interest rates.

Research also shows that the business cycle is the key driver of total returns to a commodity futures portfolio regardless of the supply backdrop. The supply cycle *changes the mix of total return*, with more return from spot-price gains and less roll return in a tight long-term supply environment, and less spot-price return and more roll return in a situation of ample long-term supply. Overall, however, as global growth strengthens over the business cycle, returns to commodity futures portfolios increase.

Lower real interest rates are supportive for commodity prices. High real yields, like those that prevailed in the United States from 1982 until about 2000, favor financial assets over nonyielding commodities, such as gold, which was in a secular bear market during that period. Since 2000, real yields have been lower than normal, and commodities have done well, enjoying their strongest bull market since the 1970s, another decade in which real yields were quite low, even negative, much of the time as inflation outpaced ever-rising nominal interest rates.

Of course, other factors influence commodity prices as well. The rapid growth of emerging markets, especially China, had a major impact on commodity prices in the 2001–2008 expansion. Intensive industrial development more than tripled China's gross domestic product (GDP) between 2000 and 2013, when it averaged over 10 percent real growth per year, turning it into the largest consumer of numerous raw materials, including copper and gold.

As China settled into a much slower growth mode, concerns that global commodity demand won't be sufficient to absorb the massive supply increases from a decade of rapid investment increased. Nevertheless, China will likely remain the biggest consumer of many commodities and an important source of commodity demand growth even as its economic growth slows to about half the rate of the 2000–2010 period and its mix of commodity demand adjusts to the new pattern of its more domestic-demand-led growth. A 5 percent annual real GDP growth rate from its current size is roughly equivalent to its output gains when it was growing over 10 percent at the peak of the commodity super cycle. What's more, countries like India have a lot of catching up to do to reach even China's current living standards. Strains on global commodity supplies are bound to occur when they do.

More generally, pressures on commodity prices tend to build when global growth is in the later stages of the business cycle before a recession. Commodity bears counter that whatever demand increase results from rising global growth, it's likely to be swamped by massive overcapacity in many commodity markets because of the investment boom that naturally followed higher prices and tightening supplies during the last decade. In this view, commodity prices are in a new secular bear market because of oversupply.

Still, as shown in Exhibit 6.1, throughout the 1980–2000 secular bear market in commodities there were cyclical price patterns, when

Exhibit 6.1 Commodities Consolidating in a New Higher Range Following 2001–2010 Super Cycle

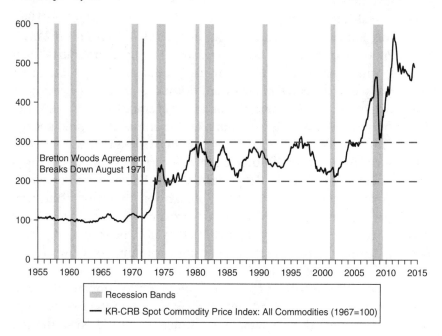

Source: Haver Analytics.

Data as of August 14, 2014.

prices generally fell during recessions and the early recovery stages, and then strengthened as expansions matured. This cyclical pattern is at the heart of the diversification benefits that commodities add to a portfolio of stocks and bonds. In fact, it's the difference in the cyclical patterns across the three broad asset classes that creates the diversification benefits that commodities add to a portfolio over the business cycle.

The cyclical pattern of commodity prices

One of the reasons research shows that an allocation to commodity futures correlates negatively with stock and bond returns is the difference between the performance of commodities in different phases of the business cycle compared to stocks and bonds. Stocks usually have their best returns of the cycle starting late in a recession, when expectations for an imminent recovery are coalescing. These high returns usually continue during the early stage of the recovery, when operating leverage generates the fastest cyclical growth in profits. For example, the first 12 months of the cyclical bull market that started in March 2009 show the Standard & Poor's (S&P) 500 price index jumped over 50 percent, its biggest 12-month gain since the start of the prior secular bull market in 1982.

Conversely, stocks anticipate recessions just as they foresee recoveries. That's why stock prices are a component of the index of leading indicators. For example, the broad stock indices peaked months before the recession began in late-2007. Bonds are also highly anticipatory. High-quality bonds like Treasuries tend to have their best returns going into recessions until the baton is passed to equities late in the recession. On the other hand, bonds usually have a tougher time when monetary policy shifts from accommodative to restrictive later in the cycle, when inflation becomes more of a concern.

It's at that point when inflation becomes a concern that commodities tend to receive the relative performance baton. This is also evident in the commodity sectors of the equity market dominated by energy and materials stocks, which tend to be relative outperformers late in the business cycle. For example, while the overall market peaked shortly before the US recession began in December 2007, the energy and materials sectors continued to move higher with commodity prices until the summer of 2008. This is evident in Exhibit 6.1, in which the breakout to a new higher secular commodity price range occurs around 2005 and continues well into the recession. More generally, inflation tends to lag behind growth, so that during the slowing phase into a recession, commodity prices are still firm because capacity utilization and demand are still near peak levels. This is the phase when equities are usually underperforming heading into their cyclical bear stage, while commodity prices are cyclically strongest.

As shown in Exhibit 6.1, commodity prices eventually fell by the middle of the 2007–2009 recession when the global economy followed the United States into the slump, and the financial crisis caused the biggest collapse in commodity prices since the 1930s. Notice that the collapse in the CRB index bottomed at the top of the old secular range that had prevailed from the late 1970s until about 2005. Oil and copper prices also retested the top of their old ranges and bounced higher, supporting the view that commodities had moved into a new, higher, secular range. Helping to support prices, the Chinese government has shown a willingness to add to its strategic commodity stockpiles when prices are low.

In any event, as a new business cycle unfolds, the economy eventually moves into the expansion phase when higher capacity utilization, lower unemployment and rising inflation pressures tend to eventually favor commodities relative to stocks and bonds.

The supply cycle

The relative cyclical performance of stocks, bonds, and commodities tends to be a demand-driven phenomenon reflecting the impact of strengthening demand running up against supply constraints. The degree of commodity price response to this obviously depends on the availability of commodity supply capacity to meet rising demand. For example, for agricultural commodities, supply issues often boil down to weather patterns that are erratic and therefore less systematic. For energy and mining commodities, in contrast, there was a highly correlated investment boom over the 2000–2010 decade in response to high and rising prices that often reflected rising marginal costs of production. Energy costs are roughly a third of production costs for other commodities, so rising energy prices are a force for rising prices elsewhere, other things equal.

The supply cycle for commodities is generally much longer than a business cycle because it takes a long time to respond to commodity price signals and to find and develop new sources of supply. For example, the supply response to the commodity price boom of the 1970s eventually created a situation of ample supply starting in the early 1980s, when a secular bear market in commodities began as a result. Despite fluctuations in demand over business cycles, supply was generally adequate to prevent unusually strong price pressures. As can be seen in Exhibit 6.1, prices were confined to a nominal range, and by 2000 were at the bottom of that nominal range that went back to the mid-1970s and breakdown of the Bretton Woods exchange-rate system. With inflation indices up substantially, commodity prices fell in real terms from 1980 until 2000.

That long period of price weakness discouraged investment, and by 2000 the world had shifted again from an ample supply backdrop to a tight supply backdrop. The ensuing commodity price bull market provided the incentives to bring on new supply, especially after 2005, when prices broke out into a new, higher long-term range. By the end of 2010, when prices peaked, worries that China's reduced growth prospects and newly developed excess supply capacity would weigh on prices combined to spark a chorus of bearish calls that the commodity super cycle was over.

That may or may not be true. What did seem clear, however, is that the incentives to invest in certain areas, like mining, were considerably diminished by 2012, and ongoing energy investment seemed to be succeeding in providing enough supply to prevent the price spikes that had curbed global growth whenever it got much above 4 percent during the prior decade.

The long supply cycle from the ample supply situation in the early 1980s that eventually transitioned to the tight supply situation of the early 2000s to about 2010, when a newly ample supply environment arose once again, covers a 30-year period. As a result, there are sufficient empirical data to contrast the returns to commodity futures as an asset class over the course of business cycles in both a tight supply and an ample supply environment.

Commodity returns during both demand and supply cycles

The results from comparing returns to commodity futures portfolios in business cycles with ample supply versus tight supply backdrops show that total returns vary across the business cycle broadly in the same pattern in both supply environments.[2] Commodities tend to provide the most diversification benefit (negative correlation) to both stocks and bonds during the slowdown phase of the business cycle, when the economy is operating at high capacity and inflation persistence is supporting commodity prices. This late-cycle diversification advantage starts slowly in the expansion phase and becomes more pronounced during the slowdown phase. It's fairly minimal during the contraction and recovery phases. These conclusions hold in both the ample supply and tight supply phases of the long-term investment cycle.

Since the economy went through the contraction and recovery phases between 2008 and 2013, it's not surprising that the diversification benefits of commodities were negligible during that period and

[2] See, for example, Damien Courvalin, Jeffrey Currie, and Michael Hinds, *The Strategic Case for Commodities Holding Strong,*, Goldman Sachs Commodities Research, April 23, 2014.

that confidence in the asset class wavered. The prime diversification advantages lie in the expansion and slowdown phases, which were yet to play out at that point.

Total returns to commodity futures portfolios are comprised of the return from changes in spot prices, the returns from rolling futures contracts, and the return from the collateral that backs the futures contracts, usually short-term Treasury bills. If the futures curve is flat through time *and* the spot price stays the same, all of the return boils down to the yield on Treasury bills. If the spot price rises over time, as is more likely to be the case in a tight future supply environment, the spot portion of the return is relatively higher compared to an ample future supply environment, in which spot prices are softening. Roll returns, on the other hand, tend to be negative in a tightening supply environment compared to an ample future supply environment, in which there is generally more backwardation in the futures curve, reflecting downward futures price pressures from expected excess long-term supply capacity. Buying a contract with a lower futures price than spot price (backwardated curve) means you sell it high when contracts expire, to purchase a lower-priced futures curve and so forth. This positive "roll" component to the total return is bigger the more backwardated the curve is. The more excessive the expected supply situation, the more backwardated the futures curve is likely to be, as producers try to hedge their future production revenues in a weakening price (excess supply) environment.

Thus, it's not surprising that the roll component is a relatively bigger share of total returns and that the spot return is a smaller component in a declining price, ample supply commodity environment. What's perhaps more surprising is that the roll return can be sufficient to keep total return attractive. This is the key to commodity returns in a range-bound long-term price environment like that between 1980 and 2000. High real interest returns on collateral also helped in that environment. Total return seems to concentrate later in the cycle in an excess supply versus a tight supply environment, which makes sense since it takes a bit more recovery and expansion to get to the peak cyclical prices (that come when commodity markets tighten) if the overall long-term supply situation is more ample.

To summarize, the diversification benefits of commodities tend to be greatest in the expansion and especially the slowdown phase of the business cycle. They are relatively insignificant in contractions

Exhibit 6.2   Correlations between Returns on Equities and a Commodity Futures Portfolio Vary during the Business Cycle

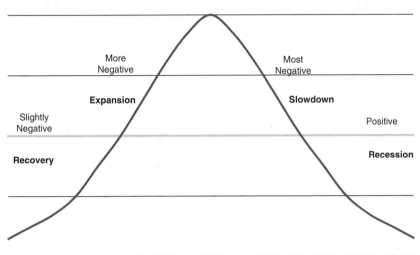

and recoveries regardless of whether the long-term supply backdrop is tight or ample. Also, in a generally tightening supply environment, more of the total return comes earlier in the business cycle from spot-price appreciation and less from roll compared with an ample supply environment. These observations are consistent with the relative performance of commodities over the past few years and are summarized in Exhibit 6.2.

Idiosyncratic diversification benefits

In addition to late cycle diversification benefits, commodities also provide a hedge against certain specific events that reduce returns on stocks and bonds. For example, having an exposure to energy can offset losses in other assets when oil prices surge. Likewise, a drought or other weather problems that cause food prices to spike can also raise inflation and slow growth, especially in developing economies, where food is a major expenditure category for the population. These types of events are not cyclical or systematic in a way that creates a regular diversification benefit from owning commodities. Instead, they are more like unpredictable disasters that require event-specific insurance. Over the years, various events have caused major spikes in

Exhibit 6.3   Oil Has Proven to Be a Good Inflation Hedge

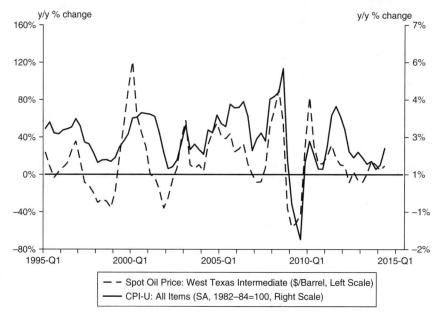

Source: Haver Analytics.
Data as of Q2 2014.

energy prices. One of the reasons commodity futures have provided equity-like returns with strong diversification benefits is the positive contribution from owning commodities during these idiosyncratic episodes, especially those associated with energy prices.

Oil investments have proven to be a particularly good hedge against inflation as well as against risks related to oil-supply disruptions associated with flaring geopolitical crises (Exhibit 6.3). For these reasons, and given the chronic risk to oil supply due to geopolitical instability, some investors prefer a commodity index that has a particularly heavy energy weight to bolster the diversification and inflation-hedge properties of the commodity component of a portfolio.

Commodities and the dollar

As noted above, voracious Chinese demand and low real interest rates were two of the main ingredients accounting for the "super cycle" in commodity prices during the 2000–2010 decade. Another component

Exhibit 6.4 Weakening Dollar Associated with Strengthening Commodity Prices and Vice Versa

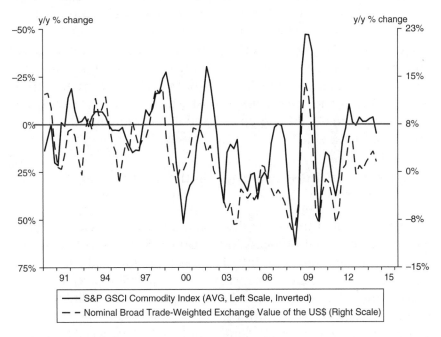

Source: Haver Analytics.
Data as of Q2 2014.

was a generally weak foreign exchange value of the dollar. Because their prices are often quoted in dollars, commodities as an asset class, and gold in particular, can be closely associated with the value of the greenback. As shown in Exhibit 6.4, the breakdown of the Bretton Woods system in the early 1970s has been followed by unusually pronounced cycles in both the dollar's forex value and commodity prices. A strong dollar has generally been accompanied by weak commodity prices, while a weak dollar is often associated with rising commodity prices. The commodity super cycle occurred during a period of dollar weakness. Gold prices averaged about $270 per ounce in 2001, down from a peak annual average of just over $600 per ounce in 1980. That two-decade bear market in gold ended when the dollar began to depreciate in 2002. By 2012, gold averaged $1,600 per ounce as the dollar had depreciated 20 percent on a broad trade-weighted basis.

One reason for the relationship between commodity prices and the dollar is the greenback's special role as a means of payment in international markets. No other currency is as widely used in the global transactions system. If the dollar falls in value against other major currencies, it means OPEC, for example, is losing global purchasing power by quoting oil at the same dollar prices. This creates an incentive to raise dollar prices for oil just to maintain constant purchasing power. This was one of the forces for big OPEC price hikes after the United States suspended the Bretton Woods payments system in 1971. Also, countries with currencies against which the dollar depreciates can afford more oil, driving up demand and causing upside pressure on prices, all else equal.

Tangible assets and secular shifts in the macroeconomic environment

As we have seen in the earlier discussion, there have been four broad macroeconomic environments in the United States since World War II. Up until the mid-1960s, inflation was fairly low and stable, with typical cyclical fluctuations between about zero and 4 percent and an average around 2 percent. Interest rates reflected that nominal environment. Then, from 1965 until about 1981, inflation trended higher and inflation expectations became untethered, playing catch-up with actual inflation. The Bretton Woods fixed-exchange rate system fell victim to this instability in the early 1970s. Interest rates rose through each cycle, but remained low in real terms until Paul Volcker arrived and reversed the trend. From the early 1980s until about 2000, *real interest rates* averaged unusually high levels as monetary policy sought to reduce inflation over several business cycles until inflation expectations were well anchored around about 2 percent, a policy known as "opportunistic disinflation." As inflation and inflation expectations declined, interest rates fell through each business cycle, with successively lower valleys and peaks. Falling interest rates drove secular bull markets in financial assets.

Exhibit 6.5 shows that tangible assets' share of household wealth over the postwar period tracked the shifts in the macroeconomic environment. In the first 20 years after World War II, inflation was low, interest rates were relatively stable, real-estate values were relatively stable, commodity prices were well behaved, and stocks were in a strong bull market. Financial assets gained share relative to tangibles in this environment mainly because stocks were extremely undervalued after the Great Depression and World War II.

Exhibit 6.5 Rising Inflation Good for Tangible Assets. Falling Inflation Good for Financial Assets. Stable Inflation Good for Both

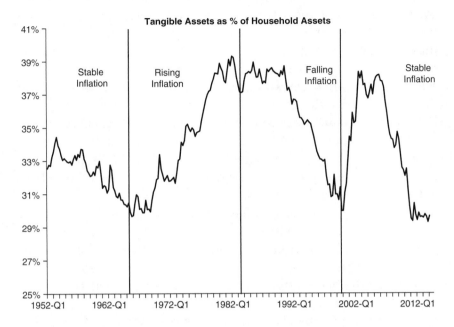

Source: Federal Reserve Board/Haver Analytics.
Data as of Q1 2014

In contrast, rising inflation during the 1965–1980 period is associated with a rising share of tangible wealth. There are several other factors behind this rise, aside from the fact that tangible asset prices rose relative to financial assets during this period. For example, people buy more tangible assets to hedge against rising inflation. Housing is the main asset for most US families. Real estate inflation accompanied the rise in general inflation especially in the late 1970s. Fixed-rate mortgages were the dominant means of housing finance at that time. Rising home values and fixed mortgage payments generated a lot of housing wealth. Financial assets like stocks and bonds were in a secular bear market during this period and lost relative value to tangible assets.

After the inflation trend reversed from up to down in the early 1980s, the new disinflation trend favored financial assets over tangible assets. Household wealth moved back in favor of financial assets during the long secular bull market in stocks and bonds during the 1980s and 1990s, until the tech bubble burst in 2000.

The fourth structural shift tracks the reflation efforts since 2000, when monetary policy has had to deal with the risk of deflation for the first time since the 1930s. The lows for policy rates since 2000 have been 1 percent in the cycle following the tech crash and zero in the cycle that culminated in the 2008 financial crisis. Low real interest rates have been necessary to keep inflation close to the Fed's 2 percent target. Negative real rates are bullish for tangible assets, especially those without a yield like gold. No yield is better than the negative yield on cash substitutes. From 2000 until about 2007, real estate did well in this environment until, like the equity bubble in the late 1990s, "too much of a good thing" caused a massive deflation in overheated home values across much of the country, sharply reducing the share of tangibles in household assets.

On balance, the reflation era has been good for both stocks and real estate, as both benefit from very low real rates. A one-time revaluation to a "new normal" lower rate environment is more of a one-off event rather than a persistent trend, however. For example, utility stocks have risen to higher multiples more comparable with their 1950s valuations when interest rates were also low and stable, and multiples were significantly higher than was the case in the higher-rate environment of the 1965–2000 era.

Yielding versus nonyielding tangibles

As in the case of individual equities, there is substantial variation in the characteristics of different tangible assets. As a result, sweeping generalizations are not always possible. For example, some equities are good inflation hedges, others are not. It depends on the mix of assets and liabilities on the balance sheet of the company, and the income and cost characteristics of the business. Inflation sensitivity varies across those dimensions. Likewise, different tangible assets have different sensitivities to the inflation and interest rate environment at any particular time. Generally speaking, however, tangible assets are a good asset class to hedge against inflation risk.

Some tangibles come with a yield and others do not. For example, gold, art, and other collectibles generally depend on price appreciation for any return. The higher interest rates, the less any given amount of price appreciation exceeds the opportunity cost of holding a nonyielding asset. Of course, as was seen in the late 1970s, price appreciation can accelerate with inflation when rising yields lag behind inflation, causing nonyielding tangibles, like gold, to provide attractive returns even when nominal interest rates are rising. In general, however, high rates are a negative for nonyielding tangibles, while low rates are more favorable as they represent a lower opportunity cost of foregone return.

Real estate and farmland are examples of tangible assets with the benefit of a potential yield. They are also sensitive to interest rates. Higher rates tend to reduce their net present value, other things equal. Still, unlike, nonyielding collectibles, they have the potential to off-set higher rate effects with revenue streams that can rise in both real and nominal terms. If rents or crop prices rise faster than inflation, real returns can rise, increasing the value of tangibles with yields. Generally speaking, over the course of the fiat-money era with inflation persistently positive, tangible assets have proven to be a useful hedge against inflation. Those with a yield have the added benefit of providing an inflation-hedged income stream.

Globalization and tangible assets

One consequence of globalization is a shift in relative valuations compared to a world in which worth is determined primarily in a national market protected from global economic forces. Nowhere is this more apparent than in the sharp rise of inequality of wealth and income in the developed countries. Rising inequality is an apparent side effect of globalization across the developed world, even in the Nordic countries that pride themselves on progressive policies to fight it.

In the United States the widening gap also reflects the greater diversity of its population. Before the world was so open to trade, lower-skilled, less-educated US workers had a stronger relative labor market position compared to today's world, in which they face much more open competition with the low-skilled, less-educated part of the population that makes up the vast majority of the world's seven billion people. The relative labor market position of this part of the US population has been weakened by globalization of the labor force. This is generally true all across the developed world, where less-skilled and less-educated workers have seen their incomes stagnate.

In contrast, there is a growing lifetime earnings premium for college graduates relative to nongraduates that is a key driver of rising inequality in the United States and other countries. Accelerating technological change underlies this need for better-educated workers. Over the past three decades, the share of US employees with a college degree has jumped from one in five to over one in three. The share of the US working-age population with a college degree is more than five times the global average.

Globalization makes a college-degreed US worker much more valuable compared to when the national workforce was competing just among itself. The jump from one in three in the US workforce to one in fifteen in the global workforce makes a college degree relatively more rare in the world market than it is in the United States, and the opportunities consequently much greater for college graduates than before. This helps explain why the premium on college education keeps growing as the world economy globalizes.

It's not just college degrees that have become more valuable in a globalizing world driven by rapid advancements in technology. Athletes, musicians, actors, filmmakers, technology entrepreneurs, and global brands of all sorts are much more valuable when the market potential is seven billion people instead of just 325 million. As a result, relatively more rare forms of human capital have seen disproportionate gains from globalization, while more common forms of human capital have become less valuable in a globalized economy.

For those at the top of the income distribution, wealth accumulation has been more rapid as globalization progresses. The number of billionaires and millionaires is growing rapidly. This is having a dramatic impact on the tangible asset market. The rarer the asset, the more intense the competition among millionaires and billionaires bidding up its price. Whether it's a trophy penthouse property in London or Hong Kong, or a sports franchise in Spain, the pool of wealth available to inflate its value is growing much faster than the underlying economy or markets for more mundane properties. Supply is relatively fixed for museum-quality art and prime location real estate. At the same time, demand is growing rapidly as globalization creates a concentration of wealth never seen before in human history in both its scale and scope. From this vantage point, a globalizing world economy is very bullish for tangible assets as more and more wealth chases too few "Picassos."

These trends are behind a massive bull market in tangible assets around the world. Billionaires are bidding up the prices of the best real estate, the priciest art, and other collectibles as rapidly rising, unprecedented wealth fights over the world's rarest collectibles. The demand is rising faster than ever before, and the supply is basically fixed. As globalization intensifies, the pressures on high-quality tangible assets are likely to build until either wealth stops expanding or prices overheat to the point at which they have to adjust.

This general phenomenon is most obvious in the upper echelons of the wealth spectrum, but it exists further down as well. More and more millionaires are created each year in the globalization process. As large numbers of people across the world are accumulating wealth as never before, their demand for tangibles, like vacation homes and precious metals, is likely to support a robust tangible asset market.

In emerging markets, like India and China, where gold has a special cachet as a store of wealth against multiple contingencies, the growing middle classes, running into the hundreds of millions of people, are likely to allocate their rapidly accumulating savings at least partly to this traditional store of value. The rapid accumulation of wealth in the wake of globalization is likely to pressure tangible asset prices as never before. The flip side of rising inequality in the rich world is rising living standards in the poor world, where people are moving out of subsistence poverty at the fastest rate in history. This is creating a rapidly growing mass market for affordable tangibles as well as the most sought-after rarities.

7

Investing for Long-Term Change: Challenging the Conventional Wisdom

So far, we have focused on cyclical patterns that recur in the US economy and their relative return implications for different asset categories. In addition, we have highlighted the important role played by secular trends in macroeconomic variables like interest rates and inflation in shaping investment returns. Of particular importance for the investment outlook is the return of interest rates and inflation to more normal historical levels from the unusually high real interest rate environment of the 1980s and 1990s, when tighter monetary policy was bringing down the trend in inflation. Restoring rates and inflation to the lower levels that prevailed in the 1950s and early 1960s has re-established some structural relationships that were disrupted by the rising inflation environment that began in the mid-1960s. Once again, dividend yields on stocks are higher than yields on most Treasury securities, and dividends have become a more important source of the overall return to equities. Credit spreads are fluctuating around a new lower mean that reflects higher profits margins, like those that prevailed before high and rising inflation started to undermine business performance. Overall, real and nominal interest rates have settled back into a "new normal, like the old normal" range.

Also important, these macroeconomic forces are operating in an underlying environment of accelerating change that is transforming the global economy at an ever-faster pace. Technological change is stimulating this transformation and driving the globalization process. While there is a natural human tendency to use the more recent past as the basis for judging trends in the economy, the evolution of the economy creates new patterns that don't make sense from this past perspective, but do yield clues about the future that often defy the consensus view of where things are headed. Understanding where things are headed is an important input to better investing, while extrapolating the past is often a disastrous approach to planning for the future, especially in an increasingly fast-changing world. It is human nature to use recent trends as the basis for future expectations. However, old conventional wisdom standards have become increasingly irrelevant for judging the future. Savvy investors try to distinguish when the past is not prologue.

Here we look at the shortcomings of some of the conventional wisdom that dominates the social narrative and focus on the role that technology and globalization are playing in shaping the dynamics of the world economy and the investment outlook. Areas of controversy with important investment implications include (1) demographics and the role of automation and artificial intelligence in the jobs of the future and potential economic growth, (2) the issue of insufficient US saving, growing government debt, and the implications of the United States being a net debtor with a persistent current-account deficit, and (3) growing income and wealth inequality, and its potential consequences and solutions. Two well-known examples of widespread misunderstanding that caused very different views about the investment environment following the Great Recession, and discussed here, surround the deceleration in the labor-force participation rate and the low saving rate in the United States. However, before we look at specific areas of controversy, we need to discuss the forces shaping the future, the secular tailwinds of change.

Surviving the future

Contrary to popular belief, it was Herbert Spencer, building on Charles Darwin's work, rather than Darwin himself, who coined the phrase "survival of the fittest." A more accurate description of Darwin's theory is suggested by another observation also often misattributed to Darwin that comes from an unknown source according to which it is not the strongest of the species, nor the most intelligent that survives. It is the one that is most adaptable to change. In the struggle for survival, the fittest win out at the expense of their rivals because they succeed in adapting themselves best to their environment.

Fitness, in essence, is defined as the ability to survive by adapting to change. The same concept applies to societies. In our view, for example, the critical factor behind the resilience of the US economy is its success in adapting to a rapidly changing world. The ability to adjust to the secular tailwinds of change will determine whether the United States can keep the preeminent position it has maintained over the past century despite threats from various periodic contenders, like the Union of Soviet Socialist Republics (USSR) during the Cold War, Japan in the 1980s, and more recently, China.

Globalization is a force for cultural convergence that tradition resists to varying degrees. The main risk is that tyrants relying on brute force overcome the "soft power" tendency toward this future. The society best able to assimilate this cultural convergence is likely to prove the dominant society in the future, and the United States has a number of advantages in this accelerating process of cultural convergence. The cultural diversity of the US melting pot essentially makes it a prototype for how the world's diverse population can live together peacefully under one government, assimilating all of the world's cultures. The difficulties of the Eurozone project since the financial crisis show how daunting this assimilation can be.

In any case, investing in a world of accelerating change is increasingly challenging as it requires "looking further than the eye can see." If everything stayed the same, that would be easy since what you see now would be what you would see later. In a rapidly changing world, however, successful investing requires anticipating change and its implications for particular asset returns. The longer the time horizon, the harder it becomes to visualize an asset's likely ultimate performance. The faster things change, the harder it becomes to see ahead.

Here we look at some major macro drivers of long-term change as a prelude to inferring some long-term investment conclusions. Ultimately, good long-term investments will include some of the beneficiaries of the secular tailwinds of change. For other investments, these same forces can be headwinds that undermine their returns or even drive them to extinction. Understanding these differences is critical to long-term investment success.

The secular tailwinds of change

Technology

Technological change is arguably the most powerful force shaping the future of mankind. Its pace has been slowly accelerating over the past few centuries and has begun to pick up speed more rapidly in recent decades. It is now approaching a critical inflection point at which change will become so rapid and powerfully transforming that in an unprecedented

Exhibit 7.1   The Secular Tailwinds of Change

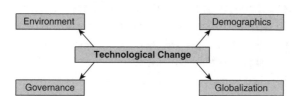

way it will strain the human capacity to think even a decade ahead. According to prominent futurists like Ray Kurzweil and Vernor Vinge, this inflection point is likely to happen in the next two or three decades. This contrasts sharply with the past, when technology evolved over centuries and, as a result, successive generations of humanity experienced similar living standards and lifestyle roles, as farmers using unchanged methods of production over multiple generations, for example.

The concept of "the technological singularity" refers to this inflection point and the emergence of superintelligence through technological means. This is in its early stages, as artificial intelligence, biological enhancement, and brain-computer interfaces are now becoming more sophisticated. The implication is a much faster-changing, harder-to-comprehend future than contemplated in the past. This means a much murkier outlook over investment horizons and a much faster pace of creative destruction that can turn a high-flying equity market winner (such as Polaroid in the 1960s) into an obsolete investment dog. When the amount of technological change packed into a year rises at an ever-increasing rate, more highfliers will become dogs more quickly unless managements can harness superintelligence to successfully ride a "faster-bucking bronco."

If we think of our five secular tailwinds in relation to each other, technological change is the prevailing wind that blows through all the others for good or ill (Exhibit 7.1). It is the most powerful and pervasive force. Understanding the other major drivers of long-term change requires to an ever-increasing degree an ability to see how technological change is impacting changes in globalization, the environment, demographics, and governance.

Globalization

One important implication of faster technological change is a faster potential pace of globalization. Over the past 200 years, the developed world has blazed a path of unprecedented prosperity by harnessing technology to raise living standards. In recent decades, developing economies, especially in Asia, have moved their people out of subsistence poverty at the fastest rate in human history by rapidly adopting the technologies that the rich world took over two centuries to create. The blueprint for development is there for all to see. Modern communication has taken it to the most remote corners of the world. Africa and the Middle East are the new frontiers where the greatest improvement in living standards is likely in the coming decades.

In the realm of economics, globalization refers to restructuring markets from local and national venues to global networks when it makes sense. More open trade of goods and services across borders is the most obvious economic benchmark of globalization. Capital flows are an increasingly globalized phenomenon. Labor flows, immigration, and rapidly increasing international travel are other signs of increasing globalization.

The potential of technology to improve human living conditions is so powerful that it is increasingly pushing up against constraints imposed largely in the realm of governance, which generally creates the main impediments to achieving faster global growth and ending global poverty. By artificially restricting economic activity, like trade, labor mobility, investment, and universal property rights, the nationalistic orientation of governance throws sand into the gears of globalization. The power of technology and the possibility of eradicating poverty much more quickly than ever before seemed possible are accelerating forces for a freer and more globalized governance structure, with fewer national impediments to progress.

From an investment themes perspective, globalization is a powerful force for change. The wind is blowing in its direction despite crosscurrents. This is largely because the potential payoffs are so huge for the mass of humanity and because the winds of technological change are strongly reinforcing the winds of globalization.

Environment

As the rich world moved from the industrial to the postindustrial stage of development, attention naturally turned to the environmental consequences of industrialization. If you are hungry, the first thing you think about is eating. Once the immediate basics are taken care of, time horizons lengthen and concerns about environmental degradation and eventual resource exhaustion start to receive more attention.

In a remarkably prescient and ambitious book, *The Next 200 Years: A Scenario for America and the World,* futurologists at the Hudson Institute laid out a vision of the long-term forces for change from their 1970s vantage point. Not surprisingly, their framework is largely built around the forces for long-term change that we identify in this chapter. Here is an excerpt from the synopsis on the cover of this book: "In this provocative work, master strategist and futurologist Herman Kahn and his associates at the prestigious Hudson Institute confront the issue of the second half of the twentieth century: whether technological and economic growth tends to destroy mankind or to improve the prospects for peace and prosperity. The population explosion, coupled with economic growth, could prove catastrophic within a century, or so say the prophets of doom; therefore, economic growth must be severely limited."

Indeed, in its initial phases, the environmental movement was, and to a certain extent still is, driven by an antigrowth zeitgeist. Books such as *Limits to Growth* argued that environmental stewardship required severe brakes on economic development, which in its extreme version would have sentenced the overwhelming majority of the world's people to permanent poverty and hunger, while the privileged few in the much-less-rich world of the time enjoyed cleaner air and water and nicer natural landscapes.

The Next 200 Years is a direct rebuttal to the intellectual fallacies of the *Limits to Growth* viewpoint, which had its peak cachet in the mid-'70s. To do this, Kahn and his associates took the secular tailwinds we discuss here and projected them out into the future with remarkable prescience, given the actual unfolding of events over the past 40 years. Fortunately, most of their more optimistic predictions have proven much more accurate than the more Malthusian views that were popular at the time, as embodied in *Limits to Growth*.

By looking at the secular tailwinds, Kahn and his associates accurately foresaw the slowdown in global population growth before overpopulation created the Malthusian nightmare many people feared at the time. Their optimistic projections on gross domestic product (GDP) growth and the rise from poverty of the world's masses have also proven surprisingly accurate over the past 40 years. Their prediction of slower growth in the rich world, as people's preferences shift from the material to leisure and other more postindustrial activities, are still underappreciated in a world in which a GDP growth fetish causes gloomy interpretations of the fact that as people get richer, they want to spend less time working. So, for example, a lower labor force participation rate and more part-time workers are regarded as structural deficiencies in the economy rather than an expression of preference for more leisure time in a much richer society.

In a much richer world, there are also more time and resources to address higher-order concerns like the environment. There is unprecedented and rapidly increasing wealth to devote to social and philanthropic causes as well. It is quite possible that eventually the private voluntary association of individuals and corporations will replace ossified and dysfunctional government bureaucracies to solve the ever-changing problems of the future, as is already evident in the rapid proliferation and success of nongovernment organizations (NGOs) devoted to fixing world problems.

The futurologists at the Hudson Institute in 1976 accurately predicted that environmental progress would occur alongside rapid economic development, as it has on balance over the past 40 years in countries that could afford to address the issue. The growing capacity to analyze bigger volumes of information is an important component of effective environmental modeling and policy, and the ability to mitigate any damaging consequences of rising global living standards seems to be a positive side effect of accelerating technological progress. Richer societies devote more resources to maintaining a positive environment, which means the global economy will evolve in the direction of a bigger environmental maintenance sector, with more opportunities for investors.

Governance

In contrast to technological progress, which transcends human nature as a sort of divine revelation, governance is more a reflection of human foibles. Most of the impediments to progress are self-imposed by the general failure to agree on needed reforms or by adopting counterproductive policies. Also, in many places governance is the coercive imposition of the will of the few on the many, which often proves disastrous and is almost always self-serving.

By governance we mean more than government. Government is a public reflection of private-sector culture and mores. The rules of society are both formal and informal, involving habit and prejudice as much as law. While these are necessary for a civilized, well-functioning society, they often serve as a mind-closing trap that prevents and deliberately blocks innovation and progress. This is the opposite of how knowledge and technology advance. Thinking outside the box creates innovations. Staying in the box is what governance is too often about.

Governance in its broad cultural sense has been evolving from the localized and tribal to the national during the past two centuries of industrialization. It is increasingly clear that globalization will ultimately force transcendence in governance from the national to the international level. This change is obviously difficult. International cooperation is slow and grudging on many issues. Even regional governance is still in the struggling stage, as the European Union (EU) clearly illustrates.

Nevertheless, a person looking at the area of modern-day Europe two centuries ago, or at the African continent and many other parts of the world, would find the world of today unrecognizable in terms of governance in all its dimensions. It seems fair to say that two centuries from now, the broad idea of governance—the rules, taboos, and habits of society and the boundaries of states—will be quite different from what we see today.

Technological change is forcing the trend toward globalized governance. The Internet allows an international vetting of moral issues that influence governance, people's view of what is right and what is not, and when something is so outrageous that they won't stand for it. Globalization involves an opening of minds to all that's out there. It is reshaping politics. While only in its infancy, global governance is already starting to coalesce in the new technology.

The US experience with cultural assimilation shows that there seems to be a human tendency to gravitate around universal preferences that will homogenize cultures to a greater extent. As a result, it seems like a safe bet that cultural, tribal, and regional differences will continue to diminish or be assimilated, as they are in the US melting pot. For investors, this means more markets will become unprecedentedly massive, as we are already seeing in many arenas.

If a private company can't keep up with change, it fails. Unfortunately, that's not as true about governments, especially those that rule by force. For the intolerant, the pressure to stop the progress of cultural assimilation is intensifying and fueling an ever-growing terrorist threat. The challenge for open societies is to minimize the coercive elements of the international governance structure that will evolve over the coming centuries.

Demographics

Governance is heavily influenced by demographics, as the Republican Party found out in the 2012 election. The pattern and speed of economic growth are also heavily shaped by demographics. Demographics affect the strain on the environment. In fact, a major reason why the analysis in *The Next 200 Years* was so much more accurate than that in *Limits to Growth* was a proper appreciation of global demographic trends and how they change at various stages of economic development. The fears of overpopulation driving the *Limits to Growth* view were based on an ignorance of very fundamental demographic analysis.

Likewise today, rapidly changing demographics are wrong-footing many economic prognosticators. As discussed above, national governance throws sand into the gears of economic efficiency and rising living standards when it creates barriers to free flows of labor, capital, goods, and services. Similarly, what appears to be a demographic problem for a nation often disappears in an open world economy. Demographics are skewed toward the aged in the rich world. They are skewed toward the young in much of the poorer developing world. This creates problems for funding entitlements in the rich world. It also leaves the poor world short of capital, which tends to have accumulated in older societies over the life cycle of population bulges such as the postwar baby boom. In the United States, for example, the retiring baby boomers make up about a third of the adult population and control about 70 percent of all wealth. This is a major source of perceived inequality. However, rather than being caused by an intrinsically unfair economic system, it is largely due to demographics. Older people need more wealth to support themselves in retirement.

Young societies need capital to enhance productivity and raise the living standard of laborers. Old societies need to live off capital, rather than labor income, to a much greater extent. This complementary mix provides a natural solution to demographic imbalances at the national level as saving-and-investment imbalances within countries can disappear when distributed globally. They disappear in economies that are open to each other, and globalization makes this possible. Immigration can also help resolve demographic imbalances.

In the next century, assuming, as seems likely, that living standards rise sufficiently in the poorer regions of the world, the global population will stabilize and age. Technology is likely to continue extending the human life span. More and more labor will be done by machines with increasingly broad intelligence and capabilities. As a result, leisure activities, which have already grown enormously in the rich world since the 1950s, will take more and more of the global population's time. It should then not be surprising that stocks of companies associated with travel, leisure, and an aging population have been some of the best performing. In fact, given all the tailwinds supporting it, this trend is most likely still in its infancy.

An older, slower growing, more internationalized population, a more interconnected global economy, and increased labor mobility are creating new problems for governments still struggling to solve the issues of the past. Whether the private sector can continue to success-fully advance living standards into the future is likely to increasingly depend on more effective governance. Unfortunately, the strains on governance are only likely to intensify in the immediate future given the accelerating pace of change and the sluggishness of government response. In the past, when these pressures have built to a breaking point, it has taken a crisis to resolve the natural tension between gov-ernance and progress. This tension is likely to remain the main risk to the "triumph of the optimists" in the years ahead.

Demography is destiny

The dominant narrative about the jobs market after the financial crisis focused on the large number of workers who were too discouraged to keep looking for work and therefore dropped out of the labor force. On both the political left and right, the declining share of the work-ing population was presented as a major economic problem. From the vantage point of the right, declining labor force participation was spun as a negative consequence of President Barack Obama's policies. On the left, it was incorporated into the "hard-times-for-the-working-class" narrative to justify more government support to address rising inequality. Yet, neither narrative stands up to the facts.

The basic problem with the dominant narrative spun around eco-nomic news is its myopia. It inserts statistics into the present-day focus without any historical perspective or insight into the trends driving the economy into the future. Instead, there is an exaggerated overem-phasis on the present. Whatever the topic "du jour" is, the economic facts are twisted to fit that current context.

The focus on inequality is a good example of the bias filtering eco-nomic data analysis. Inequality is definitely worth considering, but an alarmist discussion of the subject has crowded out more insight-ful analyses. There is more to the economy than rising inequality. In fact, standards of living are now rising rapidly for most of the world's population. Still, as political polarization has intensified in recent years, data interpretation has often had a strong political bias around an agenda. One lesson every good trader or money manager eventually learns is that political bias can be dangerous to one's "economic health." Objectivity in interpreting events and economic forecasting requires leaving one's biases out of the analysis.

But let's come back to the exaggeratedly pessimistic participation-rate interpretation. From 10 percent in October 2009 the unemployment rate fell steadily to less than 6 percent by late 2014. Throughout this process, the dominant narrative focused not on the declining number of unemployed, but rather on the fact that this decline was accompanied by a falling share of the population that was working. The judgment rendered on this growing number of people outside the workforce was intensely negative, as if there was something wrong with the economy, causing people to leave the labor force. This negative economic view influenced many would-be investors to avoid equities just when the returns were greatest.

Despite the handwringing, the weight of the evidence strongly suggested the economy was healing and profits were growing. As discussed below, demographics account for most of the decline in the labor force participation rate since 2006.[1] Also, more people are choosing to leave the labor force because they can. This is the result of the highest living standard in history, a living standard that makes it possible to work less. This is the wave of the future. Those who understood that the declining participation rate was not a sign of weakening US economic fundamentals, but rather the result of structural trends were less likely to miss the boat on one of the biggest equity bull markets in history.

What's really going on?

First, while the number of discouraged workers leaving the labor force was unusually high immediately after the financial crisis, that was not surprising given the fact that it was the worst labor market recession since the early 1930s. However, as the unemployment rate fell from 10 percent, the number of discouraged workers declined as well. In fact, just about every metric of labor market health improved steadily as policy uncertainty declined and the recovery progressed. Still, the false negative spin persisted in an effort to create the impression of no improvement. Even after all the jobs lost during the recession had

---

[1] This is corroborated by various research papers, including the Federal Reserve Bank of Philadelphia's "On the Causes of Declines in the Labor Force Participation Rate," Shigeru Fujita, February 2014.

been recovered (over 8 million), there was still a hard-core narrative of negativity that latched onto the declining labor force share of the population as its linchpin for credibility.

Instead, the US economy did what history shows it always does: it self-organized according to the new incentive structure and available mix of labor and capital. Over the long haul, as we saw in chapter 1, it creates jobs according to how many people are available and want to work. This is the labor market variant of Say's Law. The supply of labor creates its own demand. This assumes policy avoids deflationary collapses, as it has since the 1930s debacle. This means that for the long run, the relevant question is never where will the future jobs come from. It's how many people will want to work.

The key to labor supply

Because the US economy has always been able to create jobs according to how many people are available to work, cyclical setbacks notwithstanding, the issue of labor force participation is best analyzed from the supply side rather than the demand side. The false narrative, however, has tried to twist a supply-side issue into a demand-side problem. That's why it has been contradicted by the evidence and proven false. Labor force participation is mainly a supply-side issue that boils down to who wants to work and how much. The secular tailwinds of change are reshaping the answer to these questions, causing much confusion in the process.

Before my grandfather got to high school, his father died and he had to quit school to help support the family. In the early twentieth century, this was not unusual. In fact, at the turn of the nineteenth century, almost everyone worked by the time they were ten years old and few went to school after that. School breaks during the summer originated so children would be available during the peak farm work season. In a largely agricultural society, all hands were needed to survive. As industrialization moved people off farms and into cities, this began to change slowly. Going to school was a financial sacrifice for families that still depended on child labor.

In 1870, only about 2 percent of the population graduated from high school. It wasn't until my parents graduated from high school right before World War II that the high school graduation rate reached 50 percent in the United States. After rising from 2 percent to 50 percent in 80 years, the US high school graduation rate eventually peaked in the late 1960s at about 77 percent, and then began a long decline that has recently reversed. The rate passed 80 percent in 2012, and is on course to hit 90 percent by 2020.

Compulsory education has been a widespread phenomenon for less than two centuries in the United States. Initially, it was aimed at grammar school and later extended to high school. Now, more people are going to school for longer and postponing their participation in the labor force. Many young people don't get serious about a career until they are well into their 20s. Going to college has become a practical necessity for many careers. That was not true before World War II, when only a small minority of the elite could attend college. The GI Bill brought college to the masses after World War II. For most Americans, college became a part of their educational experience only during the last two generations.

The main point here is that a high early-age labor force participation rate was necessary when people used to live hand to mouth in a way most Americans cannot imagine today. Leisure time, including to study, was a rare commodity. It has become progressively more abundant over the past century, however, as living standards have risen and the necessity to work has declined. This has also created pressure and a strong trend for a more integrated life-work experience, with more jobs that satisfy individual preferences about how to spend time.

These long-standing trends have not stopped. If anything, the necessity to work is becoming less and less pressing for more and more people. Formal work in the measured labor force is becoming an option to weigh against the alternatives. The labor force participation rate for men, for example, has dropped from almost 90 percent in 1948 to less than 70 percent in recent years. In many poor countries, it's still close to 90 percent. Obviously, as income surpasses certain levels, the necessity to work diminishes because of accumulated wealth. After all, one of the main goals of humanity is to have income security so that work is more by choice and less by necessity. As more people achieve that status, they can work less.

There are several strands to this basic theme worth making explicit. For prime-age males, the world has transitioned to reduce the burden of being the primary earner. As a result of increasing work opportunities for women, female participation soared from about 33 percent after World War II to a peak of about 60 percent by 2000, when it also began to decline. The option for men to take care of the home while the spouse worked became more feasible. Retiring early relative to increased life expectancy also reduced labor force participation rates for men.

The decline in female participation since 2000 partly reflects the same factors driving prime-age male participation lower. The opportunity costs of a second person in a household taking a job have risen as childcare costs, tax disincentives, and other factors have made the net gain to a second income much less attractive for middle- and, especially, lower-income families. In addition, as per-capita incomes have risen, the need for both partners to take a job has diminished. As discussed above, in the younger-age cohort, more people have opted to postpone work in order to attend college as the payoff to a college education for lifetime earnings increases. This has caused a dramatic reduction in labor force participation for the college-age population over the past 30 years.

US per-capita income on an inflation-adjusted basis has roughly quadrupled since 1950. The marginal benefit from an extra dollar of income compared to an extra hour of leisure or an hour taking care of business at home becomes less attractive at some point. Add in the progressivity of taxes and loss of benefits, like the extended tax credit for lower-income taxpayers, and the need to work and the return to work have shifted in favor of not working, or working less.

Nowhere is this more evident than in the baby boom generation, which, as noted above, accounts for about a third of the US adult population, as well as for the bulk of the country's wealth. Most of the decline in the labor force participation rate since 2001, when the first baby boomers began to turn 55, reflects retiring baby boomers. That's because the participation rate for those over 55 (at about 40 percent) is half that of the prime-age population (81 percent) and diminishes rapidly after the age of 60. For example, while up from 11 percent in 1985, the participation rate for those 65 and over is only 18 percent. With substantial peak life-cycle wealth, many baby boomers are freer to work as a choice rather than a necessity. For many, a part-time job in an area of interest combined with income from savings and Social Security is a preferable choice to a full-time job. Tax policy penalizes Social Security benefits for those who earn too much, creating a disincentive to keep working, especially full time.

Thus, the long uptrend in the labor force participation rate from about 1965 until 1995 was driven by a young population bulge coming of age and joining the labor force with an unprecedented rise in participation by baby boom women. Various factors have exhausted that trend. By far, the biggest one is an aging population moving into retirement.

All of these factors behind the declining share of the population in the workforce reflect aging and personal choices of potential workers, given their financial need to work and the incentives that policymakers have created between working, working less, and not working. For many prime-working-age people, the marginal gains from working have fallen relative to the costs of taking a job. This is particularly true for married couples who may be deciding whether one or both should work. Given the much higher living standards possible today without working, it's not surprising that more people choose to do other things. The safety nets in most of the developed world provide a fallback position that surpasses the living standards that the vast majority of Americans faced when children routinely began working before the age of ten in the nineteenth century. These safety nets also surpass the average living standard in much of the developing world. That's why immigrants from those countries will do the work that Americans refuse. Allowing more immigration would help raise the labor force participation rate.

Should we worry about who pays for baby boomers' retirement?

Because of the intrinsically pessimistic cast of the commentary around economic issues, topics are often framed in a way that overlooks the substantive trends behind the data. We just presented an alternative view of the declining share of the population participating in the labor force. Unlike the mainstream view, which stretches the facts to present this trend in a negative light, we saw that the facts are to the contrary. In a richer society, with much-extended childhoods and life spans that are double those of a century ago, people can afford to spend much more time not working. This is a wonderful result of the progress that economic growth has brought to the developed world.

The same negative bias has permeated the discussion of the so-called burden that aged populations put on the smaller younger-age cohorts. This gloomy cast is most easily developed in a scenario in which retirees depend mainly on government pensions, like the Social Security system in the United States. The rising dependency ratio is then used to paint scary scenarios in which each younger worker is supporting increasingly more senior citizens because the pay-as-you-go financing scheme underlying Social Security is presumed to be the main source of retirement income. That, however, is an incomplete view of how retirement actually works in the United States.

In reality, Social Security is only a part of most people's retirement income. As mentioned earlier, the baby boomers make up a third of the adult population and control double that percentage of the country's wealth. That wealth generates a return, and will play a bigger role in most retirement plans than Social Security, which has become only a fallback for most people because it has been politicized rather than invested in an actuarially sound fashion like private wealth. When we consider that there has never been as large and as wealthy a generation in history as the US baby boomers, it helps to put the exclusive focus on the less significant Social Security system in perspective.

The wealth held by retirees is the main source of their retirement income. This is obvious. Nevertheless, the fact that a huge segment of the population is leaving the workforce to live on capital income has escaped the attention of commentators who bemoan the decline in the labor force participation rates and the related decline in the share of corporate income going to workers. As we described earlier, profit margins shifted higher starting in about 2001, when the first baby boomers began to turn 55 years old, the age when people start to leave the labor force. The share of employee compensation has naturally dropped off, and the share of profits has naturally risen with the baby boomers' massive wealth accumulation, retirement, and consequent dependence on capital income.

In contrast, the mainstream interpretation of higher profit margins is that workers are falling behind, and income inequality is a growing threat to be worried about. The problem with this view is that it overlooks the fact that profits and interest paid (nonlabor income) are a source of income for retirees. Those not working must rely on either transfer payments from the government, like Social Security checks, or the profits and interest generated by their savings accumulated over a lifetime of work. Because of demographics, it is inevitable that an ever-growing share of GDP will be generated by capital rather than labor as more and more of the population ages and leaves the workforce. Those who have not saved will keep working or depend on the government. For the rest, having saved allows them to collect interest on bonds and dividends on equities. As a result of the life cycle and decades of prosperity, wealth is highly concentrated at the top of the age pyramid. This is one of the main sources of perceived inequality in the distribution of wealth, but in this case it is a good thing. It allows the old to retire with dignity. After all, that is the main purpose of saving and wealth accumulation during one's working years.

All this is the natural result of a self-organizing free economy. As fewer people work and more rely on capital income, the economy is naturally transitioning to more capital and less labor input. There is no top-down Wizard of Oz directing this transition. It happens spontaneously as market signals redirect the allocation of available resources toward relatively more capital and relatively less labor. It is the result of the self-organizing gestalt process that drives the economy.

Artificial intelligence

Artificial intelligence is playing an important role in enabling this trend as it progresses, and is able to do more and more tasks previously accomplished by workers. Since 2000, a number of occupations have seen total employment levels drop by 25 percent or more as a result, including typists, telephone operators, proofreaders, telemarketers, travel agents, bookkeepers, and office assistants. Although the activities that all of these jobs entail have grown dramatically, they can increasingly be done by intelligent machines rather than people.

This is part of a long-standing shift in the nature of jobs caused by technological change. A couple of centuries ago, most Americans worked on farms. Today, only about 2 percent do. Yet, that 2 percent produces much more food than ever before, enough to feed the other 98 percent of the population and still make the United States the biggest exporter of agricultural products in the world.

Many of those earlier farmers left the farm to take factory jobs as the economy industrialized. By the 1940s, manufacturing accounted for about a third of all jobs. Since then, as in agriculture before it, that share has steadily declined to only about 10 percent. In both cases, technology made each worker more productive and reduced the need for such a large share of the workforce to produce the needed output.

In the postindustrial age, technology and artificial intelligence are progressing and taking over more and more jobs. This process of job destruction from technological progress has created angst ever since the Luddites in the early days of industrialization. Nevertheless, the pattern is always the same. Higher productivity raises incomes and creates the demand for new goods and services that are the basis for the new jobs. Since 2000, for example, the following occupations have grown by 25 percent or more: computer system managers, physical

therapists, software engineers, financial advisers and analysts, registered nurses, financial managers, physicians and surgeons, and lawyers. Clearly, these high-growth professions reflect the trends in the
economy and the population discussed here.

First, an aging population of retirees living off capital income
requires more financial advisers, lawyers, and financial managers. It
also requires more physical therapists, doctors, and nurses. The computer system management and software engineers are the "farmers" of
the twenty-first century as they create increasingly productive systems
to satisfy more demand with less labor. These new jobs that are growing rapidly generally require more education and provide higher pay
than the jobs that are being replaced by machines. That's why college
degrees are held by an ever-growing share of the employed.

Finally, as artificial intelligence takes on more and more of the
responsibilities workers have had in the past, it serves the useful function of getting more done just when there are fewer young people
coming into the labor market compared to the masses of long-living
retirees. Rather than causing a problem, more technology is exactly
what's needed today to free up more people to enjoy a leisurely life.
Fortunately, we don't have to wait for central planners to meet demand
and supply. "Mr. Market" already has, as the billions of data bits puls-
ing through the economy have organized a new gestalt that produces
more GDP with less labor and more capital. You may not see it now,
but it is happening and it will become increasingly apparent. Investors
who adapt their strategies around these economic trends will survive.
Those who don't, or who fall prey to the negative narrative twisted to
constantly find problems in the way the economy is self-organizing,
eventually go the way of the dodo bird.

Saving myths

Another area in which the conventional wisdom paints a misleading
and needlessly worrisome picture is the image of the United States as
a profligate debtor nation. Persistent current account deficits, high
fiscal deficits, low personal saving, and excessive debt owed to foreigners are all part of the underlying view that the United States borrows
too much and saves too little. This contributes to a view among some
investors that it is just a matter of time until financial Armageddon,
causing many to be fearful of investing as a result. In the meantime,
the United States continues as the biggest, richest economy on the

planet, and investment returns continue to accumulate to those who have a deeper understanding of what's going on.

As with the labor-market confusion, the conventional wisdom about saving reflects an absence of appreciation for the self-organizing nature of the US economy and its unique characteristics. People save according to their preferences for consuming now or later. They organize their finances accordingly. Similarly, businesses borrow and invest according to their assessment of the profitability of financing projects for future production. None of this gets discussed in the handwringing that projects the US economy as an overconsuming nation of deadbeats. In this view, the pundits instead offer all kinds of "solutions" to force "better" saving behavior from the top down on the presumption that their fundamental premise—that there is a saving problem—is correct. It's not. Just as the labor market takes care of itself over time, so does the savings rate.

The global savings glut

Just as globalization has reshaped the labor market, income inequality, the value of tangible assets, and most other markets, it has also changed the nature of saving and investment. In a free-floating dollar market with increasingly open world capital markets, saving and investment have taken on an increasingly global dimension. From less than $1 trillion in 1980, US assets held abroad and US liabilities owed to non-US investors have exploded to more than $20 trillion (Exhibit 7.2). At the same time, the gap between these assets and liabilities has been growing and is now in the vicinity of roughly $5 trillion. That is, the United States has a negative net worth on its international balance sheet of several trillion dollars. Ever since the late 1980s, this increasing indebtedness has been a focus for worrywarts predicting an eventual collapse in the dollar.

Without globalized markets, saving and investment are constrained to balance within national borders. However, as markets open up for both trade and capital flows across borders, the balancing occurs on a global, rather than a national, basis. This has caused a new pattern of trade and investment flows to emerge over the past 30 years. The United States has been able to deploy its high-productivity, state-of-the-art technology in direct investments all over the world. This comparative advantage garners it high returns especially in underdeveloped economies, where living standards have the most catching up to do.

Exhibit 7.2   Cross-Border Investing Explodes with Globalization

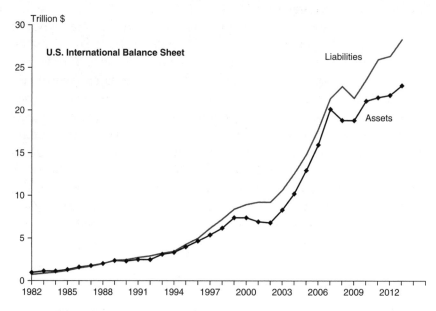

Source: Bureau of Economic Analysis /Haver Analytics.
Data through 2013.

This outflow of investment combines with a chronic trade deficit to create a big financing gap that requires foreign investors to recycle dollars back into the United States. These flows, however, allow investors from all over the world to buy US assets, like Treasuries and real estate, that are especially attractive to residents of countries in which political and foreign exchange instability make it riskier to put all one's eggs in a domestic asset basket.

Rapid growth in the developing world over the past 20 years has created a rising middle class with a vast pool of savings that didn't exist when these people were still living in subsistence poverty. Not only have incomes risen fast but saving rates are also higher in emerging markets for various reasons. Government health care, education, and retirement benefits are generally much less comprehensive in poor countries, if they exist at all. Overall economic conditions are more variable and less predictable in the early stages of development, and credit availability is more limited. For a whole host of these and other reasons, emerging market economies tend to have higher saving rates.

Thus, as the mix of global GDP has shifted dramatically over the past 20 or so years, the global saving rate has risen, reflecting the higher saving rates in fast-growing emerging markets, like China, where export-led growth policies helped create a particularly massive accumulation of savings. Initially, developed economies absorbed this savings, with countries like the United States, the United Kingdom, Spain, and Ireland, for example, enjoying consumer housing booms financed by foreign capital inflows from this rising pool of emerging-market savings. After the financial crisis, that dynamic ended, and countries like China are now struggling to deploy their huge savings pools domestically to maintain growth.

Without the extra demand from US and other developed-market consumers, the global savings glut is weighing more heavily on world growth and interest rates. Inflation is also being weighed down globally as a result. Nominal GDP at the global level is growing much more slowly, as inflation has generally come down to lower levels around the world, not just in the United States and other developed markets.

In a world with deficient demand growth because of excess savings, it's trade-surplus countries like Germany—which now has the biggest surplus in the world—that are the problem. Yet, there is a tendency to "blame" deficit countries for consuming too much and to laud surplus countries as prudent savers. Because saving is regarded as virtuous and borrowing is not, the focus remains on the wrong issue and the source of the problem remains unaddressed. The problem is everybody cannot run a surplus at the same time. On a global basis, trade has to balance. One country's surplus is another country's deficit. The pro-growth cure is more domestic demand growth in the surplus economies, not excessive austerity in the deficit countries.

In the United States, the primary source of the net debt position is the cumulating current account deficits, which generally run at about 3 percent of GDP each year. These persistent trade deficits began in the 1980s. Back then, the US deficit was the flip side of large German and Japanese surpluses. Interestingly, however, the United States has been able to run persistent trade deficits during this time without suffering the supposed ill-effects that arise from a growing net debtor position. The reasons for this suggest that the international debtor position of the United States is an advantage rather than the disadvantage that the conventional wisdom associates with persistent current account deficits. This is especially true in a world with a global savings glut.

The supposed problem with a continual US current account deficit and the associated buildup of liabilities owed to the rest of the world is the assumed drain on national income each year to service the debt owed to foreigners. At some point this drain on national income is presumed to be a debilitating restraint on domestic consumption and economic growth. The problem with this view is that instead of a net income *outflow* to service the net debtor position, the United States enjoys a persistent net income *inflow*, with the yield on its roughly $23 trillion assets held abroad more than offsetting what it has to pay the holders of its roughly $28 trillion in liabilities. As can be seen in Exhibit 7.3, the United States takes in about $200 billion more on its assets than it pays out on its liabilities.

The reason for this apparent paradox is that the mix of US assets held abroad versus the mix of its obligations to the rest of the world works in its favor. US investors own more direct investments and equities in foreign markets than foreign investors own in the United States (roughly 50 percent versus 30 percent, respectively). On the other hand, foreigners hold about 70 percent of their US investments in Treasuries, other bonds, and bank deposits, compared with about a 50 percent share of US investments in liquid and fixed-income non-US assets. The return on this riskier US-held asset mix is naturally higher

Exhibit 7.3 The United States Is "Paid to Borrow" because the World Needs Its High-Quality Assets

Source: Bureau of Economic Analysis, Federal Reserve Board/Haver Analytics.
Data as of 2014 Q1.

than the lower-risk mix of assets that foreign investors hold in the United States. Basically, the United States provides safe haven assets to the rest of the world because of its longer history of political and currency stability compared to most of the rest of the world. Switzerland just isn't big enough to satisfy this demand. With about a third of the world's financial assets, the United States is the biggest global financial market for safe, high-quality assets.

Still, US Treasuries outstanding represent only 11 percent of global private financial wealth, which was estimated by the Boston Consulting Group at $152 trillion for 2013. Their share is about 10 percent if another $6.6 trillion estimated in sovereign wealth funds are also considered, and just 8 percent of the global private and public financial wealth if only the amount of publicly held Treasuries is used in the calculation.

In addition, as the world's reserve currency used in most international transactions, the dollar supply needs to grow in line with the global economy. A 3-percent current account deficit seems to be necessary to increase the global dollar supply and prevent the greenback from constantly appreciating. When the US trade deficit gets too small and the dollar appreciates, problems start to emerge in other parts of the world.

For example, this was evident in the 1990s, when the US fiscal deficit evaporated and the US trade deficit was not providing enough greenbacks to the global economy. A succession of emerging-market crises, starting in Mexico and eventually enveloping Asia, was the result. The big Asian surpluses that accumulated from 2002 to 2007 were a response to that crisis, as countries like China pursued export-led growth to accumulate massive dollar foreign-exchange reserves and make it unlikely that such a currency crisis would happen again.

During that period of reserve accumulation, there was a growing surfeit of global savings as surplus countries such as China recycled their excess savings to countries like the United States, where lax housing finance practices encouraged excessive demand. As noted above, the evidence of an excess of global saving versus consumption was reflected in a generally falling inflation trend and declining interest rates. The solution was to bolster domestic demand in surplus countries like China and rein in lax lending practices in places like the United States. That's the pattern of the global recovery since the financial crisis. Unfortunately, because of its difficulties in forming a banking and fiscal union, Europe has been unable to rebalance favorably for world growth. Deficit countries on the periphery have been forced into depressions as Germany still pursues its record surpluses but now from outside of Europe.

In any event, the US net debtor position has sparked a lot of needless concern over the past 30 years based on preconceptions from another era, when chronic trade deficits were destabilizing in a less globalized, gold standard world. Those concerns have proven misplaced as the multitude of US investors investing abroad consistently generates better returns than entities such as the US government borrowing from abroad have to pay.

That's largely a function of the fact that the United States attracts foreign capital looking for less risk, and therefore lower returns. Treasuries are the premier example of this. The US investor has plenty of relatively safe investments at home. He seeks higher-risk, higher-return investments all over the world, especially in emerging markets. In contrast, emerging-market investors come to the United States in search of lower risk, higher-quality investments than they can find at home. As noted above, publicly held Treasuries represent just about 8 percent of global financial assets. Foreigners own $6 trillion of them (47 percent of publicly held Treasuries), which represents only about 6 percent of the financial wealth overseas. However, a large chunk of $4 trillion of Treasuries is held in official accounts, leaving only $2 trillion available for overseas *private account* holdings. This accounts for just about 2 percent of estimated overseas *private* financial wealth.

In sum, in the fixed-exchange-rate gold settlement era there was stronger pressure to balance trade on a country-by-country basis. This constrained flows of capital and goods compared to a world in which there are fewer limits on persistent trade deficits and capital is more free-flowing. This is especially true for the United States, which has the world's largest financial markets and provides the world's premier reserve currency. In essence, the United States functions as a shock absorber for the global balance of payments. By running a persistent trade deficit, the United States provides the global dollar supply that greases the wheels of international commerce.

In addition to the seigniorage benefits of providing the world's reserve currency, it turns out the United States also benefits from a positive income flow that the rest of the world pays it to supply low-yielding safe-haven assets. As global wealth grows, the downward pressure on Treasury yields could become even more intense if US fiscal deficits aren't sufficient to provide an adequate supply of Treasuries to an ever-hungry population of global investors, especially those in

increasingly unstable regions of the world. In fact, if global governance continues to deteriorate, the US safe haven will become increasingly valuable to foreign investors, just as it is to the flood of would-be
immigrants clamoring to get inside its gates.

Fiscal follies

While fiscal policy was applied with great success during the 2008–
2009 financial emergency, it has been losing its constructive role over
recent years because of political polarization. Instead of the proactive
macroeconomic policy tool described in textbooks, it has become
more of a destabilizing afterthought to the intense partisanship that
has enveloped Washington, DC.

Budget brinksmanship caused US government debt to lose its AAA
rating for the first time in August 2011. In their downgrade statement,[2]
Standard & Poor's (S&P) said, "The downgrade reflects our view that the
effectiveness, stability, and predictability of American policymaking
and political institutions have weakened at a time of ongoing fiscal and
economic challenges." After that, recurrent showdowns undermined
thoughtful macroeconomic application of fiscal policy. Increasingly,
the markets regarded erratic fiscal policy as a risk to be weighed rather
than a supportive instrument for economic progress. Similarly, at the
state- and local level—which rivals the federal government in its GDP
contribution—budget problems, often driven by politics, caused the
recovery from the financial crisis to face unusually strong headwinds as
contractionary fiscal policies weighed on the nascent expansion.

As we noted earlier, every business cycle is the same, except for
what's different. The recovery that began in June 2009 was different in
several respects. Housing, which generally leads recoveries, was missing in action because of the debacle and collapse suffered in the prior
expansion and subsequent recession. This was particularly hard on
state- and local government finances, which are closely tied to the
residential real estate cycle because of the property tax base and the
ancillary business activity around local construction. The job losses
associated with the housing depression weighed heavily on income
tax revenues. Long story short, both federal and state- and local fiscal
policies were a protracted drag on the expansion that began after the
financial crisis rather than the helpful supports suggested in economic

[2] www.standardandpoors.com/ratings/articles/en/us/?assetID=1245316529563,
August 5, 2011.

theory. Private-sector real GDP averaged 3.1 percent annual growth in the first five years of the post-financial crisis expansion. Government GDP shrank at a 1.4 percent annual rate.

Premature austerity between 2011 and 2014 at the federal level was a direct result of the political battles, which generally resolved themselves by cutting spending and raising taxes, the worst combination for a budding recovery and a major reason why the expansion was sluggish on a number of fronts. On the plus side, however, this combination caused the deficit to come down much faster than the consensus expected, considerably relieving market angst about the sustainability of the US fiscal situation.

Going forward, the stalemate is likely to continue. The problem is that most of the budget is now committed to entitlement spending, with other government activities increasingly under the budget ax. With the senior share (age 65+) of the adult population projected to grow from about 25 percent in 2015 to about 37 percent in 2039, the key to fiscal stabilization is concentrated in making healthcare and other entitlement programs more efficient and sustainable. The political polarization is focused around how to pay for this as an increasing share of the population receives benefits and pays no income taxes, while the bulk of taxes is falling on a narrowing slice of the high-income population. This is shaping up to be one of the classic problems faced by populist democracies, in which the majority votes itself more and more benefits until the taxpayers funding them move their wealth and income elsewhere and there is no more to take from. This is already happening at the state level, where high tax states with unfunded public sector postretirement programs are losing population to the faster-growing, low-tax states with sound finances.

How much is too much deficit?

While politics have become dysfunctional from a fiscal policy point of view, the stalemate brought the deficit down much faster than professional forecasters anticipated. From about 10 percent of GDP during the crisis, the deficit declined to about a fourth of that by the end of 2014 and looks to remain manageable for the rest of the decade. After about 2025, entitlements will move it progressively higher according to Congressional Budget Office (CBO) projections, which need to be taken with a grain of salt, however, given all the moving parts and the lengthy time horizon. For example, negative surprises such as wars could derail the sanguine outlook over the next decade. On the other hand, faster growth or a more enlightened fiscal and immigration policy would go a long way toward solving the future deficit problem.

In any case, the key to what's sustainable in terms of government debt is the nominal GDP growth rate. Our presumption in this book has been that the US economy needs a nominal GDP growth trend of about 4 percent to sustain its underlying debt structure (both private and public) while growing at a real trend-like 2- to 3-percent annual pace. The Federal Reserve's reflationary monetary policy appears to have restored that trend. In a 4-percent, or better, nominal growth environment, an economy can sustain deficits of that magnitude relative to nominal GDP on an indefinite basis (as the share of debt to GDP remains stable), particularly when interest rates are much lower than that 4 percent level. From that point of view, deficits don't appear to be an issue until the middle of the next decade.

In addition to the domestic sustainability of US government debt, there is also the issue of how much US debt can be absorbed by financial markets. As we saw in the previous section, if anything, the greater risk seems to be an inadequately small supply of Treasuries compared to the rapidly growing level of global wealth and the role of the United States as the world's financial safe haven despite its political dysfunction. It turns out that political dysfunction is relative, and that governance is deteriorating faster and with more ill-effects in many other parts of the world than in the United States.

Because of the likely growing demand for US Treasuries as global wealth rises, it is more likely that the United States will reach its domestic capacity to service debt before the international demand becomes a constraint on issuance. As we saw earlier, Treasuries are still a small proportion of private-sector holdings internationally compared to their role in the overall global financial market. As developed economies have reined in deficits since the financial crisis in response to debt-sustainability concerns, the supply of high-quality sovereign debt has grown more slowly, putting severe downward pressure on interest rates. Extraordinarily low US, Japanese and German government debt interest rates reflect at least in part the imbalance between the supplies and the voracious demand for high-quality sovereign paper around the world.

As long as debt grows largely in line with nominal GDP, there is little danger of a US sovereign debt crisis. The problem that arises in countries like Greece, where a severe debt crisis erupted in 2011–2012, is that investors begin to doubt the ability of the country to service its growing debt burden. Particularly important in the Greek case is that its debt is denominated in euros, which the Greek government cannot print. As the country's debt grew to the point at which it was obvious it could not make good on it, cheap foreign credit vanished, interest rates exploded way beyond its nominal GDP growth rate, and the economy collapsed in a depression. Punitive interest rates reflecting high probabilities of default make it difficult to keep rolling over government debt. This scenario is much less likely in the United States, not least because it can print its own currency to fund its debt. Still, if politicians ran deficits that required more money printing than the Federal Reserve deemed consistent with its inflation target, debt strains would emerge in the United States as well. If Congress took away the Fed's independence and forced it to print money, inflation would substitute for outright default.

All in all, debt problems are much harder to deal with if there is no growth in the economy, as Europe has been learning since the financial crisis. The economic dynamism of the United States, its stronger demographics, and better management of monetary policy should keep nominal growth from collapsing as it has in countries struggling with excessive debt payments in weak economies.

Also, while the US government has not shown as much fiscal prudence over the years as most would prefer, it has not been nearly as imprudent as critics believe, at least as far as debt accumulation to date. While painful in the short run, the fact that deficits were cut to more sustainable levels following large increases between 2008 and 2010 has greatly improved the country's fiscal outlook.

That said, from a longer-term perspective, the promise of substantial entitlements without explicit funding remains an important issue that must be addressed over the next decade in order to put US government finances on a sound footing beyond 2025.

Personal saving rate much higher than the mainstream believes

Another saving myth that feeds the dim view of the US economy is the notion that the personal saving rate has declined to unhealthy levels, leaving households vulnerable for the future and incapable of higher spending. Given the disproportionate 70 percent share of consumer spending in the US economy, this worry often caused investors to doubt return opportunities in risk assets that ultimately proved lucrative. This misunderstanding is an artifact of the way the saving rate is computed for the national income and product accounts (NIPA). Over the years, and more exactly since 1982, the discrepancy between the NIPA definition of saving and the financial reality for consumers has grown wider (Exhibit 7.4), with the NIPA measure increasingly underestimating the actual saving rate.

It turns out that a growing share of *taxed* income since 1982 is not part of personal income as measured in NIPA accounts. This includes certain taxable pensions, some contributions to social insurance programs, some small business income, and other miscellaneous income categories. Another large and growing chunk of income excluded from the NIPA measure of personal income is capital gains on the sale of assets. The problem is not that capital gains are not considered income but rather that, like the other excluded forms of income, they are part of the adjusted gross income that the Internal Revenue Service (IRS) taxes. In other words, to compute disposable income and the saving rate, NIPA accounting subtracts taxes paid on capital gains from the current income (such as salary) even though it doesn't include capital

Exhibit 7.4 Reported Saving Measure Shows Worrisome Decline. However, Accounting for *Excluded but Taxed* Income Shows Remarkable Stability

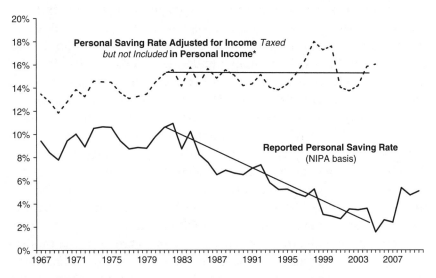

Source: BEA/Haver Analytics.

Data as of 2010.

*Data series on income *taxed but not included in personal income* were discontinued in 2005.

gains in its measure of income. This accounting mismatch causes the personal saving rate to be massively and increasingly understated.

As seen in Exhibit 7.4, if we add back the income excluded from the official NIPA saving rate, the alternative resultant saving measure shows a relatively flat or slightly rising trend since the 1960s, fluctuating around 15 percent in recent years, in stark contrast to the NIPA measure, which trended down from its 8 to 10 percent range in the early 1980s to between about 2 percent and 5 percent in recent years.

The depressed NIPA measure is the "saving rate" that generates all the judgmental media commentary about the US household saving situation. In years when it was close to zero, bleak pictures were painted of profligate US consumers who needed to save more and spend less. As noted above, this perceived inadequacy has cast persistent doubt about the health of the US economy and the investment outlook.

However, based on more consistent accounting of taxable income and taxes paid, the alternative measure discussed here shows that households seem to be saving at a fairly steady rate of about 15 percent on average. This refutes the consumer saving crisis narrative, and is more consistent with the strongly positive trend in household net worth and consumer spending, cyclical hiccups notwithstanding. This is one of many examples of how superficial analysis results in misleading conclusions in the public discourse.

To avoid an expanded accounting discussion of the various excluded forms of income, we will focus on a capital gains example to illustrate the point. Suppose Sally earns a salary of a $100,000. In addition, she has a nice gain in her stock portfolio and decides to take a $30,000 capital gain. For simplicity, let's assume her tax rate is the same on her salary income and her capital gains, say 20 percent. Finally, let's assume that she likes to save 30 percent of her after-tax income. Exhibit 7.5 shows the difference between NIPA and cash flow accounting from Sally's point of view. She saved $31,200 after paying $26,000 to the IRS and spending $72,800. That's a 30-percent saving rate on her after-tax income.

Because NIPA accounting only counts the personal income earned in the production of goods and services counted in GDP, it does not recognize capital gains as income. However, NIPA subtracts the taxes paid on capital gains from the current income earned in the production of GDP to calculate disposable income and the saving rate. After subtracting her spending, Sally now shows a mere $1,200 in saving, or less than 2 percent of her NIPA measure of disposable income. Sally feels good she saved so much. The pundits, however, see the paltry less

Exhibit 7.5 Two Ways to Calculate Sally's Saving Rate

	NIPA Accounting	Cash Flow Accounting
(+) Wages & Salary	$100,000	$100,000
(+) Capital Gains	$30,000	$30,000
(–) Tax	$26,000	$26,000
(=) Disposable Income	**$74,000**	**$104,000**
(–) Outlays	$72,800	$72,800
(=) Personal Saving	$1,200	$31,200
Saving Rate (%)=Saving/ Disposable Income	**2%**	**30%**

than 2-percent reported saving rate and pontificate about her saving problem.

Thus, as Exhibit 7.4 shows, saving behavior has been much steadier and stronger than the official measure suggests. As noted above, in addition to capital gains, several other sources of taxable income excluded from NIPA personal income have been growing as a share of taxable income so that the resultant official NIPA measure of disposable income has been shrinking, increasingly depressing the reported saving rate. People spend some of this "phantom income" that NIPA accounts exclude to pay taxes on it. As the example shows and as Exhibit 7.5 makes clear, the reported saving rate is not an indication of what most people consider saving. The more consistent measure shows a much healthier consumer saving situation. But, of course, good news does not sell.

The paradox of inequality

Another area in which the dominant narrative paints a misleading picture by focusing on a circumscribed nationalistic perspective rather than a global perspective is the subject of income and wealth inequality. The fact that income inequality has risen in the rich world over the past 20 or 30 years is the launch pad for a host of proposed top-down solutions usually overseen by the government to correct a perceived problem. Often, however, the proposals are far more likely to damage the economy than help it. For example, in his book, *Capital in the Twenty-First Century*, Thomas Piketty calls for an 80-percent tax on incomes over $250,000 and a 2-percent annual tax on net worth to slow the growth of wealth inequality. In contrast, the eminent economist Angus Deaton lays out a more optimistic vision despite, or even because, of inequality in his book, *The Great Escape: Health, Wealth, and the Origin of Inequality.* Essentially, the book describes many dimensions of improvement in most people's lives today compared to the past. According to Deaton, "people know that their lives are better and they will tell you as much."[3]

As we have pointed out several times in this book, more people are escaping subsistence poverty than at any other time in history as the poor developing economies aspire to meet the much higher living standards in the developed world, and as technology and globalization make it increasingly possible. For example, according to Hal Varian, the chief economist for Google: "one easy way to forecast the future is to predict that what rich people have now, middle class people will have in five years, and poor people will have in ten years. It worked for radio, T.V., dishwashers, mobile phones, flat screen T.V., and many other pieces of technology."[4]

So despite inequality, things are rapidly getting better for more people than ever. What accounts for this big disconnect between rapidly improving living standards around the world and the bleak prognosis offered by the inequality fixation? There are two basic aspects to the issue. First, what is really happening with inequality? Second, what are its consequences and do they warrant radical policy measures?

It turns out that from a global perspective, the evidence suggests that inequality is not rising but rather diminishing because of faster growth in the poorer developing economies, especially in Asia. If incomes are growing faster in poorer countries than richer countries, there is a catching-up taking place that is likely to continue to help converge living standards across countries over time. That is what globalization does. Contrary to the prevailing opinion, it is a strong force that reduces inequality. While this should be obvious, it has been ignored. Again, good news is hard to sell.

This fact has been verified in research by Christoph Lakner, a consultant at the World Bank, and Branko Milanovic, senior scholar at the Luxembourg Income Study Center. They find that while income inequality has become more severe at the national level for most countries, it has been falling for the world as a whole for the past 20 years because developing economies have experienced more consistent economic growth.

[3] The Great Escape, March/April 2014 CATO Policy Report.
[4] Hal R. Varian, "Beyond Big Data," *Business Economics*, Volume 49(1), January 2014, pp. 27–31.

We call this result the "paradox of inequality" as global inequality can fall even if inequality rises in each individual country. That's because faster income growth at the lowest levels lifting people out of subsistence poverty in poor countries is a more powerful force for reducing inequality than the income shifts in richer countries.

Indeed, if we just look inside one country, like the United States, we see rising inequality. As we've already discussed, this is a reflection of the more intense labor market competition in a global market versus a protected national one. Globalization and accelerating technological change divide the relative labor market worth of the US population more acutely. The top benefits, while the bottom gets hurt. Even in China, inequality has risen during the past 20 years of declining global inequality. The rapid growth and urbanization of the coastal regions during the export-led boom raised incomes faster than in the interior regions. While inequality is a growing concern in China, the country made a major contribution to reducing world inequality simply because many of its people left rural subsistence poverty for much higher incomes in factories as economic policy encouraged rapid industrialization. Its upper-income echelons did even better. China already has more billionaires and millionaires than any country except the United States. Better infrastructure and measures to stimulate services and small business in general, rather than just large government-sponsored enterprises, would go a long way toward raising incomes at the lower end of the distribution at a faster rate, narrowing inequality to a greater extent. In fact, the second aspect of inequality refers to what are the consequences and what policy measures would help address the negative effects of rising inequality.

First, as the Deaton book makes clear, inequality has not stopped human progress. To the contrary, more people's lives are improving at a faster pace. As the Varian statement about the "toys of the rich" becoming the "toys of the poor" within a decade illustrates, accelerating technological change is making this happen faster than ever before. Second, rather than government solutions to reduce inequality, what we increasingly see is government dysfunction keeping the poor from advancing even faster, and thus contributing to growing, rather than declining, inequality within national borders. Private capital is bringing "the toys of the rich" to the poor because it is profitable to do so. Also, because of the rapid acceleration in technology, the gap between the efficiency of corporate activity and the inefficiency of government activity is getting wider. Companies that cannot adapt, fail, and as a result, global corporations have shown an amazing resilience that governments can only dream of.

The various debacles in US government programs in recent years, including the implementation of the Affordable Care Act, the administration of Veteran Hospitals and the IRS administration problems, highlight the difference between a well-functioning corporate sector and the malfunctioning government sector. The incentives system works in markets much better than in politics and government, where the incentives are often quite perverse. What's more, experience both here and abroad shows that the bigger the government, the harder it becomes to manage and the more dysfunctional and counterproductive it becomes. The private sector on the other hand, has the incentive to be as lean, productive, and successful as it can be in delivering the goods to rich and poor alike, creating wealth at an unprecedented pace in the process.

As that wealth creates billionaires, those billionaires are increasingly funding NGOs and foundations to solve the world's problems. Donations from all income groups are increasingly directed to address issues that people care about but that governments have neglected despite ambitious promises and great expectations. This work is done on a voluntary basis, according to what people see as major problems. It does not require a heavy coercive hand from the state, and because it bypasses slow-moving bureaucracies, it often achieves results faster and more cheaply. Ideally, this model will become an increasing source of support to address the problems of the day. It has the added advantage that it can easily move on to the next problem after solving the first one, eliminating the difficulty that governments have with ending bureaucratic structures after a job is done.

As capital takes an increasing share of income because of the demographic and technological forces we described earlier, it is critical that more people own capital to augment the diminishing labor share of income. One approach advocated by the Piketty book is forced government redistribution from the rich to the poor. Government-run pension systems set up on a pay-as-you-go basis, like social security, and run according to prevailing political winds are defended by those who resist changing the status quo.

An alternative approach would facilitate mass ownership of capital to tie the rising returns to capital directly to a widespread ownership base. That essentially is what 401K saving for retirement allows: millions of people with direct ownership of all the US corporations. That is also what more actuarially sound public pension funds in countries like Chile and Norway do. Bypassing politics and letting people or public funds invest directly to take advantage of the rising share of income going to capital addresses the issue of rising profits and reduced labor share of income. Unfortunately, the idea of privatizing Social Security has been politically taboo based on scare tactics that point to the big one-off crashes in stock prices to obscure the fact that equities consistently provide high-single-digit returns over long stretches of time. That would be a sensible solution to improving government finances, while letting the masses share in the rising share of capital income. It's ironic that the Left is the main opponent of policy that incentivizes mass ownership of capital. After all, equalizing mass ownership of property and capital has presumably been its ultimate objective.

Exhibit 7.6 summarizes some of the long-term themes that fly in the face of the conventional wisdom. Strategic asset allocation can benefit from recognizing the positive and avoiding the negative implications of these trends, as well as from seeing through the misleading narratives that, more often than not, prove detrimental to one's financial well-being.

Exhibit 7.6 Ten Key Long-Term Investment Insights

---

(1) Lower real and nominal interest rates, more in line with 1950s and early 1960s levels (Chapter 3 and 4)

(2) Higher profit margins than during the 1965–2005 period (Chapter 4 and 5) due to:

- Lower inflation and interest rates
- Aging population dependent on asset returns rather than labor income
- Increased automation and machine intelligence

(3) Lower credit spreads more in line with the 1950s and early 1960s (Chapter 4)

(4) Higher PEs from lower risk-free real rate and lower equity risk premium (Chapter 4 and 5)

(5) Higher share of dividends in total return (Chapter 5)

(6) Dividends back above or closer to the Treasury yield (Chapter 5)

(7) Unprecedented wealth accumulation, demographics and high incomes reduce labor-force participation rate (Chapter 6 and 7)

- Leisure rises in relative value
- Environmental protection rises in relative value
- Extended childhood and education rise in relative value
- Booming high-end and aspirational markets

Continued

Exhibit 7.6   Continued

(8) Income inequality falls at global level while rising nationally (the paradox of inequality, Chapter 7).

- A rising emerging market (EM) middle class
- A slower growing developed-market middle class
- Life getting better for rich and poor

(9) Globalization rebalances national imbalances (Chapter 7).

- Aging developed markets (DMs) provide capital to younger emerging markets (EMs)
- Capital-income funds retirement for aging DMs
- Rich-world investment helps raise productivity and labor income for rising EM middle class
- Immigration helps demographic rebalancing

(10) U.S. provides model for globalized economy

- Resilient market economy
- Provides world's primary reserve currency
- Main safe haven for global investors
- Most diverse population of major economies
- Diasporas from most cultures provide testing ground for global brands
- Diversity of people living peacefully under one governance structure and rule of law
- Melting pot assimilates cultures much as globalization does

8

Lessons Learned from the Financial Crisis

The financial crisis of late 2008 and early 2009 was easily the worst systemic economic event that the United States has experienced since the early 1930s. The extraordinary measures taken to prevent it from becoming another Great Depression were largely successful. Many observers have disputed this on the basis that the claim that aggressive monetary and fiscal measures stopped something much worse relies on a counterfactual argument that can never be proven. It is certainly possible that a less aggressive intervention might have prevented the disaster many feared. It is less plausible to assert that a completely hands-off response that allowed the panic to subside on its own would have rendered a better outcome. It's the difference between putting out a house fire and letting the neighborhood burn down. Anyone who understands what happened in the early 1930s could clearly see that.

The roots of the crisis were many and deep. The Financial Crisis Inquiry Commission established by Congress to investigate the causes of the crisis focused on the more immediate sources of instability that generally involved all the players in the economy: the private financial sector that sliced, diced, and bundled the mortgage loans; regulators, who were seen as too lax, public housing policies; politicians who pressured regulators; ratings agencies; and, of course, individuals who borrowed irresponsibly to purchase homes at inflated prices without any prospects of paying back the loans. In essence, everyone was counting on home prices "that only rise and never fall."

The role of housing and housing finance was, however, the clearly dominant factor that was different in the business expansion that began late in 2001. Its size and scope drove the expansion. Yet, it did not rise out of the ashes of the 2001 recession or the 1992–2001 business cycle. Its roots were deeper. Indeed, in some crucial respects, The Great Financial Crisis was the culmination of a long-term trend toward progressively higher leverage in the US economy that arose out of the ashes of the Great Depression, exacerbated after 1992 by increasingly aggressive government policies that encouraged home buying based on ever-declining lending standards coupled with a widespread perception that home prices never really go down.

Secular roots of the crisis

After the Great Depression and World War II, Americans were very underleveraged. The debt-deflation process of a severe balance sheet recession had left them scarred and averse to the use of debt. Too many people knew someone who had been ruined in the 1930s by the plunge in asset prices and the drop in product prices and wages that made debts bigger and bigger in real terms, causing bankruptcies and widespread unemployment. Debt was a dirty word.

This all began to change after World War II when the soldiers came home to resume their peacetime roles. Home buying was encouraged under the GI Bill home loan program established in 1944 near the end of the war. Over the next 60 years, the government adopted a number of other programs and tax measures that were aimed at encouraging homeownership. Up until 1950, just under half of Americans owned a home. At the peak of the housing bubble, the homeownership rate peaked just shy of 70 percent. After the crisis, it was back to about 65 percent, which was about where it was when the long housing expansion had started in 1994 with especially aggressive public policy focused on expanding home ownership for low-income families.

In the 1950s, fear of debt began to subside. In each successive business cycle until the 2008 financial crisis, households went into the next expansion with more leverage than they had at the start of the prior expansion (Exhibit 8.1). In the early 1950s, Americans owed about 8 cents for every dollar of their net worth. By 2007, this had more than tripled to about 25 cents. Household debt rose from about 30 percent of gross domestic product (GDP) to over 90 percent during this period. The vast majority of this debt was mortgage debt secured by a principal residence.

Naturally, this could not have happened without an ever-increasing supply of credit provided by a financial sector that itself was progressively more leveraged. In fact, while leverage in the nonfinancial sector

Exhibit 8.1 Household Leverage Rose through Every Business Cycle until the Financial Crisis

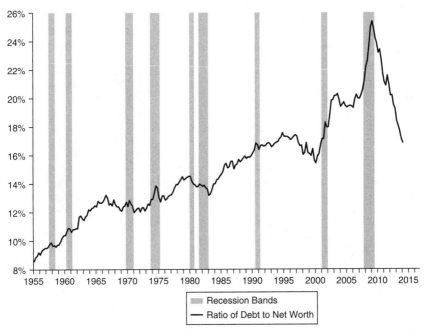

Recession Bands
— Ratio of Debt to Net Worth

Source: Federal Reserve Board/Haver Analytics.
Data as of August 2014.

generally tripled over the postwar period, it rose by a factor of more than ten in the financial sector, from less than 10 percent of GDP to over 100 percent of GDP (Exhibit 8.2). The financial sector's share of all debt outstanding rose from about 5 percent to just over 30 percent by 2008.

One reason the nonfinancial corporate sector weathered the financial crisis better than households, small businesses, financial firms, and governments was its lesser dependence on real estate, including relatively little real estate debt. The junk bond boom in the 1980s spurred a secular peak in nonfinancial corporate leverage that was corrected in the 1990s. As a result, most of these companies went into the 2008 crisis without excessive levels of debt on their balance sheets as well as with high cash balances. The recovery from the crisis was especially strong, in relative terms, for nonfinancial corporate America, and its earnings and equities enjoyed one of their best recoveries in history. This sharp contrast in performance with the highly leveraged sectors vulnerable to residential real estate prices further illustrates the

Exhibit 8.2   Financial Sector Debt Outstanding Rose More than Ten Times Faster than GDP in the Six Decades to the Financial Crisis

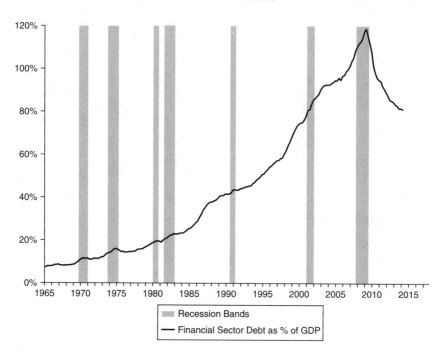

Source: BEA, Federal Reserve Board/Haver Analytics.

Data as of August 2014.

special role that housing and housing finance excesses played in the financial crisis and recession of 2008–2009.

During the 60-year period of progressively rising leverage in the household and financial sectors there was an ongoing erosion of credit standards. Twenty-year mortgages became thirty-year mortgages. Down payments fell from 20 percent to 10 percent to 5 percent and eventually to "nothing down." Car loan maturities extended from three years to five years. Income verification standards were dropped as various forms of "nontraditional" mortgages (NTMs) proliferated. These were long-run changes that made it possible for households to keep leveraging to ever higher levels and helped raise the home-ownership rate from less than 50 percent in 1950 to about 64 percent between 1980 and 1992. Then, a series of aggressive government initiatives went into effect with the purpose of putting home ownership within reach of low- and middle-income families.

The dissenting minority of the Financial Crisis Inquiry Commission characterized the shift in mortgage underwriting standards that began in the early 1990s in the following way: "Initiated by Congress in 1992 and pressed by HUD in both the Clinton and George W. Bush Administrations, the U.S. government's housing policy sought to increase home ownership in the United States through an intensive effort to reduce mortgage underwriting standards. In pursuit of this policy, HUD used (i) the affordable housing requirements imposed by Congress in 1992 on the government-sponsored enterprises (GSEs) Fannie Mae and Freddie Mac, (ii) its control over the policies of the Federal Housing Administration (FHA), and (iii) a "Best Practices Initiative" for subprime lenders and mortgage banks, to encourage greater subprime and other high risk mortgage lending." [1] A key section of the dissenting view is focused on HUD's key role in the growth of subprime and other high-risk mortgage lending.

The dissenting view from the Commission's minority focuses on the role of these government policies in increasing home ownership rates through relaxing mortgage standards. The majority view minimizes the role of government policies and instead puts more blame on regulators, like the Fed, and private financial institutions. There can be little doubt that there was plenty of blame to go around. The Commission's inquiry makes that clear. Also, it is hard to dispute the fact that, as both views carefully document, "nontraditional" mortgages played a big role in the housing debacle.

It's also clear that a lack of transparency about the holdings of subprime and other NTMs at various institutions, especially at Fannie Mae and Freddy Mac, was an important factor that made accurate risk assessments next to impossible before the crisis exploded. About half of the roughly $10 trillion in residential mortgages outstanding during the housing boom was held by these two privately owned institutions whose debt was owned all over the world under the long-held assumption that it would be backed by the US government, as it ultimately was. This incredible conflict of interest, whereby a private enterprise was for decades implicitly backed by taxpayers, had been constantly challenged by regulators and even presidents to no avail. Fannie and Freddie were the two biggest financial contributors to congressional political campaigns during the housing boom years, and as a result

---

[1] Financial Crisis Inquiry Commission, *The Financial Crisis Inquiry Report*, Dissenting Statement, p. 444. www.gpo.gov/fdsys/pkg/GPO-FCIC/pdf/GPO-FCIC.pdf.

remained impervious to the badly needed reforms to address the conflict of interest and massive moral hazard created by these privatized institutions with implicit taxpayer backing. Every president since Ronald Reagan had been pushed back by Congress when attempting to address this issue. The "crony capitalism" implicit in this massive conflict of interest was largely overlooked by the Financial Crisis Inquiry Commission, which after all, was appointed by Congress.

Former Treasury Secretary Timothy Geithner, for example, says the following about this issue in his comprehensive account of the financial crisis and its aftermath: "For example, during the Clinton years, they (Rubin, Summers, and Greenspan) all pushed for stricter regulation of the mortgage giants Fannie Mae and Freddie Mac, the government-sponsored enterprises (GSEs) that were exploiting their implicit federal backstop to load up on low-priced leverage. Fannie and Freddie had immense bipartisan influence in Congress, so reform didn't happen, but it should have."[2]

What's more, as we have already mentioned, the GSEs were much more leveraged than the most leveraged investment banks when the crisis hit. Sovereign purchasers, like the Chinese government, had bought billions of dollars of GSE paper, assuming that the Federal government was backing it. This was arguably the biggest single source of moral hazard in the financial system, allowing the poorly underwritten credit in NTMs to reach the scale that it did. Ultimately, the markets, ratings agencies, and mortgage originators did not worry about defaults because the credit risk could easily be put on GSE balance sheets where it essentially became a US government liability.

According to the dissenting report quoted above, "The fact that the credit risk of two-thirds of all NTMs in the financial system was held by the government or entities acting under government control demonstrates the central role of the government's policies in the development of the 1997–2007 housing bubble, the mortgage meltdown that occurred when the bubble deflated, and the financial crisis and recession that ensued."[3]

The heavy exposure of the GSEs to subprime credit was only revealed in retrospect because of the narrow and misleading definition of "subprime" that they used in accounting statements prior to the crisis.

---

[2] Timothy F. Geithner, *Stress Test, Reflections on the Financial Crisis* (Random House, 2014) p. 85.

[3] Financial Crisis Inquiry Commission, *The Financial Crisis Inquiry Report*, Dissenting Statement p. 456, www.gpo.gov/fdsys/pkg/GPO-FCIC/pdf/GPO-FCIC.pdf.

Only when they went into conservatorship in September 2008 was the full extent of their exposure revealed. Treasury Secretary Henry Paulson said the following when the government took them over: "I attribute the need for today's action primarily to the inherent conflict and flawed business model embedded in the GSE structure, and to the ongoing housing correction."[4]

It's understandable that the (Democratic) majority report of the Financial Crisis Inquiry Commission put the blame outside of government policies. It's also not surprising that the dissenters (Republicans) emphasized the role of government housing policy and implicitly the "crony capitalism" that made possible such an egregious deterioration in credit standards, abuse of government power, and misallocation of financial resources. Their debate, however, mainly boils down to who gets *the most* blame. There is little doubt that the systemic crisis was the result of a systematic, across-the-board breakdown in standards, through all segments of society.

Although it's clear that poorly underwritten credit on housing collateral was the primary cause of the bubble and its bursting, many critics blame the Fed's low interest-rate policy for the housing debacle. However, as we explained in our discussion of the basis for monetary policy, that policy was appropriate for meeting the Fed's inflation mandate. Poor credit standards had nothing to do with low interest rates. They were the culmination of a 60-year period of loosening credit standards that had its last gasp when the government sought to regulate and incentivize a massive unsustainable flood of subprime credit. It's not a coincidence that the crisis occurred in the financial sector, which is the most regulated part of the US economy. That regulatory control made it ripe for political interference, which unfortunately had a chilling effect on the dedicated civil servants charged with enforcing the safety and soundness of the financial system, as the statements quoted above from Treasury Secretaries Paulson and Geithner suggest. When a "party" like the housing bubble "party" between 2004 and 2007, or the technology stock bubble "party" in the late 1990s is going strong, the human, and therefore political tendency, is to sit back and "enjoy the ride." It's hard to stop it before it self-destructs, as the regulators who were pushed back when they attempted to rein in "Fanny" and "Freddie" found out.

[4] US Department of the Treasury, *Statement by Secretary Henry M. Paulson, Jr. on Treasury and Federal Housing Finance Agency Action to Protect Financial Markets and Taxpayers,* September 7, 2008, www.treasury.gov/press-center/press-releases/Pages/hp1129.aspx.

House of Debt

In their book *House of Debt*, Atif Mian and Amir Sufi, professors at Princeton University and the University of Chicago, respectively, document the concentration of new mortgage credit growth in low-income zip codes across the country during the housing bubble. They also summarize the research, showing much higher monetization rates of home equity by more highly leveraged, low-income borrowers as home prices soared during the last years of the boom, turning homes into ATM machines.

This newfound money paid for new cars, recreational vehicles, vacations, and extensive home improvements among other things. Research has also found the most extreme mortgage credit growth in cities with more inelastic housing supply, that is, where housing supply is constrained by geographic constraints that reduce the available land for new building. San Francisco or New York City would be "inelastic" cities, while Indianapolis or Dallas would be examples of more "elastic" cities in which available land would be less of a constraint on new building. Comparing high and low credit score borrowers in "elastic" and "inelastic" markets, studies find that the highest mortgage credit growth occurred in "inelastic" cities by low credit score borrowers. In "inelastic" cities, home prices in low-income zip codes rose 100 percent between 2002 and 2006, twice as much as home prices in high-income zip codes, as easy credit to low-income borrowers caused housing inflation on a grand scale.

House price growth was much more muted, as one would expect, in "elastic" cities, and the differential between house price increases in low-income and high-income zip codes was much narrower than in "inelastic" cities. Nevertheless, the growth of credit was highest in low-income zip codes in both kinds of cities, just much higher in "inelastic" cities, in which bigger price gains provided more borrowing potential. The authors focus on the higher leverage and heightened vulnerability of low-income borrowers as an explanation for the sharp fall in consumer demand during the crisis. The reliance on home equity credit to buy cars and other big-ticket items came to an abrupt standstill.

Ultimately, Mian and Sufi make a case for mortgage mitigation as a superior approach to bank bailouts in addressing such a crisis because it is a much more targeted approach for dealing with the underlying problem, which was a collapse in demand as an unprecedented number of low-income borrowers went upside down on their mortgages. While more aggressive mortgage relief would have helped, efforts toward this goal were severely hampered by the complicated way in which securitization sliced and diced mortgages. Identifying the borrower was straightforward. Tracing and identifying the end lender through a chain of intermediation was not, as legal issues rose exponentially with the number of parties involved. Unfortunately, mortgage relief efforts never got much traction because of this complication. As a result, a large swath of borrowers got stuck with high underwater mortgages that either required foreclosures, short selling, or a resurgence in home prices to cover debts and selling fees.

House of Debt refers to a plethora of research that clearly documents the role of mortgage lending to lower-income borrowers as the overwhelming source of the mortgage growth leading up to the crisis. As Exhibit 8.1 illustrates, this turned out to be the last gasp of the 60-year trend of rising leverage and deteriorating credit standards. How much of the blame for this final push toward excessive leverage goes to government-mandated polices that encouraged such lending practices and put regulatory pressure for lending to low-income neighborhoods because of the Community Reinvestment Act (CRA) and other government mandates will remain a highly politicized debate. The fact that poorly underwritten lending in low-income zip codes ultimately caused the bubble and its bursting cannot be disputed.

In any case, by 2014, the home ownership rate was back where it had started before the housing bubble, and lenders had a new mantra: if you want a loan, you have to show you can pay it back. This basic lending principle was forgotten in the thicket of increasingly sophisticated financial engineering and well-intended government policies, with disastrous consequences for the economy, financial institutions, and government finances. Once again, people were forced to accept that there are no shortcuts to prosperity.

Prescription for disaster: rising leverage and falling nominal GDP growth

While rising leverage increases risk and eventually creates a crisis when it goes too far, the macroeconomic backdrop can influence what those limits to leverage are. As we saw with the difference between the European and US responses to the crisis, pro-growth policies make deleveraging much less painful by supporting stronger cash flows throughout the economy to more easily service debt. Reflating US nominal GDP growth back above 4 percent created a more sustainable recovery by reducing the deleveraging headwinds from the financial crisis. Nominal GDP growth governs the growth of cash flows through the economy. Wage and salary growth is constrained by nominal GDP. In the early 1980s, when inflation was over 10 percent, wages and salaries grew commensurately. Such high growth cannot happen to personal income when inflation and nominal GDP growth are close to zero. Household income growth came down from double-digit levels in the early 1980s to barely positive by the financial crisis. This meant that the growth in income to pay back debt, for example, mortgage debt, increasingly fell short of the levels necessary until a default crisis eventually ensued.

Similarly, for the business sector, falling nominal GDP growth governs sales growth. During the early 1980s, sales growth was still positive during the recession because of high inflation. As inflation and nominal GDP growth trended lower over the past 30 years, sales growth slowed in line with wages, salaries, and personal income. Low inflation means low nominal sales growth, which is one reason why pessimism about business conditions has been so pervasive. Businesses look at nominal cash flow or sales growth as an important metric of performance. When sales were growing 10 percent in the early 1980s, it seemed better than when sales were growing just 2 percent in 2009. Real sales, or volumes, were weak in both cases, but money illusion helped mask the weak conditions when inflation was high. Revenues have to be considered against costs, and costs were basically eating the revenue gains in the high-inflation environment. For example, labor costs were also growing at double-digit rates in the early 1980s. While everybody felt better with double-digit gains in revenues and incomes, it was largely an illusion of revenues, incomes, and costs being elevated by high inflation.

In a low-inflation environment, people feel like the economy is worse because revenues and incomes are growing just 4 percent, for example, when inflation is averaging around 2 percent. Real growth, however, is still near potential around 2 percent and 3 percent, allowing for the unemployment rate to average around its so-called "natural rate." Job growth can be "normal" in both environments.

The long period of household debt growth that was much faster than nominal GDP growth after 1980 meant the cash flows to service debt (household incomes, tax revenues, corporate cash flows) were generally declining relative to the amount of debt. The lower interest rates that accompanied the disinflation trend helped resolve this strain for a while. Eventually, however, interest rates hit rock bottom, and the strains required reducing principal as well as the interest component of debt service. One way to reduce debt service is default. Mortgage default has accounted for the preponderance of debt reduction since the crisis, especially within the segment of lower-income households that became most overextended during the surge in NTMs. Loan growth has moderated as well, and is now more in line with nominal GDP.

Just as a 2-percent inflation target seems to be an "appropriate" goal for monetary policy, a 4-percent minimum goal for nominal GDP seems to be about right for the economy to realize its potential. With real growth of 2 percent or 3 percent and inflation of about 2 percent, credit can grow sustainably (i.e., in line with wages and the economy) at a 4- or 5-percent pace, and interest rates will fluctuate in the "new normal" range as described earlier.

Federal Reserve policy successfully achieved the 4-percent nominal GDP threshold with its extraordinary measures after the financial crisis. In contrast, weak money supply growth, deflating bank balance sheets, and fiscal austerity kept Europe on the edge of recession, allowing debt-deflation forces to fester as nominal growth remained closer to zero on the Continent. This is what happened in Japan during its lost decades. Not surprisingly, the effects of bad macroeconomic policies are evident in German Bund yields, which have plunged "Japanese style" toward zero as the market rightly senses that debt in Europe is too high to be serviced by the cash flows generated in a flat nominal GDP environment. This is a screaming signal of too-tight policy. Unfortunately, politics rather than economics has driven monetary and fiscal policy in Europe since the crisis started.

The 60-year trend of rising leverage on US financial institution and household balance sheets began to collide with the secular decline in inflation that started with Paul Volcker in the early 1980s. Nominal GDP growth reached double-digit levels during the late 1970s and early 1980s. From there it progressively declined, reaching the lowest levels since the 1930s during the financial crisis (Exhibit 8.3). Since then, aggressive monetary policy has reflated nominal growth to a 4-percent-plus trend. As seen in Exhibit 8.3., household debt outstanding continued to grow faster than nominal GDP until the financial crisis, when the US experienced its first balance sheet recession

Exhibit 8.3 Household Debt Growth Outpaced Economic Growth for 30 Years before the Crisis

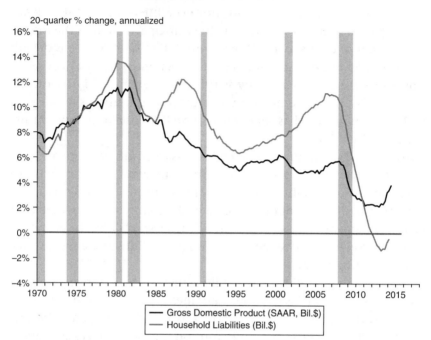

Source: BEA, Federal Reserve Board/Haver Analytics.
Data as of August 2014.

since the Great Depression. It was inevitable that the rising leverage trend would collide with the falling nominal GDP growth trend at some point. In many respects, the former was responsible for the latter.

During the first few years after the 2007–2009 recession, households continued to shrink their debt for the first time since the 1930s. Fortunately, pro-growth macropolicies supported an orderly deleveraging process instead of aggravating it as in Europe. Europe provides the counterfactual to what would have happened in the United States without macropolicy support for nominal GDP growth. As already discussed, a minimum 4-percent nominal GDP growth rate seems to be necessary to generate adequate income flows to service the high outstanding debt burden in the United States. In Europe, 2 percent, or less, nominal GDP growth seems insufficient and results in the chronic stagnation and high deflation risk that also characterized Japan before Abenomics.

"What's different this time?" The impact of the credit crisis on the business cycle

The secular deterioration in the quality of household and financial institutions' balance sheets, aided and abetted by public policies aimed at boosting homeownership, set the fundamental backdrop for the business cycle that began in late 2001, shortly after the 9/11 terrorist attacks. We have already noted that the 2001 recession was relatively muted for consumption and residential real estate, which barely flinched when the tech bubble burst. The big wealth losses were borne by the higher-income households that hold the preponderance of stock market wealth. Stock holdings are generally much less leveraged than real estate, in which the secular trend toward higher and higher leverage made the 2008–2009 financial crisis and recession much more severe. As we saw, the concentration of borrowing and home price declines was particularly devastating for low-income households that had been using growing housing wealth as a piggy bank, including for the purchase of big-ticket items like cars, that kept the expansion going. In contrast, the recession that followed the bursting of the tech bubble was much less severe and more concentrated in the nonfinancial business sector, in which extremely high valuations and overinvestment in technology companies were the primary source of excesses.

The housing stimulus that drove the 2002–2007 expansion really started in the mid-1990s, so housing had a longer-than-normal run through two business cycles as the massive growth in borrowing by previously unqualified borrowers cumulated for over a decade before falling under its own weight. The ever-growing US trade deficit during this time reflected a rising inflow of capital from emerging markets, like China, with big trade surpluses and a desire to accumulate foreign exchange reserves to preclude a repeat of the late-1990s problems during the Asian currency crisis. These countries purchased US Treasuries and GSE securities en masse with dollars earned from their burgeoning trade surpluses. This made more and more housing finance available in an increasingly destabilizing circle of lending and borrowing to weaker and weaker mortgage credits that were magically being transformed into the full faith and credit of the United States. At least that's what foreign lenders believed in order to pick up a few extra basis points of return over Treasuries by investing in GSE debt. At their peak in mid-2008, foreign central bank holdings of GSE debt reached about $1 trillion. Since then, that number has plummeted.

Despite financial crisis, the business cycle followed the usual pattern

While the once-in-a-century nature of the financial crisis played out in many special ways, reflecting the culmination of a debt super cycle, the business cycle patterns we have discussed in this book and their impact on asset values mostly played out in a normal fashion both before and after the crisis.

For example, the run-up to the late 2007 recession involved most of the cyclical patterns we have discussed. The recession only began once the Fed had tightened to the point at which the yield curve was inverted. That tightening was the response to a normal cyclical pickup in wages that was associated with a tight labor market and price inflation above the Fed's 2-percent target. Credit spreads had bottomed and began to deteriorate in a normal cyclical fashion as the economy started to lose momentum. The general stock market peaked ahead of the recession, while "late-cycle" assets like materials stocks and commodities continued to rise during the early stage of the recession.

In fact, until Lehman Brothers failed, there were some signs beginning to suggest that the recession would be over by early 2009, including aggressive cuts in the federal funds rate and a much steeper yield curve. Arguably, the collapse of Lehman caused the recession to go on for an extra six months and necessitated a much more aggressive response from fiscal and monetary policy to contain the chaos that ensued.

Similarly, once the pieces fell into place after the crisis, normal cyclical patterns emerged as the recovery began in mid-2009. Inventories were liquidated beyond what the weakness in demand justified. Too many people were laid off. Hiring and restocking became necessary once it was clear to businesses that sales were holding up sufficiently to adopt a more positive posture.

Monetary policy had to improvise because interest rates were already close to rock bottom. Quantitative easing provided the kind of extra accommodation that is typical early in an expansion. It required several rounds, but ultimately by 2014 it was clear that the economy was moving into a midcycle phase. Damage to housing and government finances created headwinds that stretched out the recovery.

Premature fiscal tightening also was a drag on the recovery, especially in 2012–2013, when budget showdowns caused a sharp contraction in the deficit and a surge in policy uncertainty that dampened business expansion and hiring plans. Fortunately, the Fed's extraordinary measures were sufficient to offset much of the fiscal drag, and the positive side effect was more sustainable federal finances.

The basic point is the extraordinary circumstances of the financial crisis did shape the recovery and subsequent expansion, yet in most respects cyclical patterns played out as they generally do. This is just one more example of the truism "every business cycle is the same except for what's different." The financial crisis was certainly different from every business cycle since the 1930s. Nevertheless, the usual cyclical patterns we have discussed in this book were to a large extent evident both before and after the crisis, providing yet again a useful roadmap to tactical asset allocation.

Many money managers lost their bearings in the midst of the financial crisis and its aftermath, as the extraordinary government policies to address the crisis fed the misleading view that disaster was looming. Instead, the waters were calmed and a fairly recognizable pattern of business cycle expansion emerged thanks to astute navigation from policymakers. Nevertheless, naysayers persisted for longer than usual as the fog lifted.

The more severe the panic and the more intense the crisis, the more likely it is to hear cries that "this time is different and the old rules don't apply anymore." Following that tack leaves a strategist rudderless. Just as rough seas incite panic, turbulent financial markets often cause investors to abandon the principles that good money management requires. Eventually, the seas calm, and this becomes apparent. Just as the tides and weather patterns provide guidance for sailors, the business cycle persists through all kinds of structural and policy environments. Dismissing cyclical patterns because "this time is different" is generally a recipe for disaster. In contrast, recognizing how cyclical patterns are altered or exaggerated by special events, like the financial crisis or an inadequate policy response to extreme financial market stress, is a powerful advantage for tactical asset allocation.

The patterns of business cycles that have persisted over centuries provide insights into the inner workings of the macroeconomy. In a free market economy, predictable human responses to incentives and the ongoing benefits from rationalizing the allocation of resources create an ever-evolving gestalt of self-organization that policy can influence for better or worse. The resilience of the US economy through the various storms of the past stands out as truly remarkable. The business cycle can test the limits of that resilience. Yet, while downturns are always painful, they help pave the way to the future by eliminating the obsolete and inefficient. The result has been an ever-rising living standard for more and more people around the world.

Bibliography

Liaquat Ahamed, *Lords of Finance: The Bankers Who Broke the World*, Penguin, 2009.

Barclays Capital, *Barclays Capital Equity Gilt Study 2014*.

Board of Governors of the Federal Reserve System, *FOMC Longer-Run Goals and Monetary Policy Strategy*, www.federalreserve.gov/monetarypolicy/.

Damien Courvalin, Jeffrey Currie, and Michael Hinds, *The Strategic Case for Commodities Holding Strong*, Goldman Sachs Commodity Research, April 23, 2014.

Angus Deaton, *The Great Escape: Health, Wealth and the Origins of Inequality*, Princeton University Press, 2013.

Elroy Dimson, Paul Marsh, and Mike Staunton, *Triumph of the Optimists: 101 Years of Global Investment Returns*, Princeton University Press, 2002.

Barry J. Eichengreen, *Golden Fetters: The Gold Standard and the Great Depression, 1919–1939*, Oxford University Press, 1996.

———, *Hall of Mirrors: The Great Depression, The Great Recession, and the Uses-and Misuses-of History*, Oxford University Press, 2015.

Financial Crisis Inquiry Commission, *The Financial Crisis Inquiry Report*, Final Report of the National Commission on the Causes of the Financial and Economic Crisis in the United States, Official Government Edition, January 2011.

Milton Friedman and Anna J. Schwartz, *A Monetary History of the United States, 1867–1960*, Princeton University Press, 1963.

Shigeru Fujita, *On the Causes of Declines in the Labor Force Participation Rate*, Research Rap Special Report Federal Reserve Bank of Philadelphia, February 2014.

Timothy F. Geithner, *Stress Test: Reflections on Financial Crises*, Random House, 2014.

Gary B. Gorton and K. Geert Rouwenhorst, *Facts and Fantasies about Commodity Futures*, Yale I.C.F. Working Paper No. 04–20, February 28, 2005.

Alan Greenspan, *The Map and the Territory: Risk, Human Nature, and the Future of Forecasting*, Penguin Press HC, 2013.

Herman Kahn, William Morle Brown, and Leon Martel, *The Next 200 Years: A Scenario for America and the World*, Morrow, 1976.

Donella H. Meadows, Dennis L. Meadows, Jorgen Randers, and William W. Behrens III, *The Limits to Growth*, Universe Books, 1972.

Atif Mian and Amir Sufi, *House of Debt*, The University of Chicago Press, 2014.

Thomas Piketty, *Capital in the Twenty-First Century*, Harvard University Press, 2014.

Jeremy J. Siegel, *Stocks for the Long Run*, McGraw-Hill, 1994.

Richard J. Smethurst, *From Foot Soldier to Finance Minister: Takahashi Korekiyo, Japan's Keynes*, Harvard University Press, 2007.

United States of America Long-Term Rating Lowered To 'AA+' Due to Political Risks, Rising Debt Burden; Outlook Negative, Standard & Poor's, www.standardandpoors .com/ratings/articles/en/us/?assetID=1245316529563.

US Department of the Treasury, *Statement by Secretary Henry M. Paulson, Jr. on Treasury and Federal Housing Finance Agency Action to Protect Financial Markets and Taxpayers,* September 7, 2008, www.treasury.gov/press-center/press -releases/Pages/hp1129.aspx.

Hal R. Varian, *Beyond Big Data,* Business Economics (2014) 49, 27–31.

Victor Zarnowitz, *What Is a Business Cycle?,* NBER Working Paper No. 3863, October 1991.

Index